FOURTH EDITION

Interdisciplinary Instruction for All Learners K-8

A Practical Guide

Karlyn E. Wood
SUNY College at Old Westbury

Pearson

Boston   Columbus   Indianapolis   New York   San Francisco   Upper Saddle River
Amsterdam   Cape Town   Dubai   London   Madrid   Milan   Munich   Paris   Montreal
Toronto   Delhi   Mexico City   Sao Paulo   Sydney   Hong Kong   Seoul
Singapore   Taipei   Tokyo

Acquisitions Editor: Kelly Villella Canton
Editorial Assistant: Annalea Manalili
Senior Marketing Manager: Darcy Betts Prybella
Production Manager: Kathy Sleys
Art Director: Jayne Conte
Cover Designer: Axell Designs
Cover Art: Nina Wood

Full-Service Project Management: Yasmeen
Neelofar/Swapnil Vaidya
Composition: GGS Higher Education
Resources. PMG
Printer/Binder/Cover Printer: Bind-Rite,
Robbinsville/Command Web
Text Font: 10/12 – TimesNew Roman

Credits and acknowledgments borrowed from other sources and reproduced, with permission, in this textbook appear on appropriate pages within text.

Many of the designations by manufacturers and seller to distinguish their products are claimed as trademarks. Where those designations appear in this book, and the publisher was aware of a trademark claim, the designations have been printed in initial caps or all caps.

Cataloging-in-Publication Data for this title can be obtained from the Library of Congress.

10 9 8 7 6 5 4 3 2 1

www.pearsonhighered.com

ISBN-13: 978-0-13-713708-4
ISBN-10:   0-13-713708-7

To Louise, Kim, Nina, and Jennifer.

*To my students and colleagues in the School of Education
at the State University of New York/College at Old Westbury.*

BRIEF CONTENTS

CONTENTS

PREFACE

Traditionally, instruction in our schools has tended to isolate the academic disciplines—or subject areas—from one another. In contrast, *interdisciplinary* instruction always *begins with a central topic, theme, or problem;* the topic is then investigated using any disciplines that can assist in the inquiry. The topics that students study can vary greatly; some are typical of those that are usually included in the social studies or science curriculum; however, topics from other disciplines, such as literature, mathematics, and the visual and performing arts can also become the basis of an interdisciplinary study.

There continues to be interest among educators in the interdisciplinary method. Interest has been stimulated by legislative steps taken by many state departments of education as well as the need to make advancement, such as those required by No Child Left Behind legislation. Since the first edition of this book, all states have prepared lists of content learning standards; those lists strongly suggest the need for interdisciplinary studies. Some curriculum mandates also stress interdisciplinary instruction. For example, the New York State Education Department currently requires teachers in Grades 3 through 6 to develop at least one interdisciplinary project with students in their classes each year. As a result, teachers and administrators are showing greater interest in interdisciplinary program designs and practical ways to plan for their implementation. Many teachers are anxious to learn exactly what interdisciplinary projects should involve and how they differ from other instructional activities.

The interdisciplinary approach has been used by early childhood teachers as a standard method of instruction for many years. Preschool and kindergarten teachers routinely plan their instructional programs around central themes, themes which are then used as much as possible in teaching daily lessons and activities. Most primary grade teachers feel that they understand the method and that they have been readied for it by their college preparatory programs. Although there is an increasing interest in interdisciplinary instruction in the intermediate grades and middle school, teachers at those levels may feel they have had less preparation and experience with the interdisciplinary approach than their early childhood colleagues.

The purpose of this book is to provide pre-service and in-service elementary and middle school teachers and administrators with a handbook that introduces the interdisciplinary method and offers practical suggestions on how to plan for and implement the method in classrooms. I have based this book partly on the materials that I have prepared for my courses in teacher education.

In the book, I have purposefully kept the theoretical chapters succinct—yet complete—so that the emphasis can be on the *thinking processes* involved in planning both *interdisciplinary* and *multidisciplinary* units—two unit types that are suitable for students at differing levels of ability.

This book is intended for use in methods courses at both the undergraduate and graduate levels; it is also appropriate for in-service courses in schools and teacher centers. The practical explanations and examples provided should prove especially helpful for teachers who have not previously studied interdisciplinary instruction and who want to learn how to get started.

College instructors who emphasize a constructivist approach to teaching and who advocate interdisciplinary methods in their social studies, science, and general methods courses can use this book to help their students understand both the theoretical and practical aspects of the interdisciplinary approach. Instructors of other methods courses, such as literacy and mathematics, will find it valuable in helping students to detect the relationships between those disciplines and comprehensive interdisciplinary studies.

To emphasize the planning processes and illustrate the essentials of those processes as clearly as possible, I have included examples for each component in the unit planning process in chapters 3 and 4. The models in this book illustrate *one* way to design interdisciplinary units—although surely not the *only* way. The point of view expressed throughout this book is that there is no single planning format that will work satisfactorily for every teacher.

New to the Fourth Edition

All references in the fourth edition have been updated. The chapters have been revised and reorganized into six chapters in the new edition to provide for a logical grouping of topics. To make the instructional resources of the previous edition easily accessible, they have been incorporated in the chapters to which each of the resources pertains. Some of the sample web designs in the third edition have been eliminated; those that are discussed or used for examples are included in the fourth edition in the chapters where they are discussed.

The lesson and unit planning components and processes follow *backward design* as the main approach to their designs. Lesson plan examples for each of the procedural protocols discussed follow the explanations of those protocols. Steps in each of the example lesson plan procedure sections are annotated to explain their purpose in the procedure design. New rubric examples are included in chapter 6 on assessment.

Organization of the Book

The first and second chapters provide the theoretical framework for interdisciplinary instruction. The first chapter discusses the theory supporting interdisciplinary instruction; it includes an outline of distinguishing features and compares the interdisciplinary approach with multidisciplinary and integrated instruction. Interdisciplinary studies are explained, and the rationale for using the interdisciplinary approach with students in elementary and middle schools is reviewed. The second chapter explains some of the requirements of teachers who plan to use the approach in elementary and middle schools. That chapter concludes with some of the challenges to the implementation of the interdisciplinary approach in today's schools.

Chapters 3 and 4 are specifically designed to teach the *processes* involved in planning interdisciplinary and multidisciplinary units. Chapter 3 details the processes involved in planning interdisciplinary units. Chapter 4 studies the multidisciplinary unit, an alternative type of unit that is particularly suitable for students in the intermediate grades and departmentalized middle schools. Both chapters include a detailed unit plan outline, followed by explanations with examples of each unit component. Complete versions of the unit plans that are partially completed in chapters 3 and 4 are provided at the end of those chapters. Chapter 3 also includes suggestions for designing learning centers for student exploration and practice in connection with units of study.

Chapters 3 and 4 can be used by teacher candidates for reference during in-class practicum sessions. Instructors will be able to use valuable class time to interact directly with pre-service teachers as they study the components of each unit planning process and design their own units.

The new chapter 5 provides information about the lesson planning processes. This chapter reviews preliminary considerations in the lesson and unit planning processes, including students' learning and development, teachers' questioning techniques, and applications of Bloom's Taxonomy.

The new chapter 6 provides information on the topic of assessment for interdisciplinary instruction. It includes information on both authentic assessment and traditional examinations. Rubrics are explained and illustrated.

In addition to reference lists, each chapter concludes with a suggested activity and a list of suggested readings related to chapter topics. The readings include early theoretical works for those who would like additional background material or who plan to undertake their own research on topics included in the chapters as well as writings that reflect current thinking and trends on those topics.

Acknowledgments

Our quest for knowledge is a lifelong pursuit in which we learn both from our experiences and one another. Teachers often play an important role in facilitating this process. For most of us, some teachers will be especially well remembered for their positive contributions. To begin, I consider myself fortunate to have been taught by the late Myrtle Cope, an exemplary master teacher. I thank her for the early influence she had on my decision to become an elementary teacher and for the example she provided me of the constructivist approach to education, a philosophy that continues to influence my teaching practice.

I would also like to acknowledge the late Roland Chatterton, a forward-thinking educator and pioneer in multidisciplinary education. Dr. Chatterton introduced me to interdisciplinary methodology; it was his patient mentoring and guidance that facilitated my own development as an interdisciplinary teacher.

I would like to thank my wife, Louise, for her patience and support as I prepared the manuscripts for each edition of the book. My colleagues in the School of Education at the State University of New York/College at Old Westbury have provided me with their support, and I thank them for their interest and encouragement throughout the project. I am especially indebted to my colleagues, Amy Hsu, Margaret Renner, Basilio Serrano, and Gareth B. Wilmott, who provided me with valuable feedback on my plans and manuscript revision drafts. I want to thank them for their time and their many helpful suggestions.

I also want to express my appreciation to my students in the School of Education at the SUNY/College at Old Westbury who have permitted me to include their lesson plans and unit plan web designs in my book.

I particularly wish to thank my reviewers for their input and suggestions: Patricia Calderwood, Fairfield University; Joyce Frazier, University of North Carolina-Charlotte; Stephen Hancock, University of North Carolina-Charlotte; Belinda Hill, Saint Martin's University; Stephen Lafer, University of Nevada-Reno; David Locascio, Longwood University; Rhonda Truitt, Catawba College; and Bruce Young, Covenant College.

I would like to acknowledge artist Nina Wood for the drawings she prepared for me that inspired and were adapted for the design on the cover of this book.

Finally, I would like to acknowledge my editors at Pearson/Allyn & Bacon: Annette Jacobs and Kathleen Sleys for their interest and counsel; Yasmeen Neelofar for her expertise and the recommendations she made throughout the copyediting process; and Swapnil K. Vaidya for his guidance and support in the final production stages of the book.

TO THE READER

When I started teaching, I had little understanding of the interdisciplinary method, and I was certainly unaware of all I would have to learn over the next few years to use it in my own classroom. As a young, inexperienced teacher, I began my career in an elementary school district that was proud of its *multidisciplinary* philosophy, where teachers were expected to use a multidisciplinary approach at every level—from kindergarten through the sixth grade. I began studying the method from the outset, but it was not until I observed the enthusiasm of the other teachers who had been using it for some time that I became committed to developing the skills I would need to carry it out myself.

Throughout the first two years, I found multidisciplinary—or interdisciplinary—teaching far more challenging than I had ever anticipated, and it is likely that I would have given the method up altogether if I had not been given a great deal of moral support from other teachers and administrators in my school. I learned from my colleagues how important it was to reserve extra time to plan for this kind of instruction and soon found myself spending countless hours after school on a task I found nearly overwhelming—trying to write plans for the interdisciplinary units I was teaching.

In those early experimental years, I paid little attention to planning *processes* and instead, spent—or misspent—most of my energy searching for the best way to write a unit plan. Eventually, I realized that I needed to learn more about the planning process itself, so in time, my concentration shifted from the *writing* of the plan to the *thinking* involved in designing an interdisciplinary unit. I had discovered that the planning process was far more important than the format of the written plan. However, my attempts to locate information on the interdisciplinary approach or the unit planning process revealed that little substantive material appeared to be available. Even the most popular instructional methods textbooks in use at our local universities had little to offer on the subject.

Seventeen years later, when I began teaching education majors in college, I found that there was still a dearth of practical material written about interdisciplinary unit planning to use with my students, so, out of necessity, I began preparing my own. To develop those materials, I drew on my classroom teaching experience with the method and focused on the sequential thought processes involved in unit preparation.

Now, after using those materials for several years, I have found them to be especially helpful for future teachers who are just beginning to learn about interdisciplinary instruction and unit planning. I have noted that when the materials are used in class, I need to spend less class time explaining the planning processes and giving repetitious verbal instructions about them. Instead, I have more time to work directly with teacher candidates as they practice designing their own interdisciplinary and multidisciplinary unit plans.

It is my hope that this book will help both pre-service and in-service teachers explore interdisciplinary instruction and the planning processes involved in it. I also hope that instructors will save valuable time by using this book and will be able to use that time to help their students become better teachers.

ABOUT THE AUTHOR

Karlyn Wood received his Ed.D. from Hofstra University and is an emeritus Professor of Humanities of the School of Education at the State University of New York/College at Old Westbury on Long Island, where he taught courses in interdisciplinary methodology and child development. He supervised and conducted seminars for student teachers and was the Chair of the Childhood Education and Literacy Department. Karlyn has also taught at the elementary level, served as a district reading consultant, administrator, and coordinator for an experimental elementary program. His publications include articles in *Language Arts, Childhood Education, The Journal of Child Development,* and *The Journal of Teacher Education.* His papers have been included in *Sociological Abstracts* and *ERIC* documents. He belongs to the American Educational Research Association, Association Montessori Internationale, the Association for Supervision and Curriculum Development, and he is a member of the Kappa Delta Pi honor society.

1 Introduction to Interdisciplinary Instruction

Water tower experiment.

OVERVIEW

This chapter provides an introduction to the interdisciplinary approach to instruction and its theoretical foundations. The essential concepts reviewed in this chapter present a framework for the planning strategies that are offered in subsequent chapters of the book. They are the following:

- Distinguishing features of the interdisciplinary approach
- Comparing interdisciplinary, multi-disciplinary, and integrated instruction
- Interdisciplinary and multidisciplinary studies: Their organization and design
- The rationale for using interdisciplinary instruction with diverse learners in elementary and middle schools

Distinguishing Features of the Interdisciplinary Approach

In 1933, a method of teaching that was strongly advocated by John Dewey involved students in "projects," investigations that required the use of more than a single academic discipline. Dewey believed that to be educative, it was necessary that such projects "present problems that awaken new curiosity and create a demand for information" (p. 218). Although it is not identical to Dewey's *project method*, interdisciplinary instruction is a problem-centered approach to the study of topics, themes, and major questions that is based largely on Dewey's ideology.

Although the interdisciplinary approach is not new, it has never been widely practiced in American schools. Today, however, there is renewed interest in this approach because of the need to find alternative ways to address state and federal mandates for improvements in student achievement and the quality of instruction. We are searching for ways to raise test scores without "teaching-to-the-test." As a result, many teachers are incorporating aspects of interdisciplinary instruction in their teaching.

A central purpose of this introductory chapter will be to examine the features of the interdisciplinary approach and the rationale for its use in elementary and middle schools. It will be suggested that the interdisciplinary approach may well be an alternative method that can help address the need to improve the quality of education in our schools, enhance personal meaning, and better meet the needs of our diverse student population.

The initial discussion will describe several distinctive features of interdisciplinary studies. These studies are organized as comprehensive instructional unit plans that are prepared using either an interdisciplinary or multidisciplinary format. An interdisciplinary study has at least four unique characteristics:

- Interdisciplinary studies are organized in comprehensive interdisciplinary or multidisciplinary unit plans that focus on a specific topic, theme, or problem.
- Interdisciplinary studies are explored by using the skills and techniques—*the ways of knowing*—associated with any academic disciplines that can inform the topic, theme, or problem under investigation.
- Interdisciplinary studies place equal emphasis on the mastery of the *processes* involved in learning about a topic, theme, or problem and the mastery of *content*—concepts, facts, generalizations, and principles.
- Interdisciplinary studies accommodate student diversity by providing for the differentiation of student investigating and reporting techniques.

Comparing Interdisciplinary, Multidisciplinary, and Integrated Instruction

Although some educators consider *interdisciplinary, multidisciplinary,* and *integrated* instruction to be identical or nearly the same, others suggest that they differ in specific ways. Interdisciplinary and multidisciplinary instruction both involve the use of "two or more academic subjects or fields of study" during the exploration of a topic or theme (Encarta World Dictionary, 1999, p. 933). Integrated instruction is similarly defined as "learning experiences organized around developmentally appropriate topics, themes, or concepts which provide opportunities for students to draw on standards from more than one subject" (Early Elementary Resources Guide, 1996, p. 23). It should be noted that the terms *interdisciplinary approach* and *interdisciplinary instruction* are used throughout this text; the two terms refer to the overall method involved in teaching both interdisciplinary and multidisciplinary units. Variations in the two unit types are explained in detail in Chapters 3 and 4.

Parker (2005) suggests that the three approaches have distinct characteristics. For example, although *multidisciplinary* instruction makes use of two or more disciplines when exploring a specific topic or theme, it maintains a somewhat greater focus on the individual disciplines involved in the study. Information from the different disciplines involved in a study is combined and reported only at the conclusion of the study (Chatterton, 1968). There is an even clearer distinction between the interdisciplinary and multidisciplinary approaches in fields other than education. For example, in the medical field, "Multidisciplinary research teams work in parallel or sequentially from their specific disciplinary base to address a common problem. Interdisciplinary research teams work jointly but still from a discipline-specific base to address a common problem" (Slatin, Galizzi, Devereaux Melillo, & Mawn, 2004, p. 62).

Integrated instruction suggests the incorporation of one subject within others. It is an instructional approach to curriculum. An example of this is found in programs that empha-size reading and writing—taught as literacy—across all disciplinary areas in the curriculum of a school; literacy skills are taught as integral and essential to each discipline. Another view of integrated instruction is found in the subject, social studies, in which several disciplines—history, geography, economics, and other social sciences—are *integrated* to form a new subject within which its several disciplines become integral parts.

Another feature of the integrated approach is that it may provide clear connections with students' lives apart from the school environment because it involves "learning constructed in an innovative and purposeful way that shows relationships between what happens within and outside of school" (Williams-Boyd, 1996, p. 179). Beane (1997) also emphasizes the social aspects of an integrated approach in his definition of it as a curriculum that "is concerned with enhancing the possibilities for personal and social integration" (p. 19).

A report to the Minnesota State Legislature by the Minnesota Board of Teaching (2006) also attempts to clarify the differences between interdisciplinary and integrated instruction:

> Interdisciplinary curriculum, which draws content from particular disciplines that are ordinarily taught separately, is different from integrated curriculum, which involves investi-gation of topics without regard to where, or even whether, they appear in the typical school curriculum at all. (p. 2)

Perhaps the most important feature the three approaches have in common is that they all involve attention to more than a single academic discipline. Therefore, they are all *interdisciplinary*. In Chapters 3 and 4, the design and planning of interdisciplinary units—which can be used at all grade levels—and multidisciplinary units—which are especially well-suited for departmentalized middle schools—are explained and illustrated with examples. The comparison of some of the main differences between these two unit types is shown in Figure 1.1.

FIGURE 1.1   A Comparison of Interdisciplinary and Multidisciplinary Units.

Description	*Interdisciplinary Unit Design*	*Multidisciplinary Unit Design*
The unit focuses on the study of a topic, theme, or problem.	X	X
The unit is appropriate for elementary grades K–3.	X	
The unit is appropriate for elementary grades 4–6.	X	X
The unit is appropriate for departmentalized middle school grades 5–8.		X
The unit is planned by a classroom teacher.	X	
The unit is planned by a departmentalized team of teachers.		X
The research process guides the development of the unit and its procedures.	X	X
Procedures of the unit parallel interdisciplinary research in fields other than education.	X	
Procedures of the unit parallel multidisciplinary research in fields other than education.		X
Students are actively involved in developing questions and suggesting areas to be researched.	X	X
The topic, theme, or problem can be subdivided for research either by discipline or sub-topic.	X	X
The unit design provides for a series of lessons and activities related to the unit topic, theme, or problem.	X	
The unit design can make provisions for student committee research.	X	X
The unit design provides for disciplinary instruction by a team of teachers.		X
Instruction in all or most disciplines is provided mainly by the classroom teacher.	X	
Instruction in each discipline is taught separately by members of a departmentalized teaching team.		X

Interdisciplinary and Multidisciplinary Studies: Their Organization and Design

The interdisciplinary approach involves students in the exploration of comprehensive interdisciplinary or multidisciplinary studies of topics, themes, and problems. Those studies have commonly been organized as *activity-centered* units for elementary and middle school students. Planning activity-centered units typically begins by first determining the specific lessons and activities that will make up the unit study. Unit objectives and assessments follow.

An alternative to activity-centered planning is *backward design,* a planning process developed by Wiggins and McTighe (2005). Backward design is a partial reverse of activity-centered planning. It involves consideration of unit objectives and assessments before deciding the specific lessons and activities the unit will include. The lessons and activities used will address those objectives and accommodate the assessments to be included. According to Wiggins and McTighe, backward design involves three stages (pp. 17–28).

> **Stage 1:** Identifying the enduring understandings, learning standards, and essential questions of the unit
> **Stage 2:** Determining unit assessment strategies
> **Stage 3:** Planning the unit learning experiences

Backward design emphasizes the long-term development of *enduring understandings* and *big ideas.* "A big idea is a concept, theme, or issue that gives meaning and connection to discrete facts and skills" (p. 5). Scientific concepts like *adaptation* and *natural selection* are examples of big ideas. Backward design unit planning engages students in the exploration of the essential questions to which the unit topics, themes, or problems are related. This is a particularly appropriate for interdisciplinary and multidisciplinary unit planning.

Both backward design and activity-centered planning have positive attributes and some potential drawbacks. Activity-centered planning is familiar to most teachers, and students usually enjoy the activities that are planned for them. However, unit assessments may tend to be limited to the development of the isolated knowledge that the individual lessons and activities develop. Assessments may not be adequately related to or assess the major unit concepts. It is possible that activity-centered plans may also focus so much on the separate lessons and hands-on activities that the unifying, interdisciplinary concepts of the unit may not become clear to students.

Backward design is a logical and intellectually sound planning process. Following it helps to ensure that all components of the unit plan are related to one another, including the learning standards, objectives, essential questions, and assessments. However, backward design is not as familiar as activity-centered planning is to many teachers. Also, some teachers may find determining the big ideas and the enduring understandings for their units difficult and evasive. Even Wiggins and McTighe warn us about this with,

> We predict that you will be somewhat disturbed by how hard it is to specify the understandings and what they look like in assessment, and how easy it is to lose sight of goals related to understanding in the midst of planning, teaching, and evaluating student work. (p. 9)

The unit planning strategies described in Chapters 3 and 4 of this text for interdisciplinary and multidisciplinary units combine features of both activity-centered and the backward design planning processes. The planning process that will be followed in those chapters involves the following components:

- Identifying the unit topic, theme, or problem
- Determining the unit objectives:
    Learning standards
    General objectives (knowledge, skills, and dispositions)
    Essential questions (thought-provoking, often divergent questions)
- Determining the unit assessment plan
- Developing the unit learning plan: describing the lessons, activities, and strategies that will be designed to address the unit objectives

See Figure 1.2 for examples of topics, themes, enduring understandings, and essential questions.

Regardless of the approach, all unit plans need to address the learning standards recommended by national professional organizations or that are required by state departments of education and local school districts. The organizational structure of the unit needs to encourage students to use any disciplines—subjects or domains—that can help them to gain a better understanding of the topic, theme, or problem they will investigate.

While many interdisciplinary and multidisciplinary studies are organized and planned to explore topics, themes, or problems associated with social studies, units can be planned that begin with any discipline, subject, or domain. An interesting and exceptionally well-developed example of an interdisciplinary study that begins with the arts and evolves to include history, literature, science, and other areas of the curriculum is *Spaces and Places* (Pappas, Kiefer, & Levstik, 2006). This is a unit for students in an upper elementary grade or middle school.

Much earlier, Elwyn Richardson (1969), an elementary teacher in New Zealand, also used the arts as the basis for his unusual interdisciplinary, crafts-oriented program. Richardson's students explored their natural rural environment and completed art projects made from raw materials found in that environment. Richardson also involved his students in interdisciplinary literacy, science, and mathematics activities related to their explorations and findings.

Using the Skills, Techniques, and Ways of Knowing in Applicable Academic Disciplines

While students are involved in studying holistic topics or themes, they are exposed to additional skills and ways of knowing inherent in the different disciplines used to investigate those topics. Although we must determine the understandings and essential questions of a study in advance, we need to encourage students to participate in the planning process. We do this by raising questions they would like to include about the topic, theme, or problem of the study. Guided by the essential questions and the topical questions they have added, students must think critically about the issues involved. They also learn to apply skills and techniques from various disciplines that can help them with their research.

FIGURE 1.2 Examples of Topics, Themes, Enduring Understandings, and Essential Questions.

Focus of Interdisciplinary Studies	Examples	
	Lower Elementary Grades	*Upper Elementary Grades and Middle School*
TOPICS	–Myself and Others –My Family and Other Families Now and Long Ago –My Community and Other United States Communities –Communities Around the World –Local History and Government	–History and Government of the United States –History and Government of Canada –Latin America –Eastern Hemisphere Nations –Exploration and Colonization of the Americas
THEMES *Note that themes can span all grade levels.*	–Changes –Culture –Human Systems –Interdependence	–Human Needs and Wants –Places and Regions –Economic Systems –Technology
ENDURING UNDERSTANDINGS	People make choices due to unlimited needs and wants and limited resources.	Constitutions, rules, and laws are developed in a democratic society to protect its citizens.
ESSENTIAL QUESTIONS	–Why has it been difficult to stimulate recycling in some communities? –How can we help others in our community? –What is a friend?	–How can we prove global warming? –What were the major causes and effects of European exploration? –In what ways can we cope with our diminishing natural resources?

Note that the above examples are common topics that appear in many state curriculums.

The interdisciplinary approach provides students with many natural opportunities to observe the connections and to note relationships among the various disciplines involved in their studies. Jacobs (1989) emphasized the importance of this characteristic for teachers as well as students, suggesting that teachers need to intentionally "apply methodology and language from more than one discipline to examine a central theme, issue, problem, topic, or experience" (p. 8).

Emphasis on Process and Content

For many years, educators have debated the relative importance of process and content. Disciplinary, subject-centered instruction often tends to focus on helping students acquire *content*—facts and general information. Another distinguishing feature of the interdisciplinary approach is that not only is there an emphasis on important *content,* but the approach also attributes equal significance to learning the *processes, skills,* and *ways of knowing* that are unique to the different disciplines, subjects, or domains.

Although no consensus exists among educators about which focus is more important, the *processes* involved in inquiry and scientific investigation are clearly important and useful in interdisciplinary and multidisciplinary studies. Teachers who use this approach tend to agree with Dewey's (1916) advice that equal importance be attributed to content and to process in student investigations. It is assumed that students need to amass facts and develop concepts while they become proficient in the application of important academic learning processes that then "become the models [they will use] for later exploratory behaviors" (Gardner, 1993a, p. 31). In this way, students gain insights about and practice the different ways of knowing.

At upper elementary and middle school grade levels, students undertake more complex forms of inquiry, using processes that naturally stimulate their higher level thinking and reasoning skills. In addition to gaining knowledge and practicing the learning processes, all students have numerous and meaningful opportunities through authentic investigations to practice their reading, writing, and computational skills.

Differentiation of Student Investigating and Reporting Alternatives

The interdisciplinary approach accommodates students' diverse strengths and learning preferences and offers many opportunities for the differentiation of instruction. Tomlinson (2001) describes four elements to be considered in the differentiation of instruction: 1) the *content* that is taught and the ways students are given to develop it; 2) the different opportunities students are given to *process* information; 3) the various ways students are encouraged to complete their culminating *products;* and 4) the way the *learning environment* is constructed to facilitate students' differing ways of working to gain information. We know that students do not all learn, nor are they able to demonstrate what they have learned, in the same ways.

"Designing and facilitating multiple paths to reach defined learning goals is one of the hallmarks of successful differentiation" (Carolan & Guinn, 2007, p. 45). When we plan for interdisciplinary studies, students are afforded many natural opportunities to follow "multiple paths" and use a variety of materials and equipment. For example, some students are capable of reading to gain information on a topic; others may need visual materials to process the same knowledge effectively. Others may profit more from other activities, such as conducting interviews, performing Internet searches, or using WebQuests. (A WebQuest is a carefully planned set of steps to be followed by students when they investigate a specific topic using the Internet.)

Differentiation in the interdisciplinary approach permits the students alternatives and opportunities to prepare their culminating reports in a variety of ways, including writing reports; organizing panel discussions or debates; presenting dramatizations; designing PowerPoint presentations; and preparing art projects. In early grades, some students may be able to report their findings by planning a puppet show, performing a dance, and so on.

In summary, features of interdisciplinary instruction that distinguish it from other educational approaches are the following:

- Units of instruction are organized to investigate topics, themes, problems, enduring understandings, essential questions, important issues, or concepts.
- The skills, techniques, and ways of knowing in applicable academic disciplines are all employed in the unit study.
- Equal emphasis is placed on the value of the processes involved in learning and the content knowledge that students gain.
- The interdisciplinary approach provides for differentiation of investigating and reporting methods that address student diversity.

The Rationale for Using Interdisciplinary Instruction for Diverse Learners in Elementary and Middle Schools

Why should an interdisciplinary approach be used for students in elementary and middle schools today? Before answering this question, consider how a group of children are likely to receive instruction about a specific social studies topic in a school with a conventional approach to its curriculum. Observe how one group was taught about the island nation of Japan during an eight-year period:

In the first grade, children usually study about families. Stories about families from several cultures around the world are read to them; one story might be about a Japanese family. A music teacher may have taught the children a Japanese folk song in the second grade and a traditional Japanese dance in the third grade. In the fourth grade, an art teacher may have had the children experiment with origami. The children also study geographic regions of the world in fourth grade, including some discussion on islands and island nations. Finally, in middle school, the children study aspects of Asian cultures, including the Japanese culture.

The sequence in the description is characteristic of a traditional, or subject-centered, approach to a social studies topic. Instead of being provided with an interdisciplinary inquiry of Japan and Japanese culture at a specific grade level, the students are offered isolated bits of information in a fragmented study that are spread across eight years. Most lessons and activities are taught to the entire class at the same time, and typically, all students are required to meet the same requirements; there is little differentiation of instruction.

At first, it may appear logical to approach a topic this way. We know that adults can internalize related information received over a period of time. However, we also know that it is more difficult for children to do so, particularly because of the differences in their cognitive development and diversity.

The general assumption of the approach described in the Japan example is that students are all able to learn in the same ways and to show what they have learned by completing identical assignments. There is little consideration for what is known about cognition in young children. For example, in 1975, Piaget and Inhelder wrote that thinking in young children is often *centered*; in the child's mind, isolated concepts and bits of information remain unrelated. Later, Gardner (1991) suggested that we know that the mind of a young child—5 to 7 or even 10 years old—is intuitive, resourceful, highly imaginative, and creative. We also know that the same mind is limited by a "tendency to stereotype and simplify. . . . It contains a swirl of symbols, scripts, theories, and incipient notions and concepts, which can be involved in appropriate ways but which also remain to be sorted out in a more secure manner" (pp. 110–111).

In view of these cognitive limitations, an important reason for using an interdisciplinary method is that by using that method, students investigate topics holistically, and there are opportunities to differentiate both in the ways students gain information and show what they have learned. The contrast with the traditional method described in the Japan scenario is evident. As a result, young students may be less likely to misinterpret and more likely to make better sense of their world.

Learner Diversity and Multiple Intelligences—Theories of Sternberg and Gardner

An especially strong argument for differentiation of instruction is evident in Sternberg's (1985) theory. Sternberg proposed that we all possess three kinds of intelligence—*analytical, creative, and practical*; these are accommodated particularly well in interdisciplinary instruction. Sternberg (2006) has also explained the importance of recognizing the diversity that exists among the ways learners process information. Sternberg has found that this is particularly important to recognize in non-mainstream cultural groups, and he supports his theory by citing examples of several cognitive and practical differences he has found among students in Alaskan Eskimo and Kenyan cultures.

Gardner's *multiple intelligences* (MI) theory expands upon Sternberg's three kinds of intelligence (1983, 1993b). Gardner initially proposed that there are at least seven areas of intelligence. Later, he added an eighth intelligence, *naturalist intelligence,* and a ninth, *existential intelligence,* both of which have since been analyzed (Kane, 1999). At first, Gardner was reluctant about including existential intelligence, and he considered it to be a *half-intelligence* mainly because the part of the brain that deals with existential questions was unclear (Gardner, 1999; Smith, 2002). Even so, Gardner (1999) seems to suggest that existential intelligence meets the criteria he has established for an intelligence area. He states: "Perhaps surprisingly, existential intelligence scores reasonably well on the eight criteria. . . . Although empirical psychological evidence is sparse, what exists certainly does not invalidate the construct" (p. 64), and he concludes that "existential intelligence . . . may well be admissible" (p. 64).

It is clear that both Gardner and Sternberg maintain that students process information in multiple ways. An interdisciplinary approach can facilitate these ways because students routinely use multiple sources of information to investigate topics and are encouraged to choose from a variety of media and methods to report their findings. In Gardner's

MI theory, human beings operate in the nine—and possibly more—intelligence areas listed in Figure 1.3.

Gardner suggests that his "theory gives educators a way of thinking about individual gifts and how to accommodate teaching to them" (Brandt, 1988, p. 34). Thus, if students are developing in any or all of these intelligence areas, they need opportunities to grow in the others. Clearly, such opportunities will occur naturally when educators link "the multiple intelligences with a curriculum focused on understanding" (Checkley, 1997, p. 11). This is a primary focus of the interdisciplinary approach. Thus, replacing isolated, subject-centered, disciplinary instruction with interdisciplinary methods in elementary and middle schools may help to facilitate optimal development for our students who have diverse abilities and ways of learning.

Although Gardner's theory is widely accepted among educators, learning theorists, sociologists, and psychologists, its acceptance is not universal. For example, Allis (1999) cites a number of social scientists who hold more traditional views of intelligence and who disagree with multiple intelligences theory. Even though there are concerns about MI theory, it continues to have considerable support among other educators and learning

FIGURE 1.3   Gardner's Multiple Intelligences.

Intelligence	Strength
LINGUISTIC, OR VERBAL, INTELLIGENCE	The ability to use language well and to learn through verbal methods such as reading, note taking, listening, writing summaries and reports, and conducting interviews
LOGICAL–MATHEMATICAL INTELLIGENCE	Using mathematics and logic, forming hypotheses, and conducting scientific inquiries
SPATIAL INTELLIGENCE	Detecting spatial relationships, noticing likenesses and differences visually, creating art and design, and thinking by visualizing in pictures
MUSICAL INTELLIGENCE	Using music as a tool for thinking, demonstrating feelings and attitudes with music, and associating thought with music
BODILY–KINESTHETIC INTELLIGENCE	Using the entire body to help master or to explain ideas and concepts
INTERPERSONAL INTELLIGENCE	Understanding others, working effectively and cooperatively with other people, and sharing tasks and responsibilities
INTRAPERSONAL INTELLIGENCE	Understanding oneself and being able to analyze one's personal performance in order to grow and change
NATURALIST INTELLIGENCE	Recognizing flora and fauna, discriminating among them, and having a sensitivity to phenomena in the natural environment
EXISTENTIAL INTELLIGENCE	Having interest in and raising questions about the meaning of life, death, and why things are the way they are

theorists, including Sylwester (1995, pp. 108–116) who prepared a comprehensive overview of MI theory indicating that it is supported by research on the human brain. Also, many teachers find MI theory to be one that is comparatively easy to relate to and apply practically in their classrooms.

Campbell, Campbell, and Dickinson (2004) have suggested that MI theory supports the interdisciplinary approach: "With MI-based teaching, discrete subject matter distinctions begin to dissolve, enabling teachers to plan interdisciplinary units" (p. 289), and interdisciplinary lessons, ones "that cross subject-area lines," accommodate students' multiple intelligences (Moran, Kornhaber, & Gardner, 2006, p. 25).

Social Interaction: Theories of Piaget and Vygotsky

Students also need opportunities for the kind of social interaction and guidance that teachers and capable peers can provide naturally in interdisciplinary studies. Piaget (1970) believed that social interaction between students and teachers was necessary to develop arbitrary social concepts, but he also cautioned about the use of too much direct verbal instruction or reliance on demonstrations in teaching, especially with very young children. Piaget believed that these approaches might inhibit the development of operational (generalizable, useful) knowledge. In particular, Piaget expressed concern about the use of excessive direct instruction in developing scientific and mathematical knowledge.

It is possible that Piaget may have attributed less importance to the value of the kind of social collaboration that is typical with interdisciplinary methods in fostering the development of some concepts. The value of social interaction in promoting optimal learning is clearer in Vygotsky's (1978, 1986) premise of a *zone of proximal development* (ZPD). According to Vygotsky, the ZPD is "the distance between the actual developmental level as determined by independent problem solving and the level of potential development as determined through problem solving under adult guidance or in collaboration with more capable peers" (1978, p. 86). In the ZPD, Vygotsky is plainly suggesting the importance of instructional methods that promote learning through social interaction among students, teachers, and peers.

Learning theorists agree with Vygotsky about the value of both culture and social interaction in the process of knowledge acquisition. A comprehensive discussion of Vygotsky's theory and the significance of social interaction for student learning is provided by Wertsch (1985), and Case's (1985) Canadian studies of early development also support Vygotsky's theory about the impact of social interaction and instruction in early childhood on children's cognitive development. Case also suggests that interdisciplinary instruction promotes children's problem-solving skills.

In *Acts of Meaning,* Bruner (1990) also discusses the importance of social interaction and the value of adult instruction and *scaffolding*—providing a temporary support system for students until they are able to work independently. In their review of Vygotsky's theory and its implications for classroom practice, Forman, Minick, and Stone (1993) provide a compelling argument for interdisciplinary studies by suggesting that such studies provide natural opportunities for students to interact with one another as well as with their teachers. The authors also stress that this kind of social interaction is essential for optimal learning.

Support from Research on the Human Brain

The interdisciplinary approach is also supported by findings from research on the human brain. In recent years, educators have been examining those findings to determine the need for changes in curriculum and instructional practice. As a result, several educators have prepared research-based materials that can be helpful for teachers.

Robert Sylwester's (1995) straightforward overview of the brain and its functions is a succinct yet comprehensive discussion of this important topic. In his book, Sylwester explains the value of helping students to make connections and detect relationships between what they are taught and their personal experiences. He also mentions teaching techniques that help to foster these links and which are often used by interdisciplinary teachers, including "debates, role playing, simulations, songs, games, films, and novels" (p. 103). Sylwester also recommends activities, such as "student projects, cooperative learning, and portfolio assessments" (p. 132), all of which address diversity in learners and are activities that are routinely found in interdisciplinary instruction.

We also know that learning is more likely to occur when the brain is not threatened. Students need to be willing to risk making mistakes in a classroom environment where they feel that they will not be ridiculed when wrong. Such a safe learning environment can also encourage students to be more honest about what they know and do not know. Honesty and willingness to admit errors are fostered in an atmosphere where the brain is not constantly defending itself from ridicule, either from peers or teachers. Willingness to admit one's errors is one of several *dispositions* or *habits of mind* that also include openness to new ideas, having a questioning attitude, being persistent at tasks, and so on (Heck & Roose, 2005; Wiggins, 1993). These are all ways of thinking that are critical to students' success and which can be fostered through interdisciplinary instruction.

Another implication for the interdisciplinary approach from human brain research indicates the need for holistic studies. It has been found that information learned in isolation tends to remain in isolation and appears to be more difficult for young students to process, recall, and use (Hardiman, 2001; Lowery, 1998; Westwater & Wolfe, 2000).

Although research on the human brain has been the topic of a number of conferences for educators and has stimulated the production of new curriculums and instructional materials, it is important to realize that there is yet no consensus about its educational implications. For example, Jorgenson (2003) has voiced concern about developing curriculum and materials based on human brain research. He recommends that "educators must recognize the limitations of the fledgling cognitive-neuroscience movement as it currently can contribute to our profession" (p. 364). Willingham (2006) has voiced similar concerns about endorsing changes in teaching based on brain research until there is evidence that such changes will make a difference.

Even though the debate over the educational applications of brain research is likely to continue, Eric Jensen (2005) reminds us of findings from brain research suggesting that the brain makes associations and constructs meaning better when it finds patterns like those that interdisciplinary, holistic methods provide. Jensen feels that, in general, interdisciplinary instruction is more meaningful at all age levels because it helps students to note relationships among the various disciplines for the topics they study. He also suggests that interdisciplinary studies may be especially meaningful to older students because they may be more capable of detecting patterns due to their greater knowledge base.

Benefits to Our Diversity of Learners and Students with Special Needs

Another important reason for using the interdisciplinary approach is its effectiveness as an alternative to traditional approaches for students with special needs. In 1975, Public Law 94-142, the Education of All Handicapped Children Act, was enacted, mandating that children with handicapping conditions be placed in the least restrictive instructional environment possible, preferably in regular classrooms. To comply with this regulation, classroom teachers began working with children who were previously taught in special classes apart from other students. At that time, most teachers had little or no preparation for their new role, so they had to experiment on their own and try creative approaches and methods in order to include—not just accommodate—their "new" students.

Many children with special needs must still spend part of the school day in special assistance settings outside their regular classrooms. Their frequent absence from the classroom can make including them in the regular program of activities difficult for teachers. The flexibility afforded by the interdisciplinary approach can help teachers overcome this problem to some extent. Because interdisciplinary units are usually completed over a period of time, not all children need to be present in the classroom at the same time, especially during periods of individual and group research and project development. Those who leave the room for special help can rejoin their classmates and work on unit assignments when they return as well as at other times during the day.

Differentiation of research and reporting techniques is also fostered during an interdisciplinary study. Students are encouraged to use a variety of resources to locate information, so those who have difficulty reading for information can use alternative methods. Such methods include interviewing; studying pictures; listening to recorded books on CDs or audiotapes; viewing DVD or videotaped programs, teacher-prepared computer or DVD presentations; films; and filmstrips. Students can also interact with computer software programs and Web sites on the Internet. Materials can be selected carefully to ensure that minimal reading is required. Reports need not be limited to writing papers or answering questions from a textbook selection. Students can use alternatives that interest them, such as performing demonstrations, painting pictures and murals, and preparing dioramas and other constructions, in order to show the concepts they have gained.

The Use of Multiple Sources of Information

In contrast to the conventional approaches, no single textbook is used exclusively in an interdisciplinary program. Classrooms are equipped with textbooks from many publishers on topics and themes in social studies, science, language arts, and other disciplines. In each classroom, the available materials are written at, below, and above grade level to accommodate as many ability levels as possible. Instead of relying on one or two sources, students consult multiple sources, helping to ensure that they will gain a more inclusive view of history and historical events.

An adequate supply of textbooks is needed for students; in fact it is often helpful to have texts in social studies and other disciplines from several different publishers available for students to use. However, textbooks alone are not sufficient for interdisciplinary studies because they "belong in the reference category, along with encyclopedias, dictionaries, and thesauruses" (Daniels & Zemelman, 2004, p. 36). Students need access to other materials, such as trade books—single topic non-fiction books—and literature related to unit topics. Multimedia items, including DVD and video programs, as well as access to the Internet can provide up-to-date information for students. Some items can usually be borrowed from public and school libraries and media centers.

A variety of materials also helps to ensure that students have access to information about the contributions of all segments of our population. Some topics require that we have resource materials in the classroom that adequately address the diversity of our people as well as historical issues, such as slavery, the Holocaust, the Armenian genocide, as well as human rights issues and world problems that are sometimes given minimal treatment or neglected in a single textbook.

The significance of this kind of exposure for students is effectively dramatized in a statement by Milagros Henriquez (1995) as she accepted an award at her graduation for outstanding work related to multicultural education. "Multicultural education is *basic* education for students in the twenty-first century." In our multicultural society, the interdisciplinary approach offers students access to information that only a rich variety of materials can provide.

Meaningful Applications of Ways of Knowing and Skills in the Academic Disciplines

Most real problems in life are investigated or solved by using more than one discipline. For example, when we purchase a new home, economics is a major factor but not the only one. Location (geography), architectural style (art), nearby educational facilities, and other community resources also need to be considered before a final decision can be made. Interdisciplinary instruction routinely and realistically follows this example by encouraging students to use the ways of knowing associated with any disciplines that can be applied logically to the topics they investigate.

We are all concerned about students' academic skills and with providing sufficient practice in those skills. In many schools, workbook and duplicated exercises may have little or no relationship to the unit studies students are pursuing at a given time. If so, those exercises are simply practice-for-the-sake-of-practice. We know that skills practice as well as the investigation of "almost any subject is best taught when it is needed to accomplish something else" (Wakefield, 1993, p. 137).

The interdisciplinary approach responds to Wakefield's suggestion because it always provides for the application of skills in meaningful contexts. As topics, themes, and problems are explored, students find that they *need* to use their inquiry skills, *need* to read for information, *need* to compose e-mail, letters, and reports, and they often *need* to give oral presentations to their class. Students use mathematical skills as they prepare charts, graphs, and maps; they make use of technology to search for information or invent new designs for their projects; they follow the scientific method while working on related science experiments and activities; and they explore drama, music, and dance and gain experience with various art media. In fact, the interdisciplinary approach can provide so many spontaneous, purposeful opportunities for students to practice their academic skills, prepare projects, and work with construction materials that teachers who have previously used artificial duplicated materials and other conventional practice items may no longer feel the need to use them as often.

Other studies have found that the interdisciplinary approach results in greater enthusiasm on the part of teachers, students, and their parents, higher attendance rates among students, and improvement in standardized test scores (Bolak, K., Bialach, D., & Dunphy, M., 2005). Teaching teams using the interdisciplinary approach in middle schools have expressed greater job satisfaction and have found that their students achieve at higher levels [Flowers, Mertens, & Mulhall (1999)].

In summary, the rationale and support for interdisciplinary instruction includes:

- Gardner's theory of multiple intelligences and the importance of social interaction in the learning process
- Support from research on the human brain
- Benefits to our diversity of learners and students with special needs
- The benefits derived from the use of multiple sources of information
- Meaningful applications of the ways of knowing and skills in the academic disciplines
- Increased enthusiasm of teachers, students, and parents and increases in scores on standardized examinations

Summary

The discussion in this chapter has attempted to clarify the underlying theoretical base and rationale and to establish the framework for designing interdisciplinary and multidisciplinary units of instruction. Chapter 2 will focus on requirements of interdisciplinary teachers and challenges to interdisciplinary programs in the schools today.

ACTIVITY

Read the following description of how two fifth grade teachers introduce a new unit on *Westward Expansion* to their classes. Consider the distinguishing features of the interdisciplinary approach that have been outlined in this chapter and the main differences between the ways the two teachers approached the same unit study.

Ryan Jackson teaches fifth grade in an urban elementary school. His students are ready to begin studying a new unit on an important topic in American history for the next several weeks. During the usual time for social studies, Mr. J. began his introduction to the topic with several questions. First, he asked the students to relate anything they know about how our country grew from the original thirteen states to its present size. One student, Emily, said that she thought that new land was bought by the United States after the Revolutionary War. Another student, Bryan, said he believed that there were wars that were fought to take over new land. Other students offered several additional ideas. While the students were contributing their thoughts, Mr. J. made a list of what the students said they knew or thought they knew on the board at the front of the room. He recorded what the students said without editing their responses or commenting about the ideas they expressed.

After the students had no additional contributions, Mr. J. stated that the new study the students would be pursuing was one that would explore what is known historically as the period of *Westward Expansion,* an important topic in American history. Then, he asked the students what they would first need to do to prepare for the study. One student, Jimmy, said that they would need to search the Internet for information. Aisha, another student, said that they would need to know what they wanted to find out before they could do that. Then another student, Katherine, said she agreed with Aisha and that they would need to make a list of some questions before they would be able to begin their study. At that point, Mr. J. explained that he also agreed that the class would need to prepare questions for the study and that making such a list would be the first task.

Mr. J. then gave the students an assignment in preparation for the next social studies period. Everyone was asked to make a list of three questions that he or she thought would be helpful in exploring *Westward Expansion.* During the next research period, their questions would be listed on the board, and discussion would be held to determine the most important questions that the class would research. He also explained that, at that time, a decision would also have to be made about how to approach the research, and he suggested two possible ways to proceed. The questions could be divided among several student committees, or everyone could undertake researching all the questions. To end the lesson, Mr. J. asked students if they had any questions about what they needed to do before the next class.

In another fifth grade class, Grace McAllister was also beginning a new study of *Westward Expansion.* She started the first lesson during her regular time for social studies by asking the students to take out their social studies textbooks. When the students appeared to be ready, Ms. M. told the students to turn to page 168 in their books, and then she asked one of the students, Michael, to read the title of the chapter on that page. Michael read: "Westward Expansion: The Growth of the Union". Ms. M. then asked the students if they had any ideas about what the title meant. One student, Allison, said that it probably meant that people were going west. Another student, Shannon, said that it could mean that our country is growing in some way. Several other students offered ideas that were similar.

Next, Ms. M. told Anthony, another student, to begin reading the chapter aloud. After he had read one paragraph, another student was asked to continue. The entire chapter was read in this manner—each student reading a paragraph at a time. At the end of the reading, the students were told to take out a sheet of paper and to answer a set of 10 questions about Westward Expansion at the end of the chapter for homework. Ms. M. also explained that answers to the questions would be collected the next day.

- How does each teacher involve students in the study of the topic?
- Which of the two classes do you think will engender the greatest interest in the topic? Why?
- Consider each of the distinguishing features of the interdisciplinary approach that are reviewed in this chapter. Which teacher has planned an interdisciplinary study? Cite evidence from the descriptions to support your answer.

REFERENCES

Allis, S. (1999, July 11). The master of unartificial intelligence: Howard Gardner's definition of "smart" still sparks controversy. *The Boston Sunday Globe,* pp. D1–D5.

Are there multiple intelligences? Retrieved January 13, 2006 from http://www.sq.4mg.com/MIcriticisms .htm

Beane, J. A. (1995). Curriculum planning and development. *Phi Delta Kappan, 76*(8), 616–622.

Beane, J. A. (1997). *Curriculum integration: Designing the core of democratic education.* New York: Teachers College Press.

Bolak, K., Bialach, D., & Dunphy, M. (May 2005). Standards-based, thematic units integrate the arts and energize students and teachers. *Middle School Journal, 31(2),* 57–60.

Brandt, R. (1988). On assessment in the arts: A conversation with Howard Gardner. *Educational Leadership, 45*(4), 30–34.

Brooks, J. G., & Brooks, M. G. (1999). *In search of understanding: The case for constructivist classrooms* (Rev. ed.). Alexandria, VA: Association for Supervision and Curriculum Development.

Bruner, J. (1990). *Acts of meaning.* Cambridge, MA: Harvard University Press.

Campbell, L., Campbell, B., & Dickinson, D. (2004). *Teaching and learning through multiple intelligences* (3rd ed.). Boston: Pearson Education.

Carolan, J., & Guinn, A. (2007, February). Differentiation: Lessons from master teachers. *Educational Leadership 64*(5), 44–47.

Case, R. (1985). *Intellectual development: Birth to adulthood.* Orlando, FL: Academic Press.

Channon, G. (1970). *Homework.* New York: Outerbridge & Dienstfrey.

Chatterton, R. (1968). *The multidisciplinary teaching of class research topics.* Merrick, NY: Merrick School District No. 25.

Checkley, K. (1997). The first seven and the eighth. *Educational Leadership, 55*(1), 8–13.

Cross-subject teaching [Film]. (1993). West Haven, CT: National Education Association. (Episode No. 4, NEA Professional Library).

Daniels, H., & Zemelman, S. (2004). Out with textbooks, in with learning. *Educational Leadership, 61*(4), 36–40.

Dewey, J. (1916). *Democracy and education.* New York: Free Press.

Early elementary resources guide. (1996). Albany, NY: University of the State of New York, State Education Department.

Encarta world dictionary. (1999). New York: St. Martin's Press.

Fizzell, R. (1984). The status of learning styles. *The Educational Forum, 48*(3), 303–312.

Flowers, N., Mertens, S. B., & Mulhall, P. F. (November 1999). The impact of teaming: Five research-based outcomes. *Middle School Journal, 36*(5), 9–19.

Forman, E. A., Minick, N., & Stone, C. A. (1993). *Contexts for learning.* New York: Oxford University Press.

Gardner, H. (1983). *Frames of mind: The theory of multiple intelligences.* New York: Basic Books.

Gardner, H. (1991). *The unschooled mind: How children think and how schools should teach.* New York: Basic Books.

Gardner, H. (1993a). *Creating minds.* New York: Basic Books.

Gardner, H. (1993b). *Multiple intelligences: The theory in practice.* New York: Basic Books.

Gardner, H. (1999). *Intelligence reframed: Multiple intelligences for the 21st century.* New York: Basic Books.

Hardiman, M. M. (2001, November). Connecting brain research with dimensions of learning. *Educational Leadership, 59*(3), 52–55.

Heck, M., & Roose, D. (2005). Dispositions as habits of body, mind, and spirit: Quaker and Native American perspectives. In Smith, R. L., Skarbek, D., & Hurst, J. (Eds.). *The passion of teaching: Dispositions in the schools.* Lanham, MD: Scarecrow Education.

Henriquez, M. (Speaker). (1995). Acceptance speech at the academic awards ceremony of the Teacher Education Program at the State University of New York/College at Old Westbury.

Jacobs, H. (Ed.). (1989). *Interdisciplinary curriculum: Design and implementation.* Alexandria, VA: Association for Supervision and Curriculum Development.

Jensen, E. (2005). *Teaching with the brain in mind* (2nd ed.). Alexandria, VA: Association for Supervision and Curriculum Development.

Jorgenson, O. (2003). Brain scam? Why educators should be careful about embracing 'brain research'. *The Educational Forum, 67*(4), 364–369.

Kane, J. (1999). *Education, information, and transformation: Essays on learning and thinking.* Upper Saddle River, NJ: Pearson/Merrill Prentice Hall.

Kornhaber, M., Fierros, E., & Veenema, S. (2004). *Multiple intelligences: Best ideas from research and practice.* Boston: Pearson/Allyn & Bacon.

Learning styles and the brain. (1990). *Educational Leadership, 48*(2), 4–81.

Lowery, L. (1998, November). How new science curriculums reflect brain research. *Educational Leadership, 56*(3), 26–30.

Michaelis, J. U., & Garcia, J. (2000). *Social studies for children: A guide to basic instruction* (2nd ed.) Boston: Pearson/Allyn & Bacon.

Minnesota Board of Teaching. (2006, January). *Report to the legislature.* Retrieved January 10, 2006 from http://children.state.mn.us/mdeprod/groups/Communications/documents/Report/008666.pdf

Montessori, M. (2002). La maestra: Lecture 2. *Communications, Association Montessori Internationale, 4,* 6–10.

Moran, S., Kornhaber, M., & Gardner, H. (2006). Orchestrating multiple intelligences. *Educational Leadership, 64*(1), 22–27.

Pappas, C. C., Kiefer, B. Z., & Levstik, L. S. (2006). *An integrated language perspective in the elementary school* (4th ed.). Boston: Pearson/Allyn & Bacon.

Parker, W. C. (2005). *Social studies in elementary education* (12th ed.). Upper Saddle River, NJ: Pearson/Merrill Prentice Hall.

Piaget, J. (1970). *Science of education and the psychology of the child* (D. Coltman, Trans.). New York: Orion Press.

Piaget, J., & Inhelder, B. (1975). *The origin of the idea of chance in children.* New York: Norton.

Reed, J. S., & Bergmann, V. E. (1995). *In the classroom: An introduction to education* (2nd ed.). Guilford, CT: Dushkin.

Richardson, E. S. (1969). *In the early world: Discovering art through crafts.* New York: Pantheon Books.

Slatin, C., Galizzi, M., Devereaux Melillo, K., & Mawn, B. (2004, January-February). Conducting interdisciplinary research to promote healthy and safe employment in health care: Promises and pitfalls. *Public Health Reports,* (119), 62.

Smith, M. K. (2002). Howard Gardner, multiple intelligences and education. In *The encyclopedia of informal education.* Retrieved from http://www.infed.org/thinkers/gardner.htm

Sternberg, R. J. (1985). *Beyond IQ: A triarchic theory of human intelligence.* New York: Cambridge University Press.

Sternberg, R. J. (2006). Recognizing neglected strengths. *Educational Leadership, 64*(1), 30–35.

Sylwester, R. (1995). *A celebration of neurons: An educator's guide to the human brain.* Alexandria, VA: Association for Supervision and Curriculum Development.

Tomlinson, C. (2001). *How to differentiate instruction in mixed-ability classrooms* (2nd ed.). Alexandria, VA: Association for Supervision and Curriculum Development.

Vygotsky, L. S. (1978). *Mind in society: The development of higher psychological processes.* Cambridge, MA: Harvard University Press.

Vygotsky, L. S. (1986). *Thought and language* (New rev. ed.). Cambridge, MA: MIT Press.

Wakefield, A. P. (1993). Developmentally appropriate practice: "Figuring things out." *The Educational Forum, 57*(2), 134–143.

Wertsch, J. V. (1985). *Vygotsky and the social formation of the mind.* Cambridge, MA: Harvard University Press.

Westwater, A., & Wolfe, P. (2000, November). The brain-compatible curriculum. *Educational Leadership, 58*(3), 49–53.

Wiggins, G. (1993). *Assessing student performance.* San Francisco: Jossey-Bass.

Wiggins, G., & McTighe, J. (2005). *Understanding by design* (2nd ed.). Alexandria VA: Association of Supervision & Curriculum Development.

Williams-Boyd, P. (2003). *Middle grades education: A reference handbook.* Santa Barbara, CA: ABC-CLIO.

Willingham, D. T. (2006, Fall). "Brain-based" learning: More fiction and fact. *American Educator, 30*(3), pp. 27–32 ff.

SUGGESTED READINGS

The following are additional recommended readings on selected topics that are included in this chapter. Some are classic writings; others are recent publications on these topics.

Learning and Diversity

The following are several classic readings on development and learning that may be found to be helpful in explaining the theories of Piaget and others.

Battalio, R. (2005, Fall). Setting the stage for a diverse audience. *Kappa Delta Pi Record 42*(1), 24–27.

Flavell, J. H., Green, F. L., & Flavell, E. R. (1995). *Young children's knowledge about thinking.* Chicago: Society for Research in Child Development, University of Chicago Press.

Forman, G. E., & Kuschner, D. S. (1977). *The child's construction of knowledge.* Monterey, CA: Brooks/Cole.

Furth, H. G., & Wachs, H. (1974). *Thinking goes to school.* New York: Oxford University Press.

Hersh, R. H., Paolitto, D. P., & Reinger, J. (1983). *Promoting moral growth: From Piaget to Kohlberg* (Rev. ed.). New York: Longman.

Phillips, J. L. (1981). *Piaget's theory: A primer.* San Francisco: Freeman.

Putnam, J. (1997). *Cooperative learning in diverse classrooms.* Upper Saddle River, NJ: Pearson/Merrill Prentice Hall.

Schwebel, M., & Raph, J. (Eds.). (1973). *Piaget in the classroom.* New York: Basic Books.

Wadsworth, B. J. (1978). *Piaget for the classroom teacher.* New York: Longman.

Wadsworth, B. J. (2004). *Piaget's theory of cognitive and affective development* (5th ed.). Boston: Pearson/Allyn & Bacon.

Instructional Methodology

The following sources support the interdisciplinary, multidisciplinary, and integrated instructional approaches.

Bruner, J. (1960). *The process of education.* New York: Vintage Books.

Charbonneau, M. P., & Reider, B. E. (1995). *The integrated elementary classroom: A developmental model of education for the 21st century.* BosBoston: Pearson/Allyn & Bacon.

Dewey, J. (1933). *How we think.* Boston: Heath.

Dewey, J. (1938). *Experience and education.* London: Collier–Macmillan.

Jacob, S. H. (1982a). Piaget and education: Aspects of a theory. *The Educational Forum, 46*(2), 265–282.

Jacob, S. H. (1982b). Piaget and education: Aspects of a theory. *The Educational Forum, 46*(3), 221–238.

Katz, L., & Chard, S. C. (2000). *Engaging children's minds: The project approach* (2nd ed.). Stamford, CT: Ablex.

Kauchak, D. P., & Eggen, P. D. (2007). *Learning and teaching: Research-based methods* (5th ed.). Boston: Pearson/Allyn & Bacon.

Kindsvatter, R., Wilen, W., & Ishler, M. (2004). *Dynamics of effective teaching* (3rd ed.). White Plains, NY: Longman.

Martinello, M. L., & Cook, G. E. (2000). *Interdisciplinary inquiry in teaching and learning* (2nd ed.). Upper Saddle River, NJ: Pearson/Merrill Prentice Hall.

Multiple Intelligences Theory

The sources listed below provide some of the initial writings about Gardner's theory of multiple intelligences.

Campbell, L., Campbell, B., & Dickinson, D. (2004). *Teaching and learning through multiple intelligences* (3rd ed.). Boston: Pearson/Allyn & Bacon.

Gardner, H. (1982). *Art, mind, and brain: A cognitive approach to creativity.* New York: Basic Books.

Gardner, H. (1985). *The mind's new science: A history of the cognitive revolution.* New York: Basic Books.

Gardner, H., Feldman, D. H., & Krechevsky, M. (Eds.). (1998). *Project Zero frameworks for early childhood education: Vol. 1. Building on children's strengths: The experience of Project Spectrum.* New York: Teachers College Press.

Kornhaber, M., Fierros, E., & Veenema, S. (2004). *Multiple intelligences: Best ideas from research and practice.* Boston: Pearson Education.

CHAPTER

2

Requirements and Challenges of Interdisciplinary Instruction

Middle school teaching team planning a new multidisciplinary unit.

OVERVIEW

This chapter provides a review of the following:

- Teaching requirements for interdisciplinary instruction
- Challenges to the development of interdisciplinary programs

Implementing Interdisciplinary Instruction:
Requirements of Teachers

What does interdisciplinary instruction require of teachers? While interdisciplinary instruction can offer an excellent alternative to more traditional methods, to be comfortable with it, we need:

- A compatible philosophy of education;
- A considerable store of knowledge;
- Excellent skills in classroom management;
- Skill in planning interdisciplinary and multidisciplinary units;
- Skills in the use of instructional technology; and
- The ability to collaborate with others in the school community.

A Compatible Educational Philosophy

A primary factor to consider when deciding to use the interdisciplinary approach is our philosophical compatibility with it. Today, the *constructivist* philosophy is one that is clearly compatible with the interdisciplinary approach. Constructivism values student diversity and advocates instruction that places students at the center of any learning. It is a democratic philosophy, and it fosters the idea that students need to process and construct knowledge for themselves. The primary role of the teacher is to provide pathways for students, and sources for them to use as they strive to gain new knowledge. The teacher assumes the role of *master learner* among students, not the one who is responsible for transmitting knowledge to them. A constructivist teacher works to differentiate instruction to accommodate the many needs of individual students. She knows and shares learning techniques and processes with her students.

Kimpston, Williams, and Stockton (1992) discuss the relationship between various philosophies of education and teaching methods. Their analysis indicates that the *experimentalist* and *reconstructionist* philosophies are also compatible with the interdisciplinary approach. This is true mainly because those philosophies also emphasize respect for student diversity and the importance of promoting the processes involved in learning. Experimentalism—often called *progresivism*—stresses the importance of considering the *whole child* and of the need for active participation and experimentation by learners in education. Reconstructionism focuses on the study of social topics which often form the basis of interdisciplinary studies. Teachers who subscribe to these philosophies are therefore more likely to feel comfortable with interdisciplinary instruction than those who do not.

General and Child Development Knowledge

We are aware of the need to develop sufficient background knowledge for the content areas we teach. In addition to a good fund of general knowledge, we also need to be skilled researchers in order to guide our students through the research processes involved in their interdisciplinary studies. It is also important to remember that our knowledge and skills can help to ensure that we are able to provide what Vygotsky (1978) has referred to as *scaffolding*—supporting students temporarily while encouraging them to become independent and to accept responsibility for their own learning as soon as they are able to do so. In a related discussion, Montessori (1912) refers to the tendency of teachers and other adults to assume the role of *servants* when working with students. She makes her point dramatically: "In reality, he who is served is limited in his independence" (p. 97). Independence can only be achieved by students when we avoid giving more help than they need by supplying answers to problems they can solve on their own.

Equally important, we need to have a thorough background in theories of learning and be able to apply our understandings of cognitive and affective development when planning for instruction. An awareness of diversity in students' thinking and reasoning abilities can help us tailor instructions more effectively for students who work at different levels. Lillard (1972) has stressed that developing observation skills is the key to such awareness; others, including Armstrong (2009) and Kornhaber, Fierros, and Veenema (2004), show practical ways to design lessons and activities that address the diverse ways students learn. Brooks and Brooks (1999) relate contemporary developmental theory with classroom practice and offer alternatives to traditional textbook learning activities that are especially useful for interdisciplinary teachers. Clearly, by making use of our knowledge of students' diverse abilities and their individual ways of learning, we can design effective interdisciplinary studies.

Classroom Management Skills

Planning, scheduling, assessment, record-keeping, and behavioral management skills are all directly related to success in managing a well-organized classroom. Several suggestions for managing student behavior are described below; discussions of unit and lesson planning strategies as well as assessment techniques are included in discussions in Chapters 3–6.

It is especially important to recognize the need to maintain appropriate student behavior in any classroom. The ability to use the interdisciplinary approach "and behavior management have a close relationship" (Johnson, Rice, Edgington, & Williams, 2005, p. 29). Management of behavior is critical for success in teaching; it is critical for interdisciplinary and multidisciplinary studies because a great deal of activity usually occurs during unit work. At those times, it is necessary to manage several student activities simultaneously. Both formal and informal work periods are needed, so we need to be flexible and willing to adapt to the unique types and levels of activity that arise. At the same time, we need to be sensitive to the often-subtle difference between student actions that are productive and those that are potentially chaotic.

Johnson, Rice, Edgington, and Williams (2005) suggest "that behavior management must involve a *proactive* rather than a *reactive* approach; teachers find that many potential problems or challenges can be prevented" (p. 32). Experienced teachers have found that the following suggestions can help improve students' behavior while maintaining a healthy emotional climate for any approach, including interdisciplinary instruction. The following suggestions are useful general guidelines for behavior management.

Maintain a Professional Approach to Discipline.   During the course of an interdisciplinary study, students frequently work together on research and projects. Certainly, it is important that they show respect for their peers during times when they are working closely together.

We can set an example for students by being polite to them. To avoid embarrassing them, we should always discipline students privately. We need to keep from demonstrating anger and be brief, but firm, when administering corrective measures.

Encourage Student Participation.   Students need to be active participants as they pursue the study of interdisciplinary topics. It is important from the first day of a school year that we invite their participation. When students find a classroom that is completely prepared with displays, pictures, charts, and so on the first day of school, they may feel that their participation is not invited.

Interdisciplinary studies offer opportunities for students to become involved in decision-making. It is not always possible for students to determine all of the topics they study due to state regulations and standards; however, it is possible "to open up a discussion in which members of the class try to figure out together why someone apparently thought the subject was important enough to be required" (Kohn, 2006, p. 257). Students can, however, be involved in deciding titles for their required interdisciplinary studies; they can participate in preparing bulletin boards, creating murals, and deciding how to display their reports, art, and construction projects. Students who share ownership of their classroom and the activities that go on in it are likely to assume more responsibility for how it is used (Pappas et al., 2006).

Develop Standards for Appropriate Behavior.   "In the first month or two in a classroom, the children and the teacher go through a period of mutual exploration and of growing trust" (Channon, 1970, p. 50). Students usually have a good general idea about what is and what is not appropriate behavior. Asking them to participate in deciding about classroom rules at the beginning of a school year is a fairly standard practice. While it can help to ensure that they at least know what the rules are, students often simply suggest the rules we already have in mind. Kohn (2006) gives us three reasons why generating rules at the beginning of a year may not be as productive as we may think:

> . . . rules turn children into lawyers, scanning for loopholes and caveats, narrowing the discussion to technicalities when a problem occurs. . . . teachers into police officers, a role utterly at odds with being facilitators of learning . . . usually enfold within them a punitive consequence for breaking them. (pp.72–73)

Whether we invite students to outline the rules or not, it will be especially important to establish our expectations for students' behavior during the frequent research periods and group activities that interdisciplinary studies require. Instead of creating lengthy lists of rules to post, it may be more useful to hold community discussions periodically to think about ways to foster positive behavior in the classroom.

Be Consistent with Behavior Expectations.   Students expect their teachers to be fair. Fairness means maintaining the class rules that have been established, avoiding favoritism, and sharing one's attention among students as equitably as possible.

Remain Alert.   Students look to their teachers for guidance. They expect us to exercise our natural authority as adults, provide clear directions, and have reasonable expectations, both for their behavior and for their academic work during the course of an interdisciplinary study. We must constantly be aware of everything that is happening in the classroom. This can be particularly difficult in interdisciplinary instruction because students often work on projects and research both individually and in groups during lengthy work periods.

Maintain Physical Proximity with Students.   During the work periods associated with interdisciplinary instruction, simply walking closer to students who are not behaving well lets them know that we are aware of what they are doing. Proximity alone can often correct minor problems, such as occasional off-task behavior or failure to share responsibilities in a committee or cooperative group activity.

Avoid Overreacting.   Try not to overreact. This is especially important when rules are broken or when students who usually behave well suddenly present a problem. At such times, we should analyze the situation before reacting.

Expect the Unexpected.   We cannot prevent surprises from ever arising when teaching. It is therefore important to be prepared for them and not be discouraged when they occur. Planning carefully will usually help us to be better prepared when something goes awry during a lesson or an activity period. Although unexpected events can be disconcerting, they can also be informative, even refreshing.

Try Different Approaches to Problem Behavior.   In an emotionally healthy classroom environment, it is usually only a few students who need constant reminding about their behavior. Although the goal should always be to help students learn to control their own behavior, we may need, at least temporarily, to accept responsibility for students who are not able or willing to do so.

Although it may be necessary to intervene and take responsibility for a student's behavior for a time, our ultimate aim must be what Maria Montessori maintained was essential in student/teacher relationships, a gradual process of transferring responsibility during which the student is helped to become "the ever more active partner and the teacher the more passive" (Standing, 1957, p. 303).

Be Creative When Handling Annoying Behaviors.   Students can become argumentative while working in committees for their interdisciplinary study. We can ask students who complain about one another to put their complaints in writing before we attempt to make judgments. Sometimes complaints seem less important to students after they take the time to write about them. Ellis (2007) recommends that teachers have students solve classroom management problems by applying the same inquiry skills they would use to investigate other problems. Doing so keeps the focus on ways to solve problems instead of focusing on who to blame.

Lesson and Unit Planning Skills

Learning how to design lessons that interest students, involve them, address their diverse styles of learning, and that provide adequate guidance are as important for interdisciplinary instruction as with other methods. A number of useful lesson planning *protocols* are already available to make the lesson planning task somewhat easier. A protocol is a useful, step-by-step method of organizing for a specific kind of instruction. Protocols have been developed for instruction in various disciplines, including areas of literacy; listening and viewing lessons; experiments in science; and for teaching skills in mathematics and other areas. Other planning procedures can help in structuring research projects and organizing field trips. These lesson planning protocols are explained along with examples in Chapter 5.

Teachers who use the interdisciplinary approach also need to be skillful in designing comprehensive interdisciplinary and multidisciplinary units of study. In the early grades, interdisciplinary unit planning requires ingenuity and creativity to design lessons related to a unit topic or theme and its objectives. Students in intermediate grades and middle school are able to undertake more sophisticated forms of research; this requires that we have a thorough understanding of research processes. Interdisciplinary and multidisciplinary unit planning are explained and illustrated with examples in Chapters 3 and 4.

Skills in the Application of Technology for Interdisciplinary Instruction

Today, it is essential that all teachers as well as those who plan for interdisciplinary instruction become skilled in the uses of technology and its many applications. Telecommunications through the computer and interactive computer programs have become essential tools for students and teachers alike. Technology is cited as a discipline in most state curriculum guides, and it is addressed in state curriculums and learning standards. Instead of teaching technology as a separate subject in elementary and middle schools, it should be integrated across the curriculum. The emphasis in schools and colleges of education is primarily on this kind of integration. Following are several ways this is evident.

Many elementary and middle schools are now connected to one another via the Internet and through networking services to colleges and universities. Video conferencing hardware is installed in some schools to promote interaction among students in many parts of the country and other countries.

Elementary and middle school students design their own Web sites, where they publish and share their ideas, writing, and projects with others. Most word processing programs can convert documents prepared by students to the hypertext markup language (HTML) format required for Web pages. Special software programs, such as *Web Workshop* from Sunburst Communications, are available in versions appropriate for students from Grade 2 to Grade 12. The software enables students to easily prepare their materials for posting on the Internet. Older students can learn to use more advanced software, such as Microsoft Front Page and Publisher.

Using the Internet, "Learners can go anywhere in the world on virtual field trips; they can perform scientific experiments; and they can engage in real-time research" (Recesso and Orrill, 2008, p. 4). Students can learn to conduct conventional searches and elaborate WebQuests for information on the topics they are investigating. A WebQuest involves more than a simple search for information on a topic because a carefully planned set of steps are followed during the search process. March (2003) explains that "a real WebQuest is a scaffolded learning structure . . ." and that "the best WebQuests inspire students to see richer thematic relationships, to contribute to the real world of learning, and to reflect on their own metacognitive processes" (p. 42).

As an important part of the search process, students learn how to locate the most reliable sources by using Web sites with Uniform Resource Locator (URL)—or Internet address—suffixes such as .org (professional organizations), .gov (government sources), and .edu (educational institutions). In addition to learning the use of suffix identification, we can teach students to apply a number of other criteria, such as contacting a Webmaster about a document or a site they are considering for a report. Kathy Schrock (2006) has prepared a helpful set of criteria that elementary and middle school students can use when they are attempting to determine the validity of sources they locate on the Internet. In addition to the URL, Schrock suggests careful perusal of other information on a Web site, such as the author and the author's credentials, the purpose of the site, documentation of sources, links to other related sites, and the date of posting.

Wikis and *blogs* provide students with opportunities to collaborate with others on projects and to voice their opinions on the interdisciplinary topics they are studying. Students can sign up for a *wiki* Web site that allows them to contribute or modify information, to raise questions, and offer suggestions to others who visit the site. It is simple to use with only three menu items. The *Edit* menu permits users to construct new Web pages or modify existing pages using simple word processing techniques; they click on *Save* to save any changes; and *Links* allows students to link new pages to others.

A *blog* is a type of Web log that can be created at a number of sites on the Internet. Students can include ideas, comment on events, or contribute other material, such as stories, poetry, and various reports. The blog differs from a wiki in that it is the sole property of the person who creates it. Thus, a wiki is useful for cooperative group efforts while the blog is an opportunity for individual students to post their work.

Students can also access electronic copies of original documents on the Internet for their research of historical topics from the Library of Congress and other Web sites. Some museum and institute Web sites include works of art and demonstrations.

As students gather information for their interdisciplinary studies, conventional technology resources are also useful, including interactive DVD programs and comprehensive electronic versions of dictionaries, thesauruses, atlases, and encyclopedias which are readily available on CD-ROM. They can utilize multimedia program resources, including the latest versions of such well-known programs as *Rainforest, Oregon Trail,* and the *Carmen Sandiego* series. Students can develop their own time lines—in either English or Spanish—with TimeLiner, distributed by Tom Snyder Productions.

To prepare reports of their interdisciplinary investigations, students can learn to use word processing, spreadsheet, and database software; accrue data from multiple sources, take notes, write papers, write letters; and make use of e-mail. They can also learn to use desktop publishing as well as Microsoft's *PowerPoint* presentation software and *Inspiration* or *Kidspiration* graphic organizers.

Resources for Teachers.   Technology offers us new interactive tools for instruction that we can use to assist the diversity of students we find in our classes today. Through the Internet and other forms of technology mentioned in previous page, we can offer students extra help and practice not always available in texts and other conventional materials.

Online services afford opportunities to exchange lesson and unit plans throughout the United States and to interact with groups of teachers with similar interests in interdisciplinary instruction. One of the most popular and helpful sources is the Kathy Schrock Web site at http://school.discovery.com/schrockguide/ which was mentioned earlier for its helpful list of criteria for evaluating Web sites. This Web site also includes other resources for teachers, such as lesson planning tools and examples, and other materials on curriculum, homework, clip art, and so on.

We can use computer presentation software and digital photography to prepare slide shows to use along with other teaching techniques. Even in the primary grades, students and their teachers can learn to use digital cameras effectively (Pastor & Kerns, 1997). Digital and video cameras may be used to record students' projects and to develop multimedia records of oral reports, field trips, and other investigations. Local organizations, such as community library systems and the United Federation of Teachers' New York City Teacher Centers Consortium, give teachers access to technical and instructional assistance to help them integrate the computer and other technology in their teaching.

Several commercial companies produce interdisciplinary units. The plans vary in quality, so if they are used, they will need to be adapted for different student groups. For example, Good Apple offers instructional materials designed specifically for young children. The New York Times Company publishes numerous instructional plans on topics suited to older groups in middle schools and secondary schools. Sunburst Communications has produced numerous programs in nearly every discipline for students at all age levels. This company is also responsible for well-known interdisciplinary units called *Voyage of the Mimi I and II*—plans that include guidebooks for teachers, a CD-ROM collection, and accompanying materials for students.

Educational television continues to play a role in some areas of the United States. For example, Public Broadcasting Service (PBS) television stations (pbs.org/teachers) offer lesson plans on historical and other topics. Some PBS stations also air educational programs designed for instruction at various grade levels. Program guides include topical references and complete descriptions of each program that are prepared in advance. PBS Teacher Source is an online service for teachers of students in kindergarten through Grade 12. The service includes pre-designed interdisciplinary problems that are offered at three general levels: Grades K–2, Grades 3–5, and middle school.

Online services devoted to educational purposes allow teachers to help students investigate topics individually, in cooperative learning groups within their classrooms, and with students in other schools. Excellent examples of such services include National Geographic's Web site (nationalgeographic.com), Smithsonian Kids (si.edu/kids), and the International Education and Resource Network (iEARN) (iearn.org).

The Internet, educational television, computer software programs, digital cameras, and telecommunications tools will supplement—not replace—other ways of teaching and learning. Teachers who plan to use interdisciplinary instruction will continue to use conventional audiovisual materials: DVD and videotape recorders, monitors, film and filmstrip projectors, overhead projectors, and audiotape recorders. Newer types of equipment, such as smart boards and liquid crystal display (LCD) projectors, are rapidly becoming standard in elementary and middle schools as well.

Collaboration with Others in the School Community

Opportunities are always possible for collaboration among teachers who use the interdisciplinary approach. Cooperation between the classroom teacher and specialists is a form of *team teaching* that can contribute significantly to the interdisciplinarity and quality of instructional units. We often work cooperatively with others in specialty areas such as art, music, physical education, special education, and with the school nurse, custodians, or others in the school environment. If specialty area teachers are notified when classroom teachers are planning new unit studies, they may be able to include lessons or activities that contribute to the study. For example, an art teacher may reserve a class period for instructing students on a papier-mâché project that relates to their current unit work. It is possible that after observing the process followed by the specialist, we may be able to use it ourselves without help in the future to generate more creative activities during another unit.

Collaboration is not restricted to cooperative work with specialists. In some elementary and middle schools, interdepartmental teams are organized. For example, a four-teacher interdepartmental teaching team may include a social studies teacher, literacy or English teacher, a science teacher, and a mathematics teacher. The team may be assigned either a block of time or separate periods in which to work with a group of students. The teachers have a scheduled time for planning in which they design interdisciplinary or multidisciplinary units, decide how to allocate the time in their block, develop the unit objectives, plan for assessment, and determine how they will each relate lessons in their classes to the unit topic or theme.

Teachers of art, music, health, and physical education may also work with the team as consultants for these special aspects of a study. Ideally, students are included in the planning sessions; this kind of student participation in the planning process has been found to have considerable value in interdisciplinary instruction (Stevenson & Carr, 1993). Inviting student participation in the planning process presents students with a working model of democratic organization. A way to organize a multidisciplinary unit by a middle school team of teachers in a departmental structure is explained in greater detail in Chapter 4.

In schools with self-contained classes, another team-teaching structure can be arranged. This structure usually involves two or more teachers who combine their classes and work cooperatively with the same students. This plan requires that teachers designate the specific areas of expertise they will offer students. The teachers can rotate serving as the main instructor while the others assist; however, all teachers are involved in teaching academic skills and processes. As in the case of departmentalized plans, teachers in self-contained teams must have time reserved in their regular teaching schedule to plan together. This time is also used to share knowledge of individual students' progress, interests, strengths, needs, and limitations in the different skill areas as well as to review the teaming process itself.

Departmental and self-contained team-teaching arrangements are both compatible with the interdisciplinary approach and are based on sound child developmental principles. Because team members work as a unit, instruction can be consistently and genuinely interdisciplinary or multidisciplinary rather than divided into unrelated disciplinary studies.

Both of these structures can be designed so that they afford teachers scheduled time to plan together and to exchange information on the progress of individual students. When a teaching team lacks administrative support or common planning time, it is far more difficult for the team to approach a study using an interdisciplinary or multidisciplinary approach. Instead, as students move from teacher to teacher, subjects are more likely to be taught in isolation.

Challenges to the Development of Interdisciplinary Programs

Many challenges confront us as teachers today, so planning for interdisciplinary instruction may not seem urgent, especially when compared with raising test scores. Accommodating an increasing diversity of learners and planning for differentiation of instruction are also some of the more significant demands we face today. Requests to change are indeed not new in our profession. In 1995, Miller listed the following:

> Teachers are told that they have to set higher standards for all students, eliminate tracking, tailor lessons to kids' individual needs (including those with various disabilities), adopt small-group and cooperative learning techniques, design interdisciplinary and multicultural curricula, work in teams with other teachers, promote "critical" and "creative" thinking instead of rote learning, attend to children's social and emotional needs, rely on "perform-ance assessment" instead of multiple-choice tests, get with the latest technology, encourage active learning in "real-life" contexts, use fewer textbooks, and, on top of everything else, become "agents of change" in their schools. (p. 2)

Some of the factors—both positive and negative—that tend to affect making changes, particularly changes that result in movement toward the interdisciplinary approach, include reluctance to change, the demands of No Child Left Behind (NCLB) regulations, the need for support from school systems, the need to involve parents and the community in decision-making, and the lack of adequate research on the interdisciplinary approach.

Reluctance to Change

Today, many teachers are currently incorporating some, if not all, aspects of interdiscipli-nary instruction in their lessons. Most of us try to include other disciplines when planning lessons in reading, mathematics, and science; it is evident that the content of social studies makes it particularly well suited to combining several disciplines when preparing lessons or units of study. Comprehensive interdisciplinary units are also planned and taught by some elementary teachers when they are provided with adequate materials and encourage-ment from their school districts. In many middle schools, teaching teams that have oppor-tunities to plan cooperatively together are teaching multidisciplinary units; each teacher on the team assumes responsibility for exploring topics through his/her disciplinary specialty. Still, the practice of interdisciplinary instruction is not universal for several reasons.

Each year, new voices add their criticisms of and recommend modifications to U.S. educational programs. Yet, in practice, most changes evolve slowly. This observation is not new; years ago, Leonard (1968) talked of the slow pace of change in education and cited several major reasons for the reluctance of some teachers to act rapidly on any changes that are recommended. Leonard's thinking is logical, and it still applies today:

> A certain caution in educational matters is quite understandable. A school child is far more complex, embodying far more variables, than NASA's entire satellite communications network. Baffled by this complexity and inhibited by a reluctance to "experiment" with children's lives, educators feel justified in clinging to methods that have been developed, hit or miss, over the centuries—even when they are shown to be inefficient. (p. 214)

Leonard's reasoning makes the cautious acceptance of changes in teaching understandable, especially if the changes suggested are extensive or if evidence from research supporting their effectiveness is insufficient. As suggested earlier, one of the principal reasons for reluctance to try the interdisciplinary approach can be attributed to a lack of adequate research by teachers and schools where it has been used. Therefore, we have little information regarding how it compares to other approaches, particularly regarding differences in the ways it addresses diversity and facilitates differential instruction. Insufficient research may well be the main reason why interdisciplinary instruction has not been considered more often by those who make decisions about curriculum matters in our schools.

The slow pace of change toward interdisciplinary instruction is especially disturbing when its potential values for students are considered, particularly those discussed earlier in this chapter. It is possible that, as state departments of education continue to add their support and recommend the approach, more school systems will encourage their teachers to try interdisciplinary instructional methods. In the future, schools that do so must undertake studies of its value and issue formal reports of their experiences.

No Child Left Behind Legislation

There has been considerable public concern for underachieving students in the United States. Responding to that concern in 2002, Public Law 107-110, the No Child Left Behind Act of 2001 (NCLB) was signed into law. This comprehensive legislation was designed to improve education for all children and particularly to address the needs of the disadvantaged school population. The law was dramatic in its scope, and it included provisions that established a new and central role for the federal government in education. The concentration for funding for NCLB was intended to be targeted to school districts with high concentrations of poor children and was designed to give greater flexibility to states in their spending of federal allotments. The main provisions of NCLB beginning in 2002 are indicated in Figure 2.1.

FIGURE 2.1 Provisions of No Child Left Behind.

Academic Year	Provision
2002–2003	Schools must submit annual report cards showing achievement and other data.
2004	"Reading First" was established to fund research-based reading programs for students in grades 1-3, with a priority for high poverty areas and an early-reading program targeted to 3-5 year-olds in disadvantaged areas.
2005–2006	Teachers in core content areas must be "highly qualified". Generally, this suggests being certified in their field.
	Annual testing is required in reading and mathematics.
2007–2008	Annual testing aligned with state standards is required in science once in elementary, middle and high school.
2013–2014	Targeted proficiency levels must be reached for all schools.

A significant provision in 2005 regarding the requirement for "highly qualified" teachers was aimed at uncertified teachers in the schools. By the year 2006, "teachers of core academic subjects are expected to have a bachelor's degree, full state certification, and proven competency in the subject areas they teach" (Darling-Hammond & Berry, 2006, p. 14). This was a first-of-a-kind federal legislation. Although most teachers involved in NCLB have been certified at the elementary, middle school, or secondary level, there is currently no special "license" to use any particular instructional approach. There is currently no special certificate in interdisciplinary instruction, yet there appears to be some movement in that direction. Interest in such a certificate can be attributed to provisions of NCLB which encourage schools to be innovative in developing their programs to improve students' test scores. For example, one state has considered the addition of a certificate in interdisciplinary instruction for middle school and K-12 special area teachers (Minnesota Board of Teaching, 2006). It is possible that other states and school districts will follow; if so, this could be the very kind of support that many teachers need in order to encourage them to explore the interdisciplinary approach.

NCLB's provisions focus primarily on reading and mathematics test scores to determine if schools are successful. However, educators are voicing their concern about the narrow focus of these provisions. Schools that do not perform well become subjected to punitive actions that affect the most vulnerable schools and students. Teachers say that they do not have time to teach lessons and units in social studies because of the considerable demands for testing required by NCLB regulations. According to Checkley (2006) "teachers, particularly in elementary school, would love to teach social studies, but they must adhere to schedules that allot time for math and reading instruction and little else" (p. 1). Teachers and students "are under excruciating pressure to improve test results, often at the expense of meaningful learning and more low-income and minority students are dropping out. . . . You can see practice tests replacing student-designed projects, children appearing alternately anxious and bored, terrific teachers quitting in disgust" (Kohn, 2003, p. 20). "Any balanced curriculum, regardless of its approach, should highlight the interconnectedness of various fields of knowledge. . . . Restoring curriculum balance to the schools will require vigorous and committed leadership" (Cowelti, 2006, p. 67). Teachers who become committed to using the interdisciplinary approach will contribute to that restoration of balance because during the course of an interdisciplinary unit, students have ample opportunities to practice all academic skills in meaningful contexts.

Is there a solution? Margaret Renner (2007), in a paper delivered at the Oxford University Round Table on Literacy, suggested five conditions that can help to correct the serious deficiencies in the accountability system of NCLB. The *promise* of No Child Left Behind can be realized:

- If educators write the policy, implement the models, and determine the levels of accountability;
- If the political agenda can be deleted from policymaking;
- If the *haves* view their responsibility in terms of preserving a generation;
- If action research drives policy and informs instruction;
- If children believe that education is about growth and development (a process) and not just scores (a product). (p. 15)

Renner stresses the need for action research and accountability: "Teachers know that data must inform curriculum . . . , that accountability like research should never result in punitive action . . . , that accountability involves differentiated instruction and the inclusion of learning styles," and "that interdisciplinary practices result in integrated knowledge" (p. 14). Yet, we can only achieve these goals with adequate support.

System Support

A number of important factors are involved in making any system-wide changes in curriculum and instructional approaches. Initially, an orderly process for instituting any change must be outlined. There are already existing models for instituting such changes. For example, Fullan (2002) and Wiles and Bondi (2007) provide insights and suggestions for educators contemplating curricular revisions. These writers include valuable outlines of the tasks involved and leadership requirements for a successful change process.

Oliva (2005) described several alternative models useful in making curricular changes. He also proposed his own model, which appears to be well suited for the shift from traditional to interdisciplinary programs. The Oliva model begins with an outline of program aims and the philosophical and psychological principles on which the new curriculum is to be based. Other steps involve an analysis of community and student needs and stating goals and objectives. Listing steps toward implementation of the new program and evaluation procedures completes the process. Oliva's model is flexible, and his suggestion that interdisciplinary programs extend across the curriculum indicates that the model not only is applicable for elementary programs, but also is applicable for introducing interdisciplinary instruction in departmentalized middle schools.

Adequate planning, staff preparation, and system-wide support are the primary keys to success in the movement toward any change in our schools. Any methodological change can place heavy demands on a school system; this is especially true of the interdisciplinary approach because both in-service preparation and new instructional materials may be needed.

If further progress toward interdisciplinary instruction is to be made, more teachers will not only need preparation for their new role, but also support to make the transition from more conventional methods. The teachers who are not currently using aspects of the interdisciplinary approach must be consulted and involved in the change process from the outset. Whenever teachers are not included in the initial decision-making steps or when administrative support is weak, the movement toward an interdisciplinary program—or any other instructional modifications—is unlikely to succeed.

The teaching staff should also be involved in selecting the topics for their interdisciplinary or multidisciplinary units to ensure that the topics studied align with their state curriculum mandates and learning standards. Teachers need time to share their unit plan designs with one another during the regular school day. Opportunities to form networks are also important so that teachers can work cooperatively to effect the changes they believe are appropriate for their students (Miller, 1995). It is clear that these kinds of collaboration cannot occur without adequate time and administrative backing.

Materials and Equipment

The staff may also need new materials. Both the kind and the quantity of instructional materials will change with interdisciplinary methods. For example, instead of having a textbook from one publisher for each child in a class, a teacher should have a collection of five or six copies of social studies and science textbooks from each of several publishers. This approach gives students access to more than one viewpoint as they research their unit topics. Purchasing the new materials will involve additional funding, which may be difficult for school systems to find today.

Teachers must have an adequate supply of trade books—single topic books—on the unit topics studied in their classes. In elementary schools, some of these books should be kept in individual classrooms; in middle schools, most materials can be centrally located in the school library or media center. The school media center should house enough books and magazines, DVD and videotape programs, films, filmstrips, and other resource materials so that students from different classrooms who study similar topics at the same time will have an adequate, up-to-date supply of resources. School librarians are especially well prepared to assist teachers and students alike in selecting materials that can assist in the study of unit topics.

All classrooms should be equipped with computers, Internet access, and an adequate supply of computer software. Teachers should have access to software catalogs from various suppliers so that they can study the many new programs that are continually being developed. Computer networking opportunities with college and university libraries and other community resources should be carefully explored and added if found to be valuable and feasible. Carlitz and Lentz (1995) offer an especially helpful list and discussion of the standards that educators should consider when they are making decisions about these networking opportunities.

The Need for Parent and Community Involvement

Any commitment to major changes in a school curriculum must also involve parents and the community. Parents are usually included in some aspects of school life, but often their participation has been limited to routine matters, such as field trip supervision, fund-raising, and involvement in parent–teacher organization activities. A somewhat more important role for parents is one that is "best interpreted to mean being consulted, having one's opinion taken seriously, and becoming part of the equation when vital decisions are made" (Marsh & Horns-Marsh, 1999, p. 152).

To support the idea of parent and community participation in the decision-making process, the National Parent–Teacher Association has included among its six Standards for Parent/Family Involvement Programs "parent involvement in school decision making and advocacy" (Sullivan, 1999, p. 43). Ray (2005) emphasizes that our students come to school from a diversity of family structures, each of which has its strengths and challenges. Whether a family is of the traditional two-parent, single-parent, foster parent, multigenerational, lesbian, or gay family structure, its members and other members of the community should be invited to participate in discussions and serve on advisory committees considering changes that may be directed toward the interdisciplinary approach to instruction. Parents also need to understand the underlying theory, so that they can help their children at home with the kinds of work that an interdisciplinary approach entails.

Bryk and Schneider (2003) have emphasized the need to build a trusting relationship among members of the school community to reduce "the sense of risk associated with change" (p. 43). Others (Ray, 2005; Manning & Lee, 2001) make more specific suggestions for inviting parents to become active participants in the decision-making process in their schools. Any movement toward instituting the interdisciplinary approach will require cooperation, support, and mutual trust on the part of those involved. Working together, a team composed of teachers, administrators, and parents can affect changes that endure.

Lack of Adequate Research

As explained earlier, reports on interdisciplinary programs in schools are rare. Lagemann and Shulman (1999) voiced their concern about this lack of research and also the need to make changes in the methods—primarily an exclusive reliance on testing—that are used to evaluate the success of programs in schools of different sizes; arrangements, such as team teaching; and approaches, including interdisciplinary instruction.

There are also missed opportunities to assess the effectiveness of such programs. In 1968, Roland Chatterton, a school district administrator in a suburban community on Long Island in New York State, produced and directed two unique documentary films illustrating a *multidisciplinary,* unit-centered instructional program that the teachers in his schools had developed. The films show a master teacher guiding a group of fifth-grade students through two research-oriented multidisciplinary units. Special area teacher–consultants in art, music, library and media, health, and physical education are observed assisting the classroom teacher and students with their research, projects, and reports.

The Chatterton films followed the students and teachers engaged in various lessons and activities throughout a 5 to 6-week multidisciplinary unit. The films intentionally left the value of this approach for the viewer to decide. Although the documentaries are both inspiring and convincing, and the method's positive results are inferred by the film director, neither film reports any research that may have been undertaken by the school system to document the value of the approach. Therefore, viewers are left to wonder if any objective evidence was collected and if there was any indication that the approach was any more effective than other methods. (Some colleges and universities have copies of these unusual films, but unfortunately, the film company that produced them no longer exists.)

Current lists of learning standards clearly indicate that many state departments of education are advocating the interdisciplinary approach. However, until more serious research studies and formal reports on the method's actual use in schools are available, movement toward interdisciplinary instruction is likely to remain slow, and some teachers will continue to be reluctant to try the method in their classes.

Summary

Teachers who use interdisciplinary instruction find it professionally challenging. To be successful, we need to become secure in the lesson and unit planning processes and in classroom management. Interdisciplinary instruction requires an extensive fund of general knowledge, child development, and theories of learning. Individual differences in learning style also require us to adapt our instruction to the ways students are able to learn best.

Even with the emphasis on testing stimulated by NCLB legislation and other challenges to it, there continues to be interest in interdisciplinary instruction. Practical aspects of the interdisciplinary approach follow in the remaining chapters. Those chapters include:

- Designing interdisciplinary units
- Designing multidisciplinary units
- Lesson planning strategies for interdisciplinary instruction
- Assessment planning for interdisciplinary instruction

ACTIVITY

Melissa Cooper teaches the fourth grade in a small elementary school in her rural community. She and the other teachers in her school have always used fairly conventional teaching methods. She recently attended a professional workshop on interdisciplinary instruction and would like to begin using it with her class. Ms. C. realizes that making such a change in her teaching will require some discussion with her administrators and that any changes she makes could affect the other teachers in her school.

Ms. C. is considering what she will need to do before she undertakes any change in her teaching in this small school. Help her to decide the following:

- What arguments should she propose to her administration for the change she wants to make?
- How should she approach other teachers who may be affected by any changes she makes in her teaching?
- What else should she consider in making the change?
- How would you respond to the three questions above if you knew that Ms. Cooper were teaching in a large inner city school?

REFERENCES

Armstrong, T. (2009). *Multiple intelligences in the classroom* (2nd ed.). Alexandria, VA: Association for Supervision and Curriculum Development.

Brooks, J. G., & Brooks, M. G. (1999). *In search of understanding: The case for constructivist classrooms* (Rev. ed.). Alexandria, VA: Association for Supervision and Curriculum Development.

Bryk, A. S., & Schneider, B. (2003). Trust in schools: A core resource for school reform. *Educational Leadership, 60*(8), 40–44.

Carlitz, R. D., & Lentz, M. (1995). Standards for school networking. *T.H.E. Journal, 22*(9), 71–74.

Channon, G. (1970). *Homework.* New York: Outerbridge & Dienstfrey.

Chatterton, R. (1968). *The multidisciplinary teaching of class research topics.* Merrick, NY: Merrick School District No. 25.

Checkley, K. (2006, May). Social studies jockeys for position in a narrowing curriculum. *Education Update 48*(5), pp. 1–2, 8.

Cowelti, G. (2006). The side effects of NCLB. *Educational Leadership, 64*(3), 64–68.

Darling-Hammond, L., & Berry, B. (2006). Highly qualified teachers for all. *Educational Leadership 64* (3), 14–20.

Ellis, A. K. (2007). *Teaching and learning elementary social studies* (8th ed.). Boston: Pearson/Allyn & Bacon.

Fullan, M. (2002). The change leader. *Educational Leadership, 59*(8), 16–20.

Johnson, D. D., Rice, M. P., Edgington, W. D., & Williams, P. (2005). For the uninitiated: How to succeed in classroom management. *Kappa Delta Pi Record, 42*(1), 28–32.

Kimpston, R., Williams, H., & Stockton, W. (1992). Ways of knowing and the curriculum. *The Educational Forum, 56*(2), 153–172.

Kohn, A. (1998). *What to look for in a classroom and other essays.* San Francisco: Jossey-Bass.

Kohn, A. (2003). Almost there, but not quite. *Educational Leadership, 60*(6), 26–29.

Kohn, A. (2006). *Beyond discipline: From compliance to community* (2nd ed.). Alexandria, VA: Association for Supervision and Curriculum Development.

Kornhaber, M., Fierros, E., & Veenema, S. (2004). *Multiple intelligences: Best ideas from research and practice.* Boston: Pearson/Allyn & Bacon.

Lagemann, E. C., & Shulman, L. S. (1999). *Issues in educational research: Problems and possibilities.* San Francisco: Jossey-Boss Publishers.

Leonard, G. B. (1968). *Education and ecstasy.* New York: Delacorte Press.

Lillard, P. (1972). *Montessori: A modern approach.* New York: Schocken Books.

Manning, M. L., & Lee, G. (2001). Working with parents: Cultural and linguistic considerations. *Kappa Delta Pi Record, 37*(4), 160–163.

March, T. (2003 December/2004 January). The learning power of WebQuests. *Educational Leadership 61*(4), 42–47.

Marsh, F. E., & Horns-Marsh, V. (1999). For the record. *Kappa Delta Pi Record, 35*(4), 152.

Miller, E. (1995, January/February). The old model of staff development survives in a world where everything else has changed. *The Harvard Education Letter, 11*(1), 1–3.

Minnesota Board of Teaching. (2006, January). *Report to the legislature.* Retrieved January 10, 2006 from http://children.state.mn.us/mdeprod/groups/Communications/documents/Report/008666.pdf

Montessori, M. (1912). *The Montessori method.* New York: Frederick A. Stokes.

Oliva, P. F. (2009). *Developing the curriculum* (7th ed.). Boston: Pearson/Allyn & Bacon.

Pappas, C. C., Kiefer, B. Z., & Levstik, L. S. (2006). *An integrated language perspective in the elementary school* (4th ed.). Boston: Pearson/Allyn & Bacon.

Pastor, E., & Kerns, E. (1997). A digital snapshot of an early childhood classroom. *Educational Leadership, 55*(3), 42–45.

Ray, J. A. (2005). Family friendly teachers: Tips for working with diverse families. *Kappa Delta Pi Record, 41*(2), 72–76.

Recesso, A., & Orrill, C. (2008). *Integrating technology into teaching: The technology and learning continuum.* Boston: Houghton Mifflin.

Renner, M. (2007) Spring. NCLB—A Triage Experience. *Long Island Education Review, 7*(1), 9–14.

Schrock, K. (2006). Critical evaluation survey: Elementary school level; Middle School level. In *Kathy Schrock's guide for educators.* Retrieved on January 22, 2009 from http://school.discovery.com/schrockguide/eval.html

Standing, E. M. (1957). *Maria Montessori: Her life and her work.* New York: New American Library.

Stevenson, C., & Carr, J. F. (Eds.). (1993). *Integrated studies in the middle grades.* New York: Teachers College Press.

Sullivan, P. (1999). The PTA's national standards. *Educational Leadership, 55*(8), 43–44.

Vygotsky, L. S. (1978). *Mind in society: The development of higher psychological processes.* Cambridge, MA: Harvard University Press.

Wiles, J., & Bondi, J. (2007). *Curriculum development: A guide to practice* (7th ed.). Upper Saddle River, NJ: Pearson/Merrill Prentice Hall.

SUGGESTED READINGS

The following are additional recommended readings on selected topics that are included in this chapter. Some are classic writings; others are recent publications on these topics.

Change in Education

Ashton-Warner, S. (1963). *Teacher.* New York: Simon & Schuster.

Barth, R. S. (1974). *Open education and the American school.* New York: Schocken Books.

Channon, G. (1970). *Homework.* New York: Outerbridge & Dienstfrey.

Comer, J. (2004). *Leave no child behind: Preparing today's youth for tomorrow's world.* New Haven, CT: Yale University Press.

Dennison, G. (1999). *The lives of children: The story of the First Street School.* Portsmith, NH: Boyton/Cook.

Epstein, J., Sanders, M. G., Simon, B. S., Salinas, K. C., & Van Voorhis, F. L. (2009). *School, family, and community partnerships: Your handbook for action* (3rd ed.). Thousand Oaks, CA: Sage.

Gross, B., & Gross, R. (1969). *Radical school reform.* New York: Simon & Schuster.

Hentoff, N. (1966). *Our children are dying.* New York: Pitman.

Holt, J. (1964). *How children fail.* New York: Delta.

Holt, J. (1967). *How children learn.* New York: Pitman.

Holt, J. (1989). *Learning all the time.* Reading, MA: Addison-Wesley.

Holt, J. (1969). *The underachieving school.* New York: Pitman.

Kohl, H. (1988). *36 children.* New York: New American Library.

Kohn, A. (1999). *The schools our children deserve: Moving beyond traditional classrooms and "tougher standards."* Boston: Houghton Mifflin.

Kozol, J. (1990). *The night is dark and I am far from home* (New Rev ed.). Boston: Houghton Mifflin.

Pines, M. (1967). *Revolution in learning: The years from birth to six.* New York: Harper & Row.

Postman, N., & Weingartner, C. (1969). *Teaching as a subversive activity.* New York: Delacorte Press.

Reeves, D. B. (2006)). Of hubs, bridges, and networks. *Educational Leadership 63*(8), 32–38.

Richardson, E. S. (1969). *In the early world: Discovering art through crafts.* New York: Pantheon Books.

Sadowski, M. (1995). Moving beyond traditional subjects requires teachers to abandon their "comfort zones." *The Harvard Education Letter, 11*(5), 1–5.

Silberman, C. E. (1970). *Crisis in the classroom: The remaking of American education.* New York: Random House.

Classroom Management

Arends, R. I. (2007). *Learning to teach* (7th ed.). Boston: McGraw-Hill.

Bandura, A. (1997). *Self-efficacy: The exercise of control.* New York: W.H. Freeman.

Charles, C. M. (2008). *Building classroom discipline* (9th ed.). Boston: Pearson/Allyn & Bacon.

Charles, C. M., & Senter, G. W. (2008). *Elementary classroom management* (5th ed.). Boston: Pearson/ Allyn & Bacon.

Cooper, J. M. (2006). *Classroom teaching skills* (8th ed.). Boston: Houghton Mifflin.

Edwards, C. H. (2008). *Classroom discipline and management* (5th ed.). Hoboken, NJ: John Wiley.

Holt, L. C., & Kysilka, M. (2006). *Instructional patterns: Strategies for maximizing student learning.* Thousand Oaks, CA: Sage.

Hoover, R. L., & Kindsvatter, R. (1997). *Democratic discipline: Foundation and practice.* Upper Saddle River, NJ: Pearson/Merrill Prentice Hall.

Jones, V., & Jones, L. (1995). *Comprehensive classroom management: Creating positive learning environments* (4th ed.). Boston: Pearson/Allyn & Bacon.Landau, B. M. (2004). *The art of classroom management.* Upper Saddle River, NJ: Pearson/Merrill Prentice Hall.

Marzano, R. J., & Marzano, J. S. (2003). The key to classroom management. *Educational Leadership 61*(1), 6–13.

Moore, K. D. (2009). *Effective instructional strategies: From theory to practice* (2nd ed.). Thousand Oaks, CA: Sage.

Ormrod, J. E. (2009). *Essentials of educational psychology* (2nd ed.). Upper Saddle River, NJ: Pearson/ Merrill Prentice Hall.

Ornstein, A. C., & Lasley, T. J. (2004). *Strategies for effective teaching* (4th ed.). Boston: McGraw-Hill.

Powell, R. R., McLaughlin, H. J., Savage, T. V., & Zehm, S. (2001). *Classroom management: Perspectives on the social curriculum.* Upper Saddle River, NJ: Pearson/Merrill Prentice Hall.

Putnam, J. G., & Burke, J. B. (1992). *Organizing and managing classroom learning communities.* New York: McGraw-Hill.

Queen, J. A., Blackwelder, B. B., & Mallen, L. P. (1997). *Responsible classroom management for teachers and students.* Upper Saddle River, NJ: Pearson/Merrill Prentice Hall.

Traynor, P. L., & Traynor, E. (2005). *Got discipline? Research-based practices for managing student behavior.* Irvine, CA: EduThinkTank Research Group.

Educational Philosophy

Duck, L. (1994). *Teaching with charisma.* Burke, VA: Chatelaine Press.

Ozmon, H., & Craver, S. M. (2008). *Philosophical foundations of education* (8th ed.). Upper Saddle River, NJ: Pearson/Merrill Prentice Hall.

Educational Technology

Allen, S. M., Dutt-Donner, K. M., Eini, R. F., Chuang, Hsueh-Hua, & Thompson, A. (2005/2006, January). Four takes on technology. *Educational Leadership 63*(4), 66–71.

Caruso, C. (1997). Before you cite a site. *Educational Leadership, 55*(3), 24–26.

Cummins, J., & Sayers, D. (1995). *Brave new schools.* New York: St. Martin's Press.

Davis, A. P., & McGrail, E. (2009, March). The joy of blogging. *Educational Leadership 66*(6), 74–77.

Doyle, A. (1999). A practitioner's guide to sharing the Net. *Educational Leadership, 56*(5), 12–15.

Lewin, L. (1999). "Site-reading" the World Wide Web. *Educational Leadership, 56*(5), 16–20.

Newby, T. J., Stepich, D. A., Lehman, J. D., & Russell, J. D. (2006). *Instructional technology for teaching and learning: Designing instruction, integrating computers, and using media* (3rd ed.). Upper Saddle River, NJ: Merrill/Prentice Hall.

Ryder, R. J., & Hughes, T. (2000). *Internet for educators* (3rd ed.). Upper Saddle River, NJ: Merrill/ Prentice Hall.

Williams, B. (1996). *The World Wide Web for teachers.* Chicago: IDG Books.

Woronov, R. (1994, September/October). Six myths (and five promising truths) about the uses of educational technology. *The Harvard Educational Letter, 10*(5), 1–3.

Team Teaching

Hanslovsky, G., Moyer, S., & Wagner, H. (1969). *Why team teaching?* Upper Saddle River, NJ: Pearson/ Merrill Prentice Hall.

Vars, G. F. (1969). *Common learnings: Core and interdisciplinary team approaches.* Scranton, PA: International Textbook.

Vars, G. F. (1987). *Interdisciplinary teaching in the middle grades: Why & how.* Columbus, OH: National Middle School Association.

Williamson, R. (1993). *Scheduling the middle level school to meet early adolescent needs.* Reston, VA: National Association of Secondary School Principals.

3 Designing Interdisciplinary Units

*Students involved in research
for their interdisciplinary unit.*

OVERVIEW

This chapter explains a process for planning interdisciplinary units for students at all grade levels. Examples are provided for each step in the process. The focus of this chapter is on the following:

- An introduction to interdisciplinary unit planning
- The context for learning—first consideration in planning for instruction
- An outline for an interdisciplinary unit plan
- A description of the interdisciplinary unit planning process with explanations and examples
- An interdisciplinary unit plan example

Introduction to Interdisciplinary Unit Planning

Interdisciplinary units are especially suitable for students in elementary schools and where a class works together under the direction of one teacher who assumes responsibility for instruction in all or most subjects. Planning an interdisciplinary unit requires considerable time and skill. Poorly planned units generally resemble an assortment of loosely connected lessons and activities that may lack clear objectives and direction the kind of unit planning Jacobs (1989) refers to as the *potpourri approach*. When a unit is not well planned, the results are likely to be disappointing, and discourage us from using the method altogether.

Student Involvement in the Planning Process

In a democratic classroom, students should be given opportunities to participate in the design of an interdisciplinary study and to have their questions, suggestions, and special interests incorporated as a unit develops. However, we need to assume the major responsibility for the plan for guiding the planning process to ensure that all applicable disciplines are included that will assist exploration of the topic.

Students also need to be helped to note the relationships between the various disciplines and the central topic, theme, or problem of their unit study. Although our long-term goal should aim to help students become independent in planning their studies, it is important to monitor their involvement carefully and proceed slowly until the students have developed adequate skill with the process. Gardner (1995) emphasizes this idea:

> The educator of the future needs to walk a fine line—always encouraging the youngster to stretch, praising her when she succeeds, but equally important, providing support and a non-condemnatory interpretative framework when things do not go well. Eventually, aspiring creators can supply much of this support, scaffolding and interpreting framework for themselves. (p. 15)

Encouraging Students to Develop a Variety of Abilities

All students are unique in their mental makeup, learning styles, and abilities. Gardner's (1993) proposition that "people have different cognitive strengths and contrasting cognitive styles" (p. 6) suggests that students should have opportunities to develop simultaneously in more than one cognitive area. Therefore, if we consider their *multiple intelligences,* young students should be encouraged to undertake inquiries and to use reporting methods that do not depend exclusively on their linguistic ability. Instead, music, art, drama, movement, natural exploration, and thoughtful questioning can also be used by students to investigate and to demonstrate their mastery and application of knowledge.

A model program, called the *Key School,* followed this kind of program using a multiple intelligences approach to the curriculum. According to Gardner (1993), students in the context of that program participated on a regular basis in the activities of computing, music, and bodily–kinesthetics, in addition to exploring topic-centered curriculums that embodied the standard literacies and subject matter. Each student participated in an apprenticeship-like *pod,* where he or she worked with peers of different ages and a competent teacher to master a craft or discipline of interest (p. 113). Students at the Key School investigated several multidisciplinary topics each year, including those with titles, such as *Patterns, Connections, The Renaissance—Then and Now,* and *Mexican Heritage.*

For many young students, inquiries that rely exclusively on reading can be difficult, particularly if relatively few resources on the unit topic are available for them to read independently. Instead, in addition to reading materials, early childhood classrooms should offer an environment with a rich and abundant supply of other types of reference materials and learning activities, similar to a Montessori *prepared environment* (Lillard, 1972; Montessori, 1964). This type of environment fosters active involvement with learning materials and increased participation in activities (NCSS Task Force, 1989) (Standing, 1957). When young students are developing concepts, hands-on learning activities are more helpful than using abstract materials which rely heavily on their linguistic and mathematical abilities. These hands-on, concrete opportunities are especially important for special needs students.

Students who have specific talents—artistic, musical, physical, linguistic, mathematical, and so on—should be challenged to undertake forms of inquiry that use their special abilities. Those who can read for information and prepare written reports should be encouraged to do so. Some students, even in the lower elementary grades, may also be able to complete aspects of genuine research during their units. As an interdisciplinary unit reaches its conclusion, culminating activities can help the students summarize the concepts they have gained from their study.

The Context for Learning: The First Consideration in Planning for Instruction

All learning takes place in a context. So, before beginning the interdisciplinary unit planning process, it is important to consider the context for learning in which the new unit will be taught. This is one of the most important factors in the process of planning for any instruction. The context includes consideration of students' developmental abilities, their background knowledge, academic skills, special talents, interests, limitations, multiple intelligences, behavior, and interactions with one another. The context also includes available materials and equipment as well as the physical classroom environment and our own teaching skills.

Cognitive Development: Levels and Abilities

We first need to consider the critical match between the cognitive abilities of the students in our classes and the new facts, concepts, generalizations, and important understandings we hope they will gain from a new interdisciplinary study. Estimating students' thinking and reasoning abilities prior to teaching helps to minimize the chance that they will meet with frustration. Even before the second or early third grade, some students develop fairly sophisticated thinking and reasoning abilities, especially if they have had adequate instruction and opportunities to interact with adults and competent peers.

Nevertheless, as suggested earlier, students in the early elementary grades benefit from direct, hands-on experiences. These concrete experiences can easily be brought to primary-level interdisciplinary studies in a number of ways. Young students can conduct their own inquiries and experiments in science and use concrete materials to help them develop unit concept objectives. They improve their spatial skills by working with art media and designing projects to show some of the concepts they are gaining. Young students can paint murals; make collages and dioramas; and work with papier-mâché, play dough, and clay to form artifacts and other constructions related to their interdisciplinary unit topics.

We can also provide concrete experiences for young students by organizing field trips, especially to places where they are permitted to interact physically with real objects as well as make observations. Music is also a pathway to learning for many students, and we can offer opportunities to learn about the world through singing, experimenting with simple musical instruments, and listening to recordings. The only techniques that are not defendable for these young students, from a developmental viewpoint, include substituting teacher demonstrations, lectures, and whole-class oral reading exercises for the kinds of concrete learning experiences young students can handle for themselves.

Knowing students both developmentally and academically is always more difficult early in the school year than later on. Even so, in the early months, we should try to estimate their readiness for the interdisciplinary units we plan to teach. Piaget (1955, 1966, 1970, 1973, 1974, 1976) often stressed the importance of recognizing that, at all age levels, students' thinking characteristics have a significant effect on the kinds of academic work that they can do. Piaget's research also led him to conclude that thinking and reasoning in the primary grades was dominated by *preoperational thought*—a pattern of thinking that tends to be egocentric, centered, irreversible, and non-transformational (Phillips, 1981; Piaget & Inhelder, 1969). For many years, Piaget's unchallenged research led us to believe that all young children were highly egocentric and that their thinking was extremely centered during the early childhood years.

Since Piaget completed his work, contemporary researchers (sometimes referred to as *neo-Piagetian* and *post-Piagetian* researchers) have found that Piaget had underestimated the abilities of children in the preschool and early elementary years (Flavell, 1985). These researchers have found young children to be less egocentric than Piaget believed. Also, Piaget never considered the impact of social interaction as seriously as Vygotsky (1986) and post-Piagetian researchers. In Chapter 2, several of these researchers were cited, including Bruner, 1990; Case, 1985; Checkley, 1997; Forman, Minick, and Stone, 1993; Gardner, 1991, 1993; and Wertsch, 1985.

Piaget's work can still provide us with important information about children's intellectual growth and development, but one fact is clear: Contrary to Piaget's belief, intellectual development appears to proceed continuously, and cognitive development is influenced considerably by our culture and by instruction. Santrock (2008) affirmed this notion: "Most contemporary developmentalists agree that children's cognitive development is not as grand stage–like as Piaget thought" (p. 383). Information is processed, and learners improve steadily in their ability to absorb and store knowledge from their environment (Berk, 2008).

Interdisciplinary units for students in the upper elementary grades can follow the same basic structure as those designed for younger students. However, they will differ in both the quantity and the level of work that is required. (Note that *multidisiplinary* units, which are explained in Chapter 4, offer an appropriate alternative approach to unit studies for students in the upper elementary grades and middle school.)

Affective and Psychomotor Development.   Development in the affective and psychomotor domains should also be considered as a part of the context for learning. Knowledge of students' dispositions, their individual feelings, attitudes, temperaments, and ways of interacting with others are valuable information when we are planning a unit. Information about motor coordination, health, and physical development is also important, particularly when we are planning outdoor activities, field trips, or are planning to include food.

Background Knowledge.   Equally important is learning as much as possible about the students' experience and knowledge background. New information in a study can be assimilated only if it builds on students' existing knowledge base. To minimize frustration and failure, we must ensure that students have a foundation for any new material they are expected to learn.

Other Factors.   Other factors to consider are students' interests and academic skills, especially skills in reading, writing, and research. The availability of adequate supplies of appropriate learning resource materials is also important. In addition to books, other media resources are required for thorough investigations of most topics. These resources include relevant magazines; newspapers and magazines; computer software programs; teacher-prepared presentations; DVD and videotape programs; and access to the Internet and networking facilities.

We must ensure that students have the equipment, technology, and materials required for their research, constructions, art projects, and science experiments. A detailed description of the thinking process that a group of teachers may experience as they work together to select a unit topic is given in Perkins's interesting and informative scenario on this important task (Jacobs, 1989, pp. 67–76). In the scenario, a group of teachers is meeting to select a topic for their interdisciplinary unit. After choosing a topic, a web design of the unit is prepared and other important details needed for teaching the unit are discussed and agreed upon.

In summary, planning for any instruction, including interdisciplinary units must take into consideration the context for learning. This context includes many factors that need to be thought about while developing an interdisciplinary unit plan. Among other factors are students' cognitive, affective, and psychomotor development; their academic skills; interests; background knowledge; multiple intelligences; school facilities; and available equipment and supplies.

Interdisciplinary Unit Plan Outline and Design

Most teaching methods textbooks include unit plan outlines. Perusal of those outlines reveals that there is a lack of consensus on format. For example, the emphasis in one text may be on unit objectives; another may mainly list resources; and still another may suggest that units are simply a collection of lesson plans or hands-on activities.

The unit plan format recommended in this book includes related content learning standards; general objectives—the knowledge (understandings), skills, and dispositions the unit will promote; essential questions that will guide the study; a learning plan that includes a web design of the plan and descriptions of lessons, experiments, field trips, and other activities to be included in the unit; the unit assessment plan; and a list of essential materials. The process for designing the unit plan is sensitive to *backward design,* a process (Wiggins and Tighe, 2005) that was described in Chapter 1. The unit plan outline lists components found in familiar outlines, such as those in the *topic study* unit plan by Charbonneau and Reider (1995) and the Jacobs model (1989).

The first time we plan an interdisciplinary unit, it can be described as an *initial unit plan.* This plan is the preliminary plan for the unit prior to teaching it for the first time. In an *initial unit plan,* instead of complete lesson and activity plans, the unit learning plan only needs to include descriptions of those lesson and activity ideas. The reason why preparing complete lessons can be delayed is simply that after introducing the unit, it may be decided that some of the lessons or activities will not be used at all. The descriptions will provide enough information so that complete lesson plans can be prepared if and when it is decided that they will be included in the study.

Only one complete lesson needs to be planned for an initial unit, the lesson that will be used to introduce the unit to the students. The introductory lesson should be designed so that it encourages students to begin responding to the unit topic, theme, or problem. We want to stimulate their interest in the study. Students' reactions during that lesson can guide us as we make decisions about how to proceed. We may decide that some of the ideas we have in our lesson descriptions will not be appropriate or that there are ideas for other activities suggested by the students that will need to be planned and included.

Lesson and activity planning are discussed in Chapter 5. In that chapter are guidelines for a number of different lesson planning protocols that are helpful when developing complete lesson plans. It is important to keep in mind that interdisciplinary units are flexible and dynamic and always open to modification. Each time the unit is taught to a new group of students, plans for additional lessons and activities can be added to the design if needed.

The process explained in next page provides information needed to design an interdisciplinary unit plan. The interdisciplinary unit plan outline that will be followed during the discussion includes the items listed in Figure 3.1.

This basic outline can be used to design interdisciplinary unit plans for students at all elementary grade levels. The outline will be used as a template for the discussion of the interdisciplinary unit planning process in the remainder of this chapter.

The discussion that follows will explain and illustrate with examples the process involved in designing an *initial* interdisciplinary unit plan. The format of the unit plan outline is one that includes traditional components. The recommended sequence for planning the different sections of the plan in this chapter reflects *backward design* (Wiggins and McTighe, 2005), a sequence that differs from conventional unit planning practice. Those differences are indicated in Figure 3.2 in next page.

Although we can use our individual preferences for sequence when planning the various components of the unit, it is essential that all the unit sections relate to one another once the plan is completed. For example, the learning standards must relate directly to the knowledge, skills, and dispositions listed in the unit general objectives. The standards and

FIGURE 3.1   Interdisciplinary unit plan outline.

Topic:

Level:

Estimated Unit Length:

Learning Standards:

General Objectives:

Knowledge

Skills

Dispositions

Essential Questions:

Learning Plan:

Unit Web Design

Descriptions of Lessons and Activities

Assessment Plan:

Materials:

Materials for Students

Informational Resources for Teachers

FIGURE 3.2   Differences between conventional and recommended practice in designing interdisciplinary unit plans.

Process Step	*Conventional Practice*	*Recommended Practice*
1	Determine topic, theme, or problem.	Determine the topic, theme, or problem.
2	Plan a sequence of learning experiences—lessons and activities.	Determine the general objectives: –knowledge (understandings) –skills –dispositions
3	Determine the unit content learning standards.	Identify the content learning standards to be met.
4	Determine the general objectives.	Prepare possible essential questions.
5	Determine unit assessment strategies.	Prepare the unit assessment plan.
6	List the unit materials.	Prepare the unit learning plan: –Construct a unit web design of brainstormed lessons and activities. –Write descriptions of the lessons and activities included in the web design.
7		List the unit materials.

general objectives must be addressed by the lessons or activities in the learning plan; the essential questions must also relate to the general objectives and learning standards as well as the lessons and activities; the lessons and activities must help to develop the knowledge, skills, and dispositions that are listed in the general objectives; and so on. See an example below in which a learning standard, general knowledge objective, and an essential question are clearly related to one another.

> *Learning Standard*   Students will recognize the needs and distinguishing features of various animal and plant species.
> *General Objective: Knowledge*   Living things need sunlight, nutrients, air, water, and shelter in order to survive and be healthy.
> *Essential Question*   How can living things be helped to live and grow healthfully?

No matter where we begin to plan, whether we start with the content learning standards of the unit, or we brainstorm lessons and activities, we must ensure that once the unit plan is completed, there is internal consistency across the various components, that their relationships are clear.

For illustrative purposes, an example interdisciplinary unit plan on the season of *Spring* will be developed for students in the second grade. (Note that the complete *Spring* unit plan can be found at the end of this chapter.) The following paragraph describes the context for learning for which the *Spring* unit is designed. Note that it includes information about the students' previous study and background for the new unit. Their thinking, academic abilities, social characteristics, special needs, and talents are also stated.

> The students in this heterogeneous group of second graders are mainly preoperational in their thinking and reasoning abilities. They will need concrete experiences whenever possible to help them develop concepts. Some students in the group can read for information; however, most have not yet developed independent reading levels adequate for many of the books and other resources available on most topics for students at this grade level. Socially, members of the class get along well with one another, although occasional conflicts and minor behavioral problems occur. Four students have special needs: one is physically handicapped, and one has been diagnosed with a specific learning disability; another has a special talent for mathematics and another for art. Others have strength in music. This year, the class has recently completed a unit that focused on learning about their local neighborhood, and their most recent interdisciplinary unit, "Our School," expanded their knowledge of concepts related to their neighborhood. It is early spring in an elementary school in the northeastern United States, and many students have indicated their interest in the weather changes they have noticed.

Next, the task for planning each section of an interdisciplinary unit plan will be explained. Each explanation will be followed with examples from the *Spring* unit plan.

Determining the Topic, Theme, or Problem of the Unit

Explanation of task: How do we select suitable topics, themes, or problems for interdisciplinary units? Two developmentally based approaches to this task that are used by publishers of elementary textbooks follow. The same approaches are also evident in state curriculum guides and lists of learning standards. Using the first approach, the *expanding environments—or widening horizons—approach*, topics are ordered according to students' developmental levels. Young children initially study topics that are within their personal experience and about which they have considerable prior knowledge. For example, in the primary grades, social studies topics begin with the study of self and family; later, students study their school and neighborhood. Older students study regions, states, nations, and cultures in the Eastern and Western Hemispheres. To use the widening horizons approach in selecting topics for a particular grade level, we can usually rely on those that are listed in state curriculum guides and textbooks in science, social studies, and other disciplines.

Some educators have criticized the exclusive use of the *expanding environments* approach for selection of topics for interdisciplinary units. For example, Ravich (1988) contends that by following that approach, teachers limit students to simple, familiar topics that may fail to challenge or motivate them. This concern is reasonable today because before they enter school, many young children are exposed to the wide range of information offered via television and other media. However, if we keep this idea in mind when selecting topics to study, the widening horizons approach can still provide a useful general guide.

The second approach to selecting topics involves the development of concepts. In Bruner's (1963) *spiral curriculum,* children may be exposed to the same concepts and basic ideas at each grade level. In 1963, Bruner stated that "A curriculum as it develops should revisit these basic ideas repeatedly, building upon them until the student has grasped the full formal apparatus that goes with them" (p. 13). Each year, new and more complex aspects of these concepts and ideas are introduced as students become developmentally ready to understand them. For example, the concept of *community* can be taught at every grade level. As students become intellectually ready, they can be exposed to more sophisticated understandings of this concept. Bruner's approach is compatible with and complements the expanding environments approach. Whereas the expanding environments approach centers on the selection of the topics to be selected, the spiral curriculum approach involves developing fundamental key concepts and understandings those topics can help to develop.

The spiral curriculum approach supports *backward design,* the approach to unit planning discussed earlier and that is recommended by Wiggins and McTighe (2005). Using backward design, the study of any topic needs to assist in developing *enduring understandings* by engaging students in investigating *essential questions* on that particular topic. (See Chapter 1, Figure 1.1 for examples of enduring understandings and essential questions.)

A number of appropriate topics, themes, and problems for each grade level are usually listed in state curriculum guides. For example, in New York State, there are *Core Curriculum* guides for each subject area; the guides explain very clearly the content that is expected to be taught at each level. Other states have similar publications. Teaching the topics listed in the guides helps to ensure that students are exposed to the information they need in order to meet state standards. The guides are not intended to restrict us from teaching about other topics. Over the course of an academic year, it may be possible to study additional topics, themes, or problems that are not included in the state guides.

The title of the unit example in this chapter is *Spring*; however, another title may be assigned that is more interesting to the students or that reflects what will be happening during the study. Determining a distinctive unit title can usually be accomplished easily. Students will often be able to think of a title they like. Offering students a chance to suggest their own title is a good way to stimulate their interest and help them become invested in their study. In reality, the study belongs to them, so feeling a sense of ownership is important. The students can suggest titles during a class meeting, or individuals can write suggested titles on slips of paper and put the slips in a suggestion box. A class vote can be taken to select the final title. Students can also create artwork for the title so that it can be displayed in the classroom throughout the study. The title can be made from cutout letters, be written with crayon, be painted on a long strip of paper, or be made from other suitable materials.

The length of the unit will depend on the topic and other factors, such as the amount of interest it engenders in students. Interdisciplinary units for early childhood may range from a few days to one or more weeks. In other elementary grades, most interdisciplinary studies take at least three or four weeks; many require more time. In middle school, a unit may require four to six weeks or more. An example of the topic, level, and estimated length of the *Spring* unit plan follows.

Topic: Spring (Possible titles: Spring, Signs of Spring, Spring Is Here, Spring Changes)

This topic was selected because it offers young students a number of opportunities to have direct experiences related to the concept and the process of "change," an important concept in both social studies and science.

Level: Grade 2. This unit is designed for students in the second grade; it can also be adapted for students in Grade 3.

Estimated Length: 3–4 weeks

After selecting a topic for the unit, other sections of the unit can be prepared. The order for developing the different sections is optional, but it is again emphasized that the various sections must be consistent with one another when the unit plan is completed.

Determining the Unit General Objectives

Explanation of the task: Prepare a list of general objectives. General objectives should include the knowledge (understandings), skills, and dispositions that the unit will aim to develop. The content learning standards of the unit will be directly related to these objectives. The following are example general objectives for the *Spring* unit plan:

General Objectives

This unit will assist in developing the following knowledge (understandings), skills, and dispositions.

Knowledge
Students will understand that:

■ Seasonal changes are signaled by changes in the earth's environment.

Skills
Students will expand their skills for:

■ Observing, collecting, and recording data about natural phenomena.

Dispositions
Students will demonstrate:

■ Willingness to share in decision-making and use of materials.

Determining the Unit Content Learning Standards

Explanation of the task: Prepare a list of the major content learning standards the unit will address. Content learning standards are the overall, long-term goals toward which the unit is expected to contribute. Learning standards are gleaned from lists at the national, state, and local levels. Include only the most significant standards that the interdisciplinary unit addresses. The selected standards give direction to the study and are related to the important knowledge, skills, and dispositions to be developed and assessed in the unit. Two examples from the *Spring* unit plan follow. Note that most learning standards included in this text are those developed by and included with permission from professional organizations or state departments of education; others are generic, similar to the generic learning standards prepared by committees in local school districts.

Learning Standards

This unit will contribute to the development of the following learning standards.

Students will:

- Use a variety of technological and informational resources to gather and synthesize information and to create and communicate knowledge *(National IRA/NCTE Standards for the English Language Arts, Standard 8, reprinted with permission of the International Reading Association www.reading.org).*

- Recognize that various substances and physical phenomena in the environment can be distinguished by their unique characteristics *(generic standard).*

Preparing the Essential Questions of the Unit

Explanation of the task: Essential questions are the main questions of the study. Prepare essential questions and other questions that define specifically what students should gain from their unit. In this section, we state mainly those that are defined as *essential*; however, we can also include other questions that we believe to be important and that will be addressed in some ways in the unit. Wiggins and McTighe (2005) describe an essential question as one:

> that lies at the heart of a subject or a curriculum (as opposed to being either trivial or leading), and promotes inquiry and uncoverage of a subject. Essential questions thus do not yield a single straightforward answer (as a leading question does) but produce different plausible responses about which thoughtful and knowledgeable people may disagree. (p. 342)

The following are two examples from the *Spring* unit plan.

Essential Questions

The following questions form the basis of the Spring study:

- What changes in our neighborhood are signs of the spring season?

- How can animals and plants be helped to live and grow healthfully?

Preparing the Unit Assessment Plan

Explanation of the task: When an interdisciplinary unit is taught, the assessments in each of the lessons and activities will provide information regarding their individual contributions to the development of unit general objectives, learning standards, and related essential questions. However, more comprehensive measures will be needed for the unit as a whole. Those measures are the student requirements and performances stated in the unit assessment plan. Using those assessments, we can determine the ability of students to respond to the unit's essential questions and the extent to which they have met the standards and general objectives of the unit.

Not only do we want to know if students can recall information from their unit work but, more importantly, if they can apply that new knowledge in some practical ways. Assessments can include the usual examinations and papers, but some assessment techniques need to involve applications, interpretations, and creative work. These techniques may include preparing original designs, completing projects using various art media, keeping journals, constructing original models, designing presentations, planning and conducting original experiments, and so on.

Observations of students can also help to assess their ability to work together, to use equipment properly, and to assess their own work. Students' products can become part of individual portfolios that include both completed work and work that is in progress. It is important to specify in the assessment plan how each of the assessments is linked to one or more essential questions of the unit. An example from the assessment plan in the *Spring* unit plan follows.

Assessment Plan

The following will provide a specific assessment for the unit:

■ Students will paint a mural that presents a summary of the signs of spring that they find while on a field trip walking in their local neighborhood. During the field trip, they will draw sketches of new plant growth or other signs of spring that they notice. Their individual sketches will be transferred and enlarged on the mural. *(The drawings and mural will demonstrate that the students have detected and prepared a visual summary of signs of spring in their local neighborhood.)*

Preparing the Unit Learning Plan

Constructing the Unit Web Design of Brainstormed Lessons and Activities.

Explanation of the task: The *web design* is a graphic that shows the disciplines that will be involved in the unit as well as brief descriptions of lessons and learning activities that address the standards, general objectives, and essential questions of the unit. A web design can be prepared by hand or with a computer by using drawing software or drawing tools available in some word processing programs. Software is also available that is specifically designed for web construction, such as *Inspiration,* from Inspiration Software, Inc. in Portland, Oregon.

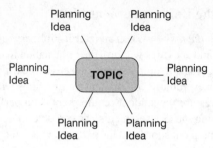

FIGURE 3.3   Model for a unidirectional web design.

Web designs are charted in two ways. One approach uses a *unidirectional* design pattern, one that begins with the topic at the center of the web design. Circling the topic are the different disciplines that the unit will involve. Radiating out from each discipline are related lessons and activity ideas. Pappas, Kiefer, and Levstik (2006) and Stephens (1974) use variations of the unidirectional arrangement for their web designs. See the model for this type of design in Figure 3.3 and an example unidirectional web design for the topic, *Transportation* in Figure 3.4.

Careful examination of the unidirectional design will reveal a weakness in this model from the perspective of interdisciplinary instruction. The unidirectional design fails to indicate any of the interdisciplinary relationships that exist among the various disciplines, lessons, and activities. Adding interconnecting lines creates a branching or *multidirectional* design, one that has the appearance of a true web. Charbonneau and Reider (1995) and Jacobs (1989) use web designs that are multidirectional. Multidirectional web designs show graphically the interrelatedness of the disciplines, lessons, and activities we plan to include in a study. See Figure 3.5 for a model of the multidirectional web design and Figure 3.6 for an example for the topic, *The United States Constitution*. Additional examples can be found in the appendix.

Before beginning to construct the web design, it can be helpful to prepare three lists: (a) a list of disciplines, (b) a list of interdisciplinary areas of concern, and (c) a list of instructional media, strategies, and techniques. These lists can assist us during the process of brainstorming ideas for lessons, activities, and performances that address the unit objectives and that ensure unit interdisciplinarity. An example of several possible lists is shown in Figure 3.7.

At first, including in these lists abstract areas—such as political science, global issues, and future studies—for students in the primary grades may seem questionable. However, young students have a natural curiosity about people in other parts of the world and often express concern about the natural disasters, conflicts, and environmental problems they hear about. Although such students may have some difficulty comprehending global issues, teachers can supply explanations and offer to discuss these issues, using terms that the students can understand. These explanations may help allay the fears that young children sometimes develop about world problems.

In the primary grades, students also enjoy thinking about both the past and the future. All history is in the past, which sometimes makes it a difficult subject for the very young to fully comprehend. Nevertheless, early childhood units can include aspects of history.

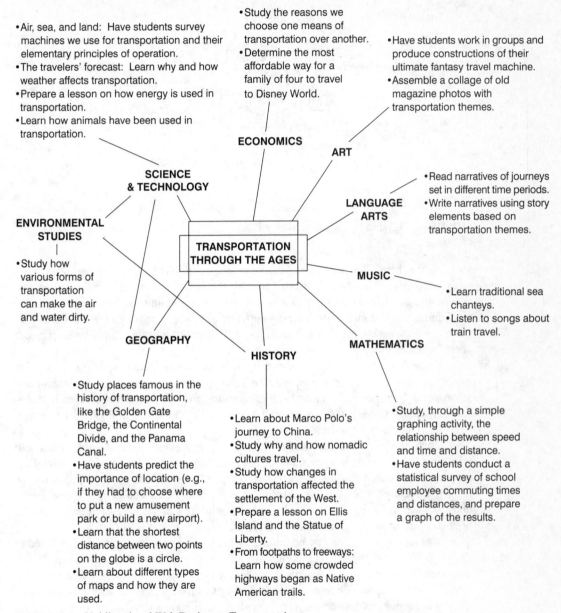

- Air, sea, and land: Have students survey machines we use for transportation and their elementary principles of operation.
- The travelers' forecast: Learn why and how weather affects transportation.
- Prepare a lesson on how energy is used in transportation.
- Learn how animals have been used in transportation.

- Study the reasons we choose one means of transportation over another.
- Determine the most affordable way for a family of four to travel to Disney World.

- Have students work in groups and produce constructions of their ultimate fantasy travel machine.
- Assemble a collage of old magazine photos with transportation themes.

ECONOMICS

ART

SCIENCE & TECHNOLOGY

LANGUAGE ARTS

- Read narratives of journeys set in different time periods.
- Write narratives using story elements based on transportation themes.

ENVIRONMENTAL STUDIES

- Study how various forms of transportation can make the air and water dirty.

TRANSPORTATION THROUGH THE AGES

MUSIC

- Learn traditional sea chanteys.
- Listen to songs about train travel.

GEOGRAPHY

HISTORY

MATHEMATICS

- Study places famous in the history of transportation, like the Golden Gate Bridge, the Continental Divide, and the Panama Canal.
- Have students predict the importance of location (e.g., if they had to choose where to put a new amusement park or build a new airport).
- Learn that the shortest distance between two points on the globe is a circle.
- Learn about different types of maps and how they are used.

- Learn about Marco Polo's journey to China.
- Study why and how nomadic cultures travel.
- Study how changes in transportation affected the settlement of the West.
- Prepare a lesson on Ellis Island and the Statue of Liberty.
- From footpaths to freeways: Learn how some crowded highways began as Native American trails.

- Study, through a simple graphing activity, the relationship between speed and time and distance.
- Have students conduct a statistical survey of school employee commuting times and distances, and prepare a graph of the results.

FIGURE 3.4   Unidirectional Web Design on Transportation.

Today, we know that by selecting a variety of materials—not only textbooks—and by providing opportunities for students to use a variety of media and individual working styles, we can help them to master some concepts once thought to be beyond their understanding.

In the primary grades, students can usually relate better to historical events and concepts when they are discussed by using terms such as *long ago* and *a long time before we were born.* Young students can relate personally to these terms because they have special

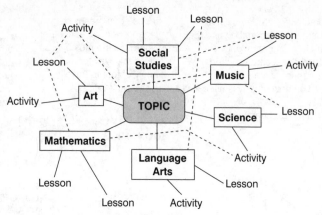

FIGURE 3.5   A multidirectional web design.

meaning for them. The concept of *future* can also be problematic for young minds. Still, young students are naturally interested in what the future will be like for them; they can and should be encouraged to think about it. Both the past and the future become more meaningful when students use learning aids, such as time lines, to plot historical events. Time lines can easily include each student's birth date as a meaningful personal reference point for the historical events that are studied.

Some disciplines and interdisciplinary areas overlap or include similar material. For example, human relations and conduct are components of psychology, sociology, and anthropology. Human relations and values clarification issues are both included in multicultural studies. Other categories or items can be added to the lists in Figure 3.7 to reflect new areas, special interests, and concerns.

The web design is a simple drawing showing at a glance what the unit includes. It also serves as a reminder when more detailed descriptions of each lesson or activity are prepared for the unit learning plan. Later, complete lesson plans can be written for the ideas that are used when the unit is taught. The beginning of a web design for the *Spring* unit is shown in Figure 3.8. It includes only a few ideas that the have been charted as the brainstorming step begins in planning the unit.

At this point, we are just beginning to plan, so only a few activities are listed in the web. The main topic is centered, with several disciplines listed around it. So far, we have planned to take the students on a walking field trip in their local neighborhood to look for signs of spring. Students will use their observational skills to search for the signs. They will record their observations by drawing individual pictures; some of the pictures will later be transferred to a mural. The purpose of the mural is to help the students summarize the signs of spring they have observed while on their walk. We will read stories about spring to the students and will give a lesson on reading a thermometer, a lesson that will prepare students for recording daily temperature changes for several weeks during the unit.

Several academic disciplines and intelligences have been considered at this point in the unit development: making drawings of observations, having a planning discussion

TECHNOLOGY

- Using the internet, students will research Francis Scott Key and find a recording of the national anthem.
- Students will design a spreadsheet of the original states, indicating the number of senators, representatives, and electoral votes.

LANGUAGE ARTS

- Students will study, then rewrite the Preamble using their own words.
- Together, have students create a class Constitution that they will illustrate and display.
- Have students write a short biography on a person involved in the making of the Constitution. (Review the research process.)
- Have students keep a journal of current government activities (news articles) and make connections to the Constitution.
- Write a newspaper article covering the 1787 Constitutional Convention.

MATHEMATICS

- Teach a lesson on time lines. Then have the students create a time line of the ratifications and amendments to the Constitution.
- Teach a lesson on fractions in connection with the 3/5ths compromise.
- Calculate the distance each delegate had to travel to get to the convention.

MUSIC

- Students will listen to "The Star Spangled Banner," and discuss what they think it means.
- Students will write a song based on the three branches of government, using the melody of the national anthem or Yankee Doodle.

THE UNITED STATES CONSTITUTION

HISTORY & GOVERNMENT

- Play Constitution Jeopardy with the biographies of famous people the students have researched.
- Teach a lesson on the Great Compromise and discuss the differences between the Senate and the House of Representatives.
- Discuss the original Articles of Confederation and why they did not work well.
- Have a class discussion on how the Constitution affects our daily lives; then have the students write a short related essay.
- Divide the class into three groups to research the three branches of the government and to report back to the class.

DRAMA

- Students will study the drama "1776."
- Have students design costumes and sets and reenact part of the debate.

ART

- Have students design a mobile depicting the three branches of government.
- Have students make a collage of images and phrases from the Constitution.
- Students will create a bulletin board of the Preamble.
- Using cardboard boxes (appliance size), students will create mini-museums for artifacts related to the Constitution.
- Teach a lesson on calligraphy. Have students use it in various projects during the unit.

SCIENCE

- Students will investigate inventions of the 1700s.
- Have students study the work of Benjamin Franklin.
- Students will conduct experiments on electricity.

GEOGRAPHY

- Have students practice their mapping and research skills by creating and labeling a map of the United States in 1787.

FIGURE 3.6   A multidirectional web design: The U.S. Constitution.

FIGURE 3.7 A list of disciplines, general areas of concern, media, teaching strategies, and techniques.

BRAINSTORMING ASSISTANTS		
Disciplines	*Concerns*	*Media, Strategies, & Techniques*
anthropology	career education	art projects
economics	citizenship	audio recordings
geography	civics	charts and graphs
history	consumerism	computer programs
language arts	current events	constructions
listening	ecology	demonstrations
reading	family living	dioramas
speaking	future studies	experiments
writing	global studies	field trips
mathematics	health	films
performing arts	human behavior	filmstrips
dance	human rights	group discussions
drama	Internet	Internet resources
music	learning styles	interviews
psychology	political science	multimedia
science	multicultural studies	murals
sociology	space exploration	presentations
technology	substance abuse	reports
visual arts	values clarification	research
skills lessons	software	surveys
timelines	video programs	DVD programs

in preparation for the field trip, learning to read a thermometer, and working together on a mural. Only the basic idea for each lesson or activity appears in the web design, just enough information to use as a reminder if the idea is used.

The brainstorming step and construction of the web design help to set parameters for the study and provide an overview of its possible development. As the *Spring* web continues to grow, additional ideas are charted. Interconnecting lines are added to indicate some of the interdisciplinary relationships among the various lessons and activities. As indicated in Figure 3.9, additions (dotted boxes) to the original web design indicate that the students will keep a record and prepare a graph of daily temperature readings.

Additions to the original design also show that the students will listen to musical selections that have spring as a theme; the same musical selections will then be used for a movement activity. We will include social studies lessons about any spring holidays

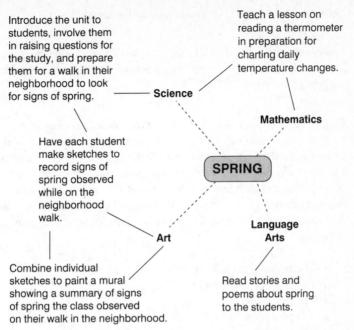

FIGURE 3.8 Initial stage in developing the web design for an interdisciplinary unit on "Spring."

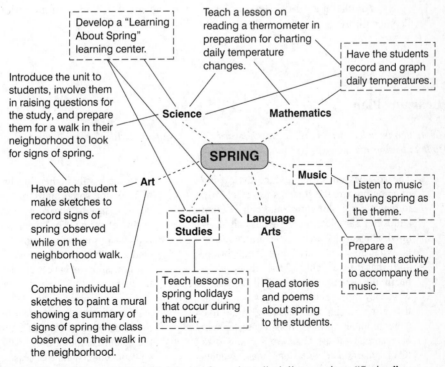

FIGURE 3.9 Additions to the initial design for an interdisciplinary unit on "Spring."

that occur while the students are involved in studying the spring season. (Additional ideas are included in the web design for the complete *Spring* unit plan at the end of this chapter.)

Describing Lessons and Activities in the Unit Learning Plan.

Explanation of the task: The lesson and activity ideas shown in the web design are stated so succinctly that, later, we may have difficulty remembering exactly what we had in mind. Therefore, in this section of the unit plan, we expand on each idea. Whereas the web design is an overall view or schematic of the unit and its interdisciplinary connections, the descriptions provide the details that will be needed when complete lesson plans are prepared. In order to be most useful, each description should provide information about the following:

- The learning standard it addresses
- Its main purpose (or objective)
- The key question it addresses
- The procedure to be followed
- The multiple intelligence areas it addresses
- How it will be assessed

An example of one lesson description and the description of an optional learning center for the *Spring* unit follow.

Learning Plan

(Note that in order to avoid repeating the words "lessons and activities," the following descriptions refer to both lessons and activities as lessons.*)*

- The first lesson will introduce the *Spring* unit and prepare the students for a field trip to look for signs of spring and collect plant and water samples in their local neighborhood. The key question for this initial lesson is: What do we already know about spring, and what do we want to learn about it? To begin the lesson, students will be asked what they believe they already know about the spring season and what they would like to learn about spring. Their responses will be recorded on the first two sections of a KWL chart. The questions that students raise will help to determine some of the goals for the spring unit. The students will then be told that later in the week, they will be taking a walk in their local neighborhood to look for some signs of spring. It may be necessary to clarify what is meant by a "sign" of spring. The students will be asked if they can suggest some signs that they will find. Finally, the students will be given permission slips to have signed before taking the walk.

  This introductory lesson addresses aspects of the following learning standards: Students conduct scientific inquiries using the scientific method of investigation; and students understand that seasons of the year, weather, and climate are determined by physical changes in the environment. Because this lesson involves a discussion, it will mainly involve students' linguistic intelligence. The lesson will be assessed by examining the lists of what students believe they already know and questions they have about the spring season.

■ Optionally, in addition to the above lessons for the *Spring* unit, prepare a learning center with at least ten activities for the students to complete independently. One activity could include examining additional samples of water taken from various sources in the local neighborhood and writing descriptions of and/or drawing pictures of what the students observe. If frogs' eggs are available, samples may be collected and placed in the learning center for the students to observe. Books or other materials at the students' reading levels on the development of frogs from eggs into tadpoles and adult frogs should be placed in the learning center. Activities in

the center may also include reading and preparing short reviews or reactions to other books, stories, and poems; creative writing; listening to music; and mathematical problem-solving. Each activity should have a task card to explain directions.

The learning center provides students with independent work to extend practice with the concepts that they are studying during the unit in the areas of science, music, language arts, and mathematics. Learning center activities can address learning standards in several disciplines; the specific standards will depend on the kinds of practice available in the center. Depending on the actual activities included, the learning center will provide for experiences that involve most of students' multiple intelligences. *(See Figure 3.10 for a way to organize the Spring learning center.)*

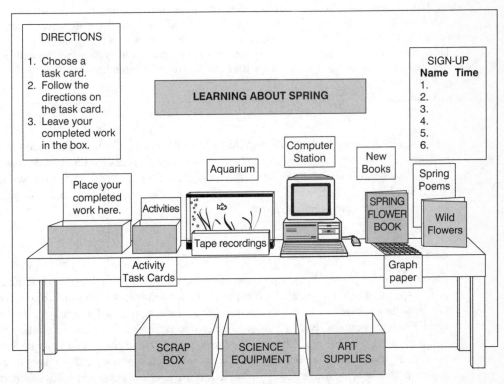

FIGURE 3.10   Model for a Learning about Spring learning center.

FIGURE 3.11 Teaching Assistant on Planning for a Field Trip.

Planning For a Field Trip

A field trip activity will take more than one class session. Before designing introductory lesson plan for the spring unit plan, an overview of a suggested three-phase procedure will first be delineated.

Organizing a field trip: A logical organization for a field trip is similar to the process involved in any research activity. It involves three phases—planning (preparation for the trip), researching (the field excursion), and reporting (a follow-up session to review what has been learned). The three phases are explained below:

Phase I: Before taking a field trip, students plan their excursion with guidance from their teacher. Questions about what students would like to learn at the field site are elicited from students and recorded for reference during the trip. Teachers may want to add other questions that they feel are important. Each student should have a copy of the questions raised during the discussion to take along on the field trip. Permission slips are distributed with instructions for returning them before the day of the trip. Several parents are usually invited to assist on the day of the trip.

Phase II: On the day of the field trip, students attempt to gain answers to their questions and to learn other related information while at the field site. They use their lists of questions at the site and note answers to their questions.

Phase III: Finally, when students return to their classroom, they discuss and record what they gained from the trip. This discussion is guided by the initial questions that were raised. Some questions may not have been answered; other information that was not planned for can be included during the discussion. The teacher then assists the students in summarizing what they learned from their field trip. This summary may take the form of an outline that students then copy for their records.

These lesson and activity descriptions add to the basic information provided in the web design, and they facilitate the preparation of complete plans for those ideas that are actually used when teaching the unit. *(Review Figure 3.11, Teaching Assistant on Field Trips, and Figure 3.12, Teaching Assistant on Learning Centers, for additional information about planning for those activities.)*

Listing the Unit Materials

Explanation of the task: List major materials needed for the unit in this section of the unit plan. Two lists should be prepared: (a) materials to be used with students and (b) materials that provide background resources for teachers. Some materials for use with students rapidly become outdated, and new ones may become available. Therefore, when the initial unit is planned, a simple list indicating the types of texts, trade books, and other materials for student use will suffice until the unit is taught. Each time the unit is retaught, new materials that become available can be added to the list, including addresses of Internet

FIGURE 3.12   Teaching Assistant for Designing a Learning Center.

Teaching Assistant on Learning Centers
Learning centers can often be included in the design of an interdisciplinary unit. They provide students with interesting and highly motivating materials and activities for exploration and for extra practice with skills that have previously been taught. One important point to remember is that learning center activities do not replace instruction; they cannot teach students something that is completely new. Learning centers are especially useful for stimulating creative writing and individual work with various art media. Learning centers for younger children can also provide materials for self-exploration prior to formal instruction in areas such as science and mathematics.

There are several types of learning centers. Simple, interactive centers can be constructed using a simple bulletin board display with pockets. The pockets hold written directions for tasks or problem-solving activities that the students select to work on independently. This type of learning center may be one of the easiest for students in middle schools to use because they usually move from class to class during the day. Students can take a simple task card with them to complete when they have time during another part of the school day.

Learning centers can also be displayed on an empty shelf or another surface in the classroom. In more elaborate centers, the materials and activities to be used are arranged on a table or a group of tables in a designated area. Space may be provided for students to work at the center, or they can be directed to take the activities from the center to their seats or another part of the classroom. The specific form used for a learning center always depends on its purpose and the classroom space available for its setup. See Figure 3.10 for a model of a learning center for the *Spring* unit.

Developing a learning center requires a considerable amount of planning and preparation. Following several important steps in designing a learning center will help to ensure its effectiveness:

- Decide on its purposes; determine if the center activities will be primarily for exploration or for practice.
- Decide on a title for the center. When the learning center is used with an interdisciplinary unit, the title can be the unit topic or a related topic.
- Determine the specific activities to be included. They can be a variety of interdisciplinary tasks, explorations, problems to be solved, construction activities, science experiments, readings, research, writing, and other activities that relate to the center's purposes and are appropriate for the students who will use it.
- Prepare task cards. **Task cards** provide specific directions needed to complete each activity. The sample task card shown below has directions for a group of fourth-grade students who are studying a research-oriented interdisciplinary unit on deserts in the United States.

Desert Collage
In this activity, you will make a collage to show what you have learned from watching a video on the Mojave Desert.

Directions:
1. Use the video tape recorder and television monitor to watch the tape, entitled "The Mojave Desert."
2. Using materials from our scrap box, prepare a collage that shows something specific you feel you have learned from the video program.

(Continued)

FIGURE 3.12   Teaching Assistant for Designing a Learning Center.   Continued

---

3. Take a sheet of construction paper from the supply section in the learning center. Write your name on the back of the paper. Paste, glue, tape, and other supplies for your work are kept in our supply closet. Take paint and paint brushes if you would like to use them.

4. Be prepared to explain your collage during one of our regular "forums" at the end of each day this week.

- Provide space for and assemble the equipment and materials needed for the activities. Art supplies; science equipment; computers and computer software; DVD programs, videotape programs and viewing equipment; tape recordings; filmstrips; textbooks and trade books; charts and diagrams; picture collections; duplicated worksheets; and any other items that may be needed should be supplied at or near the center.

- Prepare a schedule—a sign-up sheet or teacher-prepared list—to ensure that all the students will have an opportunity to use the center during a certain time.period.

- Develop a record-keeping device for assessing students' use of the center activities and for monitoring their participation. A simple checklist of students' names and learning center activities is usually adequate for this purpose. See Figure 3.4 for a sample checklist.

- Designate a place where students can leave their completed work.

- Decide how to introduce the learning center to the class. Most students thoroughly enjoy using learning centers, and they may want to begin as soon as they see it appear in the classroom. A thorough introduction can clarify routines and guidelines for using the center and help to deter problems that can arise from misuse of the activities or materials. A set of directions should be prepared for students to read before they work with any of the learning center activities. Figure 3.10 shows an example of a directions poster.

Clearly, learning centers can especially be effective for providing elementary students with opportunities to work independently on new skills that have been taught and on tasks related to their interdisciplinary units.

---

resources (URLs), computer software, multi-media presentations, DVD and videotape informational programs, and other media. The names of people who have been helpful as consultants or as guest speakers can also be included. Most of the usual art and other consumable materials need not be listed. Examples from the *Spring* unit plan follow:

Unit Materials
Materials for Students
ABC Teach. *Spring activities*. Retrieved from http://www.abcteach.com/directory/seasonal seasons/spring/

Selection of children's books on spring from the school and public libraries
Computer software and CD-ROM titles featuring information on the seasons and nature

Information Resources for the Teacher
Brewer, D. (2001). *Wrens, dippers, and thrashes*. New Haven, CT: Yale University Press.
Gogerly, L. (2005). *Spring*. Vero Beach, FL: Rourke.

Summary

Preparation of the various sections of the interdisciplinary unit plan as explained and illustrated above will generate all the information needed to write an *initial* unit plan. The complete the unit plan for the *Spring* unit is presented below. The format and outline of the completed plan reorders some of the material produced during the planning process to provide a familiar and logical organizational framework for the plan.

In order to begin teaching the *Spring* unit, a plan for the lesson that will be used to introduce it will need to be designed. The design of the first lesson or activity is a key factor in determining the success of any interdisciplinary unit. Before beginning to plan the lesson, we will again need to consider the students' background knowledge, academic skill levels, and developmental characteristics as well as the social makeup of the class. The purpose of any introductory lesson is to inform students of the unit topic and attempt to engage their interest in the new study. General principles of teaching and learning can help to guide the lesson design. Three especially important principles follow:

- To be adapted, new information must build the students' existing knowledge base.
- Students need to construct their own knowledge, using their different cognitive strengths, through direct experiences whenever possible and through opportunities to interact with adults and competent peers.
- Motivation is stronger if unit activities and lessons capitalize on the students' interests, working styles, and learning styles.

Usually, one of the lessons indicated in the web design can be further developed to introduce a new unit. The introductory lesson for the *Spring* unit involves the first phase of a field trip in which students will walk through their neighborhood to look for signs of spring. The complete plan for that lesson is included in Chapter 5; it is the example lesson used to illustrate the KWL protocol.

Interdisciplinary Unit Plan Example

Topic: Spring

Possible Titles: Spring
Signs of Spring
Spring Is Here
Spring Changes

(Note that this topic was selected because it offers young students a number of opportunities to have direct experiences related to the concept and the process of "change," an important concept in both social studies and science.)

Level
Grade 2. *This unit is designed for students in the second grade; it can also be adapted for students in Grade 3.*

Estimated Unit Length: 3–4 weeks
Learning Standards
This unit will contribute to developing aspects of the following learning standards.

Students will:

- Conduct scientific inquiries using the scientific method of investigation.
- Understand that seasons of the year, weather, and climate are determined by physical changes in the environment.
- Develop an understanding of the scientific method of investigation and apply it to investigations in science.
- Be knowledgeable about and make use of the materials and resources available for participation in arts in various roles *(Arts Standard 2, by permission of the New York State Education Department).*
- Use a variety of technological and informational resources to gather and synthesize information and to create and communicate knowledge *(National IRA/NCTE Standards for the English Language Arts, Standard 8, reprinted with permission of the International Reading Association www.reading.org).*
- Understand how to use simple instruments to measure and record such qualities as distance, size, weight, and temperature.
- Recognize that materials and objects in the environment possess unique characteristics.
- Recognize the needs and distinguishing features of various animal and plant species.
- Construct records of data they collect and detect patterns observed in those records.
- Recognize that various substances and physical phenomena can be predictive of environmental changes that occur throughout the year.
- Respond critically to a variety of works in the arts, connecting the individual work to other works and to other aspects of human endeavor and thought *(Arts Standard 3, by permission of the New York State Education Department).*
- Use spoken, written, and visual language to accomplish their own purposes e.g., for learning, enjoyment, persuasion, and the exchange of information *(National Standards for the English Language Arts, Standard 12, reprinted with permission of the International Reading Association www. reading.org).*

- Actively engage in the processes that constitute creation and performance in the arts—dance, music, theatre, and visual arts—and participate in various roles in the arts *(Arts Standard 1, by permission of the New York State Education Department).* Be knowledgeable about and make use of the materials and resources available for participation in arts in various roles *(Arts Standard 2, by permission of the New York State Education Department).*
- Exhibit responsible personal and social behavior that respects self and others in physical activity settings *(Reprinted from Moving into the Future: National Standards for Physical Education (2004) with permission from the National Association for Sport and Physical Education (NASPE), 1900 Association Drive, Reston, VA 20191-1599).*
- Use observation to collect information and draw conclusions about physical phenomena.
- Understand the different ways people of diverse racial, religious, and ethnic groups, and of various national origins have transmitted their beliefs and values *(National History Content Standard 1B, National Center for History in the Schools/UCLA http://nchs.ucla.edu).*
- Prepare original designs and materials using their previous knowledge.
- Be able to use technology to create original plans and constructions.

General Objectives

This unit will assist in developing aspects of the following: knowledge (understandings), skills, and dispositions.

Knowledge

Students will understand that:

- Seasonal changes are signaled by changes in the earth's environment.
- Scientific inquiry involves raising questions, hypothesizing about some phenomena, investigating, organizing data collected, and reporting results to others.

- Various phenomena, including the weather and seasonal changes, can affect people's feelings and inspire works of art, music, and literature.
- All living things have distinctive characteristics that distinguish them from one another.
- Living things need sunlight, nutrients, air, water, and shelter in order to survive and be healthy.
- Sound is produced by vibrating objects in the environment.
- Some celebrations and holiday events, which people observe in different ways, are associated with the season of spring.

Skills
Students will expand their skills for:
- Developing plans for scientific investigations.
- Observing, collecting, and recording data about natural phenomena.
- Constructing graphs to record data.
- Using various instruments and materials needed for scientific investigations.
- Creating art with various media.
- Designing and constructing models.
- Creating original stories and poems.
- Following the conventions of grammar, syntax, spelling, and punctuation when writing.

Dispositions
Students will demonstrate:
- Appropriate behavior that is respectful of others in a variety of settings.
- Willingness to share in decision making and use of materials.

Essential Questions
The following questions form the basis of the Spring study:

- What changes in our neighborhood are signs of the spring season?
- How can we investigate scientific problems?
- How are people affected by changes in the seasons, and how are those effects demonstrated in art, music, and literature?
- In what ways are living things alike and different from one another?

- How can living things be helped to live and grow healthfully?
- What causes a sound to be made?
- What are some holiday celebrations associated with the spring season, and why are they celebrated?

Unit Web Design: (see Figure 3.13)

Learning Plan: Descriptions of Lessons and Activities:
(Note that in order to avoid repeating the words "lessons and activities," the following descriptions refer to both lessons and activities as lessons.)

- The first lesson will introduce the *Spring* unit and prepare the students for a field trip to look for signs of spring and collect plant and water samples in their local neighborhood. The key questions for this initial lesson are: What do we already know about spring, and what do we want to learn about it? To begin the lesson, students will be asked what they believe they already know about the spring season and what they would like to learn about spring. Their responses will be recorded on the first two sections of a KWL chart. The questions that students raise will help to determine some of the goals for the spring unit. The students will then be told that later in the week, they will be taking a walk in their local neighborhood to look for some signs of spring. It may be necessary to clarify what is meant by a "sign" of spring. The students will be asked if they can suggest some signs that they will find. Finally, the students will be given permission slips to have signed before taking the walk.

  This introductory lesson addresses aspects of the following learning standards: Students will conduct scientific inquiries using the scientific method of investigation; and students will understand that seasons of the year, weather, and climate are determined by physical changes in the environment. Because this lesson involves a discussion, it will mainly involve students' linguistic intelligence. The lesson will be assessed by

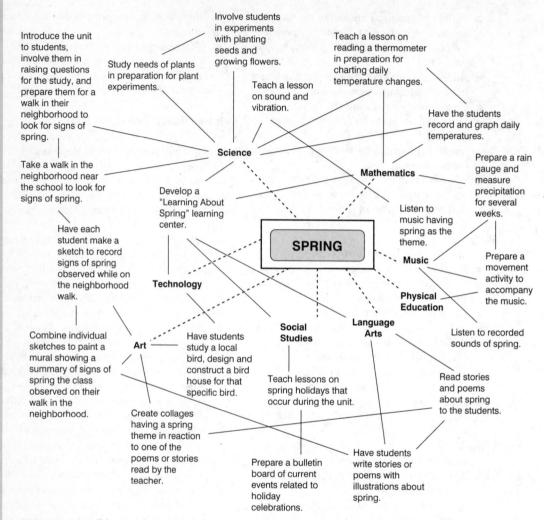

Introduce the unit to students, involve them in raising questions for the study, and prepare them for a walk in their neighborhood to look for signs of spring.

Take a walk in the neighborhood near the school to look for signs of spring.

Have each student make a sketch to record signs of spring observed while on the neighborhood walk.

Combine individual sketches to paint a mural showing a summary of signs of spring the class observed on their walk in the neighborhood.

Study needs of plants in preparation for plant experiments.

Involve students in experiments with planting seeds and growing flowers.

Teach a lesson on sound and vibration.

Teach a lesson on reading a thermometer in preparation for charting daily temperature changes.

Have the students record and graph daily temperatures.

Prepare a rain gauge and measure precipitation for several weeks.

Science

Mathematics

Develop a "Learning About Spring" learning center.

Listen to music having spring as the theme.

SPRING

Music

Prepare a movement activity to accompany the music.

Technology

Physical Education

Art

Have students study a local bird, design and construct a bird house for that specific bird.

Social Studies

Language Arts

Listen to recorded sounds of spring.

Teach lessons on spring holidays that occur during the unit.

Read stories and poems about spring to the students.

Create collages having a spring theme in reaction to one of the poems or stories read by the teacher.

Prepare a bulletin board of current events related to holiday celebrations.

Have students write stories or poems with illustrations about spring.

FIGURE 3.13   Diagram for a complete interdisciplinary unit plan on the season of "Spring."

examining the lists of what students believe they already know and questions they have about the spring season.

■ The second phase of the field trip experience will offer the students opportunities to be involved in the work of scientists. It will involve data gathering in response to the questions and suggestions about the signs of spring that students raised during the introductory lesson. The key question of this lesson is: What evidence can we find that indicates the change of season from winter to spring? On the day of the field trip—a walk through the neighborhood to look for signs of spring— drawing paper and pencils will need to be taken for the students so that they can make sketches of any signs of spring that they notice: animals, birds, insects, and so on. Stop occasionally and encourage the students to observe for signs of spring and to make sketches. Also, have containers for students to collect specimens of plants and samples of water to take back to the classroom for examination.

This lesson will address aspects of the following learning standard: Students will develop an understanding of the scientific method of investigation and apply it to investigations in science. The lesson mainly involves students' naturalistic and spatial intelligences. Notations of the items that are detected by students, their sketches, and the samples they find during the field trip will provide assessments for this lesson.

- Phase three of the field trip will explore the key question: How can the information and items we have collected from our field trip be organized and summarized? After returning to the classroom from the neighborhood walk to gather information and samples, have the students transfer and enlarge their sketches to a large sheet of mural paper. Involve the students in arranging the pictures on the mural. Using art media to record the signs of spring that the students have noted on a mural will develop a visual summary of the signs of spring that have been observed.

This lesson will address aspects of the following learning standards: Students will be knowledgeable about and make use of the materials and resources available for participation in arts in various roles *(Arts Standard 2, by permission of the New York State Education Department);* and students will develop an understanding of the scientific method of investigation and apply it to investigations in science. It will involve students' spatial, linguistic, and naturalist intelligences. Completion of the mural summarizing the signs of spring students have located and observation of the students' use of art materials will provide assessments for this lesson.

- Students will be involved in activities that make use of the plant specimens brought

back from the neighborhood walk. The key question to be explored for these investigations is: How can the plants and water samples we have collected be distinguished from one another? First, the students will have hands-on experiences examining the plant specimens. They will be encouraged to observe each plant specimen carefully to determine its size, colors, and other distinguishing features and to record their findings. A slide will be prepared for each of the water samples collected. Students will examine the different samples under a microscope and draw pictures of their observations to note the differences in samples from different locations. These activities will give students opportunities to use equipment such as microscopes and measuring devices as they explore properties of plant and water specimens; they will also have experience recording their findings.

The activities will address students' logical–mathematical and naturalist intelligences and aspects of the following learning standards: Students will use a variety of technological and informational resources to gather and synthesize information and to create and communicate knowledge *(National IRA/NCTE Standards for the English Language Arts, Standard 8, reprinted with permission of the International Reading Association www.reading.org);* students will develop an understanding of the scientific method of investigation and apply it to investigations in science; students will understand how to use simple instruments to measure and record such qualities as distance, size, weight, and temperature; and students will recognize that materials and objects in the environment possess unique characteristics. The students' records of plant features and drawings of water samples will be used to assess these activities.

- Give the students opportunities to conduct their own experiments to determine the basic needs of the plants collected while on their neighborhood walk. The key question for these experiments is: How can living things be helped to live and grow healthfully? Begin by having the students suggest what they believe plants need to live. The students will probably have different ideas, and it is possible that some students will not include all the essentials. Next, help individual students set up experiments to test their individual ideas about what plants need. Collect a number of small plants for students to use for their experiments. It is likely that some may fail to control variables when conducting their experiments. When this happens, let the students perform their experiments, then raise questions to help them understand that they need to test one variable at a time. Replicate experiments when needed. These experiments can help students discover the basic needs of the plants and give them opportunities to design and carry out their own scientific investigations.

The experiments address some aspects of the following learning standard: Students will develop an understanding of the scientific method of investigation and apply it to investigations in science. It will involve students' naturalist, logical–mathematical, and intrapersonal intelligences. To assess the experimentation activities, students will be observed to note their accuracy in conducting their experiments with the plants, and the students' interest in participating and caring for their plants.

■ After students have determined the basic needs of plants, teach a lesson on planting flower seeds. The key question of the lesson is: How should plant seeds be sown in order to develop into healthy plants? Use marigold seeds because they will grow rapidly and easily under proper conditions. As a first step in this lesson, guide students in reading a selection in their science book or other source on planting seeds. After reading the selection, the students should decide the conditions needed for growing the seeds and be given time to collect necessary materials, such as soil and containers. Assist the students as they plant their seeds. Ask the students to observe the plants each day and keep a record by writing about or drawing the changes that they observe. Students should measure and chart the height of their plants each week after the seeds have sprouted. Later in the spring, the students can take their plants home when the marigolds are mature enough for transplanting. This science lesson offers students a concrete experience in raising and caring for growing plants.

The lesson will address aspects of the following learning standards: Students will understand how to use simple instruments to measure and record such qualities as distance, size, weight, and temperature; and students will recognize the needs and distinguishing features of various animal and plant species. Students' logical–mathematical and naturalist intelligences are involved in the lesson. The lesson will be assessed by observing students' accuracy in applying the process they have learned for planting seeds and the records they maintain during the growth of their plants.

■ The key question for this lesson is: How do we read an outdoor thermometer to determine the temperature? In preparation for this lesson, install an outdoor thermometer near one of the classroom windows, and teach students how to read the thermometer. Practice reading the thermometer with the students for several days. This will prepare the students for keeping a daily temperature record for the remainder of the *Spring* unit. Divide the students into three groups: one group will be responsible for reading and maintaining a list of temperature readings early in the morning; the second group should take readings at noon; and the third group should check temperatures at the end of the school day.

This lesson addresses aspects of the following learning standard: Students will understand how to use simple instruments to measure and record such qualities as distance, size, weight, and temperature. It involves students' logical–mathematical and linguistic intelligences. Students' records will be examined to assess their ability to read and record the temperature daily at the times specified for each group.

- This lesson also involves measurement and maintaining a record. The key question of the lesson is: How can we determine the amount of rain that falls during a period of precipitation? Ask the students if they can think of any way we can determine how much rain has fallen after it has rained. It may be possible for the students to devise a method. Ultimately, however, a rain gauge will be needed, so a simple gauge using an untapered glass container with its depth measured in inches or centimeters will be sufficient. Have the students practice reading different amounts of water in the container. Locate the rain gauge in an outdoor area near the classroom for students to inspect after each period of precipitation. Have students record the amounts of water collected by the gauge in their notebooks following each period of precipitation throughout the *Spring* unit. At the end of the unit, have students compute the total amount of precipitation that has fallen during their study of spring. Optionally, use the different amounts of precipitation to create other addition and subtraction problems for students to solve. This lesson will provide students with opportunities to read, measure, and maintain records, and compute amounts of precipitation over several weeks.

This lesson addresses aspects of the following learning standards: Students understand how to use simple instruments to measure and record such qualities as distance, size, weight, and temperature; and students will construct records of data they collect and detect patterns observed in those records. The lesson involves students' logical–mathematical and naturalist intelligences. Assessment will involve examination of the completeness and accuracy of students' records and computations of precipitation.

- This lesson will introduce the students to graphing. The key question of this lesson is: What do bar graphs recording our records of the daily temperature and rainfall during our study of the spring season show us? After students have collected and recorded temperature and precipitation records in their notebooks for at least two weeks, teach the students how to prepare simple bar graphs to chart the daily temperature and rainfall readings they have been recording. Students should continue adding new readings to their graphs throughout their *Spring* study. At the conclusion of the unit, ask the students to decide what the records tend to show about the temperature in spring and the amount of rain that has fallen. (Note that it is anticipated that there will be a gradual rise in the temperature if normal conditions prevail.)

This lesson addresses aspects of the following learning standard: Students will construct records of data they collect and detect patterns observed in those records. The lesson involves students' logical–mathematical and naturalist intelligences. Assessment will involve examination of students' graphs and their explanations of what they think the graphs show about the current spring season regarding changes in temperature and amounts of precipitation.

- Conduct a lesson on the natural sounds in our environment during the spring season. The key question of the lesson is: What sounds of spring can be determined by using only our sense of hearing? Prepare a recording of natural sounds that prevail during the spring months, such as birds chirping, children playing outside, and water rushing in a stream. Have the students listen to the recording and identify each of the sounds.

This lesson addresses aspects of the following learning standard: Students will recognize that various substances and physical phenomena can be predictive of environmental changes that occur throughout the year. The lesson involves students' naturalist and linguistic intelligences. Assessment will involve students' accuracy in determining the natural sounds they hear.

- The key question of the next lesson is: What do we think about or feel when we hear music that has a spring theme? Select recordings of music having spring as the theme. Include at least one classical and one other piece to play for the students. Have the students comment on what the music makes them think about or feelings it evokes. After discussing some of the students' reactions, give them the choice of either writing in their journals about what the music makes them think about or feel or creating a poem or drawing a picture that represents their thinking. The purpose of this lesson is to promote students' interest in music and to help them realize that the sounds we hear can stimulate different thoughts and feelings.

   This lesson will address aspects of the following learning standards: Students will respond critically to a variety of works in the arts, connecting the individual work to other works and to other aspects of human endeavor and thought *(Arts Standard 3, by permission of the New York State Education Department);* and students will use spoken, written, and visual language to accomplish their own purposes e.g., for learning, enjoyment, persuasion, and the exchange of information *(National Standards for the English Language Arts, Standard 12, reprinted with permission of the International Reading Association www.reading.org).* The lesson involves students' musical, linguistic, and spatial intelligences. Assessment will involve observations of the students' verbal reactions to the music, their journal writing, poems, and drawings.

- Involve the students in an impromptu creative movement or dance activity accompanying the music. The key question of this lesson is: How can we show our reactions to music with our bodies? After listening to one of the music recordings having the spring theme, invite the students to invent different ways to move to the music. Some

students will be likely to use rhythmic patterns; others may perform large muscle movements or acrobatics, so this activity may be safer in the environment of a gymnasium or outside. This lesson will provide opportunities for the students to interpret the music individually in a movement exercise.

This lesson will address aspects of the following learning standards: Students will actively engage in the processes that constitute creation and performance in the arts dance, music, theatre, and visual arts and participate in various roles in the arts *(Arts Standard 1, by permission of the New York State Education Department);* and students will exhibit responsible personal and social behavior that respects self and others in physical activity settings *(Reprinted from Moving into the Future: National Standards for Physical Education (2004) with permission from the National Association for Sport and Physical Education (NASPE), 1900 Association Drive, Reston, VA 20191-1599).*

The lesson mainly involves students' musical, intrapersonal, and bodily-kinesthetic intelligences. Assessment will involve observations of the students' movement interpretations, their willingness to participate, and their interactions with one another during the exercise.

- The next lesson will be to help student learn how sound is produced. The key question of the lesson is: How is any sound produced? In this lesson, various vibrating objects will be used to help students discover that all sound is caused by vibration. Several objects, such as a drum, stringed instrument, a stretched rubber band, and others will be sounded as students observe. The students will be asked to decide what happens to each of the objects when it makes a sound.

   This lesson will address aspects of the following learning standards: Students use observation to collect information and draw conclusions about physical phenomena; and students recognize that materials and objects in the environment possess unique characteristics. The lesson will mainly involve students' logical–mathematical intelligence. Assessment of the lesson will involve noting the accuracy of students' verbal explanations regarding the cause of sound.

- Select and read an adaptation of a short story related to the spring theme, *The Proud Little Apple Blossom* (Andersen). The key question for this listening lesson is: How does the apple blossom change during this story? Follow the guided listening protocol when reading to the students in order to encourage their involvement in the lesson. Provide a purpose for listening to the reading; then, hold a discussion after the reading, raising questions about its content. (Guided listening is explained in Chapter 5 along with an example lesson plan for that protocol.) After the reading, have students write their own story or poem about spring, and have the students illustrate their writing with a drawing or painting. As an alternative, have students create collages to display that reflect the story. These listening, creative writing, and art activities provide students with opportunities to develop their listening skills and to express themselves by using a variety of forms. Using their completed work, assist the students in preparing a bulletin board display. Encourage the students to make decisions about how to arrange the display.

  This lesson addresses aspects of the following learning standards: Students use spoken, written, and visual language to accomplish their own purposes e.g., for learning, enjoyment, persuasion, and the exchange of information *(National IRA/NCTE Standards for the English Language Arts, Standard 12, reprinted with permission of the International Reading Association www.reading.org);* and students are knowledgeable about and make use of the materials and resources available for participation in arts in various roles *(Arts Standard 2, by permission of the New York State Education Department).* The lesson will involve students' linguistic, intrapersonal, and spatial intelligences. Assessment of the lesson will include observations of the students' listening skills and their facility when using art materials; a rubric will be constructed to assess students' writing. *(Note that this lesson can be repeated with different stories, books, and poems several times over the period of the unit.)*

- Teach a lesson on a holiday that occurs while studying the *Spring* unit. The key question for this lesson is: Why do we celebrate this holiday, and how do different people observe it? Select an appropriate multimedia program (DVD, video, or film) about the holiday to show and discuss for this lesson. The visual presentation should be selected to provide the students with insights about how the holiday originated and the different ways people in our multicultural society celebrate it. Conduct the lesson by following the guided viewing protocol. (The guided viewing protocol is explained in Chapter 5 along with an example lesson plan.) Provide a purpose for viewing the program; then, raise questions about it in a discussion at the end of the activity. Keep the lesson informal, emphasizing the information provided about the holiday. After the lesson, begin preparing a spring holiday current events bulletin board. Invite students to look through magazines and newspapers in the classroom to find articles and pictures about the holiday studied in the lesson. The local newspaper may be most meaningful to the students because it will contain items on familiar local events. Collect items for the display, and have the students decide how to set it up. Periodically, discuss new items that students locate with the class. The study of a spring holiday and discussion of related local current events should help the students realize that their community has activities that are related to this holiday which occurs during spring season. *(Other holidays that occur during the spring season can also be studied, and information about those holidays can be included in the bulletin board display.)*

The holiday lesson and display mainly address aspects of the following learning standard: Students understand the different ways people of diverse racial, religious, and ethnic groups, and of various national origins have transmitted their beliefs and values *(National History Content Standard 1B with permission from the National Center for History in the Schools, UCLA http:// nchs.ucla.edu)*. This viewing and current events lesson involves students' linguistic, spatial, interpersonal, and intrapersonal intelligences. Assessment of the lesson will involve observations of the students' participation in the discussions during the lesson and their contributions to the current events display. *(Note that lessons following a similar procedure on other spring holidays can be added.)*

■ Conduct a lesson on the Carolina wren—or another bird—that is found in the northeast during the spring season. The key question of this lesson is: What are the characteristics and needs of a Carolina wren? Help the students to learn about its food, size, color, and its nesting habits by preparing a PowerPoint presentation that includes photographs and information about the Carolina wren. The lesson will be conducted by following the guided viewing protocol during which guided questions are raised about this bird and its needs. After the presentation, involve the students in considering what materials and design would be necessary to build a birdhouse that would attract the wren. Next, ask the students to create their own designs or divide the class into groups of three to develop designs for a proposed wrenhouse model. Next, using their designs, have students construct model wrenhouses from cardboard, wood scraps, or other simple materials that are available. After the models have been constructed, give students an opportunity to explain their constructions orally to the class; the reasons for their particular designs should be included in their explanations. The lesson involves the

students in experiences in science, technology, and art.

The wren study, birdhouse design, and construction will address aspects of the following learning standards: Students will recognize the needs and distinguishing features of various animal and plant species; students will prepare original designs and materials using their previous knowledge; and students are able to use technology to create original plans and constructions. The experiences in this lesson will involve students' naturalist, spatial, and intrapersonal intelligences. Assessment of the lesson will include a short quiz on the wren, observations of students' participation in the wrenhouse design process, and a rubric to evaluate students' oral explanations of their designs.

■ Optionally, in addition to the above lessons for the *Spring* unit, prepare a learning center with at least ten activities for the students to complete independently. One activity could include examining additional samples of water taken from various sources in the local neighborhood and writing descriptions of and/or drawing pictures of what the students observe. If frogs' eggs are available, samples may be collected and placed in the learning center for the students to observe. Books or other materials at the students' reading levels on the development of frogs from eggs into tadpoles and adult frogs should be placed in the learning center. Activities in the center may also include reading and preparing short reviews or reactions to other books, stories, and poems; creative writing; listening to music; and mathematical problem-solving. Each activity should have a task card to explain directions. *(Refer to Figure 3.13, Teaching Assistant on Designing a Learning Center, which appears earlier in this chapter.)*

The learning center provides students with independent work to extend practice with the concepts that they are studying during the unit in the areas of science, music, language arts, and mathematics. Learning center activities can address learning standards in several disciplines; the specific standards will depend on the kinds of practice available in the center. Depending on the actual activities included, the learning center will provide for experiences that involve most of students' multiple intelligences. *(See Figure 5.7 for one way to organize the learning center.)*

Assessment Plan

The following will provide specific assessments for the unit:

- During the initial lesson for the unit, the students will prepare a list of questions for the *Spring* study. This is the important first step in studying any topic. They will also perform experiments on plants and study water samples taken from various locations in their local neighborhood. Students will prepare graphs of temperature changes and maintain records of precipitation during the period of the unit. *(The students' questions, experiments, and record-keeping will indicate that they have gained insights about how to investigate a topic or problem.)*

- Students will paint a mural that presents a summary of the signs of spring that they find while on a field trip walking in their local neighborhood. During the field trip, they will draw sketches of new plant growth or other signs of spring that they notice. Their individual sketches will be transferred and enlarged on the mural. *(The drawings and mural will demonstrate that the students have detected and prepared a visual summary of signs of spring in their local neighborhood.)*

- Students will listen to stories, poems, and music having a spring theme. They will write their own stories or poems and prepare drawings that represent their reactions and thinking about the season of spring, and they will participate in a movement activity accompanied by music having spring as the theme. *(The listening lessons, creative writing, and art will help to indicate students' understanding that the spring season affects people, their literature, and art.)*

- Students will examine and prepare records of the distinctive features of the different plant specimens collected during their field trip. *(These investigations of plants will demonstrate that the students notice and can express the differences in the plants they examine.)*

- Students will plant seeds and care for them to maintain healthy plants during the period of the unit. They will study an example of a bird that is found in their area during the spring season, the Carolina wren, pass a quiz on the needs of that bird, develop designs, and construct models for a birdhouse that would attract a wren.

- During a lesson on the cause of sound, students will discover that sound is caused by a vibrating object by observing that each of several objects and instruments vibrate when they are made to produce sounds. The students will also listen to and identify sounds of nature that are typical in their local environment during the spring season.

- After studying holidays that are celebrated in their community during the spring season, students will prepare a display of current events that reflect any of the holiday celebrations. The students will look for pictures and articles in their local newspaper to include, and they will help to arrange the display.

In addition to the above specific assessments:

- Students will be observed for their interest, participation, listening skills, their general behavior, cooperation, and sharing of materials, and their accuracy in conducting experiments.

- Maintain anecdotal records of observations about each student's general work habits, working and learning style preferences, cooperation when working with others, and ability to learn through experiential activities.

- Keep a journal throughout the unit of work. Include observations of activities and lessons that appear to be most helpful in developing the unit objectives. Also, note the need for revisions in the unit plan—areas that need to be strengthened and additional activities that may be offered to meet students' individual learning styles.

- Administer an examination at the conclusion of the unit to assess facts, concepts, and generalizations developed in the study. The examination may be given orally for students who have difficulty reading the questions. Students should achieve a minimum passing grade of 75 percent.
- Each student will be required to maintain a unit portfolio. Create rubrics for assessing any papers or project work to be included in the portfolio. Students will be involved in selecting the following materials for their portfolios:

Samples of written work or work in progress, including creative writing and any written reports
Examples or photographs of the mural and individual art
A journal maintained by the student
Records kept on daily temperature and precipitation
Examinations

Unit Materials
Materials for Students
ABC Teach. *Spring activities.* Retrieved from http://www.abcteach.com/directory/seasonal seasons/spring/
Andersen, H. C. *The proud little apple blossom (adapted).* Retrieved from http://www .apples4theteacher.com/holidays/spring/ short-stories/the-proud-little-apple-blossom .html

A DVD, CD, or videotape program on the needs of plants (to show after children conduct their own experiments with plants)
A selection of children's books on spring from the school and public libraries
A teacher-prepared computer slide presentation on wrens
Computer software and CD-ROM titles featuring information on the seasons and nature
Marigold (or other annual) seeds for planting
Materials for experiments with plants
Microscopes
Outdoor thermometer
Recording of spring sounds (teacher prepared)
Recordings of music and environmental sounds
Rulers
Tuning fork

Informational Resources for Teachers
Bobick, J. E., & Balaban, N. E. (Eds.). (2003). *The handy science answer book* (Rev. & expanded ed.). Detroit, MI: Visible Ink Press.
Brewer, D. (2001). *Wrens, dippers, and thrashes.* New Haven, CT: Yale University Press.
Gogerly, L. (2005). *Spring.* Vero Beach, FL: Rourke.
Phillips, R. (1978). *Trees of North America and Europe.* New York: Random House.
Rosen, M. (1990). *Spring festivals.* New York: Bookwright Press.
Smith, James (consultant with the local weather TV channel) Weinstein, E. W. (1999). *Vernal equinox.* Retrieved from http://scienceworld. wolfram.com/astronomy/VernalEquinox .html
Williams, J. (1997). *The weather book* (2nd ed.). New York: Vintage Books.

ACTIVITY

Allison Ramirez is a teacher in an urban community in the Midwest. She is planning an interdisciplinary unit on industrial growth in the United States for students in her fourth grade. Two of her *knowledge* level general objectives are the following:

Students will understand that geographic factors and natural resources in the United States influenced the inventions, particularly in transportation and communication, during the 1800s and 1900s.

Students will understand that immigrants to the United States during the 1800s and 1900s made significant contributions to the growth and development of the United States.

Complete the following tasks which are related to the two understandings expressed in these knowledge level general objectives for the unit:

1. Study your state's learning standards in social studies to locate a content learning standard that addresses each of the two understandings.
2. Write essential questions related to each understanding.
3. Devise assessment plans to help determine the students' achievement of each understanding.

Finally, write a description of a lesson or activity that will help students develop each of the two understandings.

REFERENCES

Berk, L. E. (2008). *Infants, children, and adolescents* (6th ed.). Boston: Pearson/Allyn & Bacon.

Bruner, J. (1963). *The process of education.* New York: Vintage Books.

Bruner, J. (1990). *Acts of meaning.* Cambridge, MA: Harvard University Press.

Case, R. (1985). *Intellectual development: Birth to adulthood.* Orlando, FL: Academic Press.

Charbonneau, M. P., & Reider, B. E. (1995). *The integrated elementary classroom: A developmental model of education for the 21st century.* Boston: Pearson/Allyn & Bacon.

Checkley, K. (1997). The first seven . . . and the eighth. *Educational Leadership, 55*(1), 8–13.

Flavell, J. H. (1985). *Cognitive development* (2nd ed.). Upper Saddle River, NJ: Prentice Hall.

Forman, E. A., Minick, N., & Stone, C. A. (1993). *Contexts for learning.* New York: Oxford University Press.

Gardner, H. (1991). *The unschooled mind: How children think and how schools should teach.* New York: Basic Books.

Gardner, H. (1993). *Multiple intelligences: The theory in practice.* New York: Basic Books.

Gardner, H. (1995, January 6). Creating creativity. *The Times Educational Supplement,* No. 4097, p. 15.

Jacobs, H. (Ed.). (1989). *Interdisciplinary curriculum: Design and implementation.* Alexandria, VA: Association for Supervision and Curriculum Development.

Lillard, P. (1972). *Montessori: A modern approach.* New York: Schocken Books.

Montessori, M. (1964). *The Montessori method.* New York: Schocken Books.

NCSS Task Force. (1989). Social studies for early childhood and elementary school children preparing for the 21st century: A report from NCSS Task Force on Early Childhood/ Elementary Social Studies. *Social Education,* 53, 14–23.

Pappas, C. C., Kiefer, B. Z., & Levstik, L. S. (2006). *An integrated language perspective in the elementary school* (4th ed.). NY: Longman.

Phillips, J. L. (1981). *Piaget's theory: A primer.* San Francisco: Freeman.

Piaget, J. (1955). *The language and thought of the child.* New York: Meridian.

Piaget, J. (1966). *Judgment and reasoning in the child.* Totowa, NJ: Littlefield, Adams.

Piaget, J. (1970). *Science of education and the psychology of the child.* (D. Coltman, Trans.). New York: Orion Press.

Piaget, J. (1973). *To understand is to invent.* New York: Grossman.

Piaget, J. (1974). *Understanding causality.* New York: Norton.

Piaget, J. (1976). *The grasp of consciousness.* Cambridge, MA: Harvard University Press.

Piaget, J., & Inhelder, B. (1969). *The psychology of the child.* New York: Basic Books.

Ravich, D. (1988). Tot sociology. *American Educator, 12*(3), 38–39.

Santrock, J. W. (2008). *Children* (10th ed.). Boston: McGraw-Hill.

Standing, E. M. (1957). *Maria Montessori: Her life and her work.* New York: New American Library.

Stephens, L. S. (1974). *The teacher's guide to open education.* New York: Holt, Rinehart & Winston.

Vygotsky, L. S. (1986). *Thought and language* (New rev. ed.). Cambridge, MA: MIT Press.

Wertsch, J. V. (1985). *Vygotsky and the social formation of mind.* Cambridge, MA: Harvard University Press.

Wiggins, G., & McTighe, J. (2005). *Understanding by design* (2nd ed.). Alexandria VA: Association of Supervision & Curriculum Development.

SUGGESTED READINGS

The following readings provide additional background material for the topics included in this chapter.

Unit Planning

Armstrong, T. (2009). *Multiple intelligences in the classroom* (3rd ed.). Alexandria, VA: Association for Supervision and Curriculum Development.

Ellis, A. K. (2007). *Teaching and learning elementary social studies* (8th ed.). Boston: Pearson/Allyn & Bacon.

Katz, L., & Chard, S. C. (2000). *Engaging children's minds: The project approach* (2nd ed.). Stamford, CT: Ablex.

Kauchak, D. P., & Eggen, P. D. (2007). *Learning and teaching: Research-based methods* (5th ed.). Boston: Pearson/Allyn & Bacon.

Messick, R. G., & Reynolds, K. E. (1992). *Middle level curriculum in action.* White Plains, NY: Longman.

Post, T. R., Ellis, A. K., Humphreys, A. H., & Buggey, L. J. (1997). *Interdisciplinary approaches to curriculum: Themes for teaching.* Upper Saddle River, NJ: Prentice Hall.

Roberts, P. L., & Kellough, R. D. (2008). *A guide for developing interdisciplinary thematic units* (4th ed.). Upper Saddle River, NJ: Prentice Hall.

Wadsworth, B. J. (1978). *Piaget for the classroom teacher.* New York: Longman.

Learning Centers

Fisk, L., & Lindgren, H. (1974). *Learning centers.* Glen Ridge, NJ: Exceptional Press.

Fredericks, A., & Cheesebrough, D. (1993). *Science for all children: Elementary school methods.* New York: Harper Collins.

Isbell, R. (1995). *The complete learning center book.* Beltsville, MD: Gryphon House.

Kaplan, S. N., Kaplan, J. B., Madsen, S. K., & Gould, B. T. (1980). *Change for children: Ideas and activities for individualizing learning.* Glenview, IL: Scott Foresman.

McClay, J. L. (1996). *Learning centers.* Westminster, CA: Teacher Created Materials.

Opitz, M. F. (1994). *Learning centers: Getting them started, keeping them going.* New York: Scholastic.

Poppe, C. A., & Van Matre, N. A. (1985). *Science learning centers for primary grades.* West Nyack, NY: Center for Applied Research in Education.

4 Designing Multidisciplinary Units

*Student researchers meeting
with teachers.*

OVERVIEW

This chapter reviews the process for planning a multidisciplinary unit for students in the upper elementary
grades and middle school. The focus of the chapter is on the following:

- An introduction to multidisciplinary unit planning
- Development in middle childhood and early adolescence and the design of multidisciplinary units
- An outline for a multidisciplinary unit
- A description of the multidisciplinary unit planning process for students in elementary
  classrooms and departmentalized middle schools with explanations and examples
- A multidisciplinary unit plan example

Introduction to Multidisciplinary Unit Planning

In Chapter 1, it was explained that in most fields, the significant difference between approaching a study from an *interdisciplinary* or *multidisciplinary* approach is that in multidisciplinary studies, a research team works together to plan the study of a topic in which the members have a mutual interest and some expertise to contribute. However, once the study is planned, the team members work independently from one another. They each use techniques typical of their individual disciplines to explore their individual disciplinary aspects of the research. Individual members report their findings to the group at the end of the study.

A multidisciplinary approach to instruction parallels this model. All students in a class study the same topic, theme, or problem. However, unlike the procedure in an interdisciplinary study—where all students work on the same or similar tasks—the multidisciplinary unit is subdivided for research purposes. Student committees are formed to assume responsibility for researching and reporting to the class only a part of the study. The topic can be divided along disciplinary lines—as it is in multidisciplinary research in other fields—or the topic itself can be separated into sub-topics. Four key features of the multidisciplinary unit structure are the following:

- The topic, theme, or problem of the unit is subdivided for research either by discipline or sub-topics.
- Students work on committees to study the contributions from different disciplines or sub-topics. While all instruction is the responsibility of the classroom teacher in an elementary classroom, in departmentalized schools, several teachers work with the same students and meet in classes organized by discipline.
- Students are actively involved in developing questions and suggesting areas to be researched.
- The research process guides the development of the unit and its procedures.

As students mature, their changing developmental abilities allow them to undertake studies that are increasingly more demanding and sophisticated. Most students at the upper elementary and middle school levels have developed adequate research, reading, and writing skills for the academic work required by multidisciplinary studies. At these grade levels, we can usually find more independent-level reading and other resource materials prepared on topics for student research.

Multidisciplinary studies offer an especially appropriate alternative to interdisciplinary units and are specifically well adapted for students in the upper elementary grades and departmentalized middle schools. Students are organized to serve on separate disciplinary committees—history, geography, science, mathematics, economics, health, music, art, and so on. A multidisciplinary unit can also be divided into sub-topics instead of by discipline. Each committee researches only that part of the study pertaining to its discipline or sub-topic. For example, in the multidisciplinary unit plan example at the end of this chapter, the topic *Principal Deserts in the United States* is divided into four sub-topics that include the four largest desert regions in the United States. Each student committee is responsible for only one of those regions. At the conclusion of the unit, committees assemble and report their findings to other members of their class.

In departmentalized schools, multidisciplinary units are taught by teams of teachers. The study is separated by the disciplines taught by the various team members. In the beginning, the team works together to decide the learning standards and other components of the unit plan and to determine the student committees that the unit will require, the general assignments, and culminating activities. One teacher will then assume responsibility for introducing the new unit to the students; this will often be the social studies teacher because multidisciplinary topics are often associated with that subject. After the unit is introduced, each teacher on the team will work with the same group of students but separately in their individual disciplines. For example, the social studies teacher on a team will teach aspects of a unit that involve history, geography, economics, civics, and citizenship; the English language arts teacher will include literature and elements of writing related to the unit topic; the science teacher will explore contributions from the sciences; and so on. Individual team members use methods and techniques that are suited to their disciplines.

In the next section of this chapter, multidisciplinary unit planning will be explained and illustrated with examples. Note that because most of the components of the unit that will be developed are the same as those for interdisciplinary units, this discussion will avoid repetition of detailed explanations of learning standards, general objectives, and essential questions that were covered in Chapter 3. Instead, the emphasis in this chapter will be on the aspects of those components that are unique to multidisciplinary units, such as organizing the study by discipline or sub-topic and the structure of student committees.

Multidisciplinary Unit Plan Outline and Design

Planning a multidisciplinary unit includes the following:

- Consider the context for learning in which the unit will be taught.
- Determine the topic, theme, or problem of the unit.
- Determine the general objectives of the unit—the knowledge, skills, and dispositions that will be fostered.
- Determine the learning standards that the unit will address.
- Determine the essential questions that will guide the study.
- Prepare the unit assessment plan.
- Prepare the unit learning plan: Construct a unit chart of student research committees, areas for committee research, and disciplinary teachers' instructional tasks; and write descriptions of lessons and activities.
- Prepare a list of important materials that will be required.

The format of a multidisciplinary unit plan includes related learning standards; general objectives—the knowledge, skills, and dispositions the unit will promote; essential questions; unit learning plan; assessment plan; and a list of materials. While the process involved in planning a multidisciplinary unit follows the *backward design* unit planning process (Wiggins and McTighe, 2005) described in Chapter 1, the organization of the unit plan outline (Figure 4.1) is one that may be more familiar to those who have previously followed other unit planning outlines.

Note that the sequence followed when planning the various components of a multidisciplinary unit plan can differ depending on individual teaching preferences and styles. For example, we can begin with any component of the unit: general objectives, learning standards, ideas for lessons and activities, essential questions, assessments, and so on. However, in the end, the standards, general objectives, essential questions, and unit assessments, and the lessons and activities of the unit must all be related.

Considering the Context for Learning

The context for learning—as explained in Chapter 3—involves students' developmental, academic, and social characteristics as well as the available facilities and materials in the school. The majority of students in the upper grades and middle school will have achieved what Piaget and Inhelder (1969) describe as *concrete operational thought.* This pattern of thinking and reasoning allows students to deal with more abstract concepts and systems of concepts provided they have the opportunity to relate these concepts to personal or direct experiences. Although Piaget also believed that some students in middle childhood approach *formal operational thought*—a type of thinking that involves genuine hypothetical thought—during their adolescent years, post-Piagetian researchers suggest this is not typical of most students at this level (Santrock, 2008).

FIGURE 4.1 A Multidisciplinary unit plan outline.

Topic:

Level:

Estimated Unit Length:

Learning Standards:

General Objectives:
  Knowledge
  Skills
  Dispositions

Essential Questions:

Learning Plan:
  Unit Chart
  Disciplinary Instructional Tasks
    Instruction:
      Activities:

Assessment Plan:

Materials:

Socially, older students usually enjoy working in groups with their peers where they can share tasks and become involved in making decisions. Under our direction, the students can learn to organize a research topic into manageable parts by discipline or subtopic. An important part in planning a unit involves determining the disciplinary or topical student committees that can be formed for the study. The specific disciplines involved will depend on the learning standards, general objectives, and essential questions to be addressed in the unit.

Ordinarily, older students can read better than students at earlier grade levels. It is therefore somewhat easier to provide them with more suitable independent reading and other resource materials. Their improved skills also enable them to make increasing use of computer and other technology resources, local and distance networking, and Internet services. In middle school, students continue to need opportunities to acquire knowledge by using their individual working and learning styles and multiple intelligences (MIs).

The following is an explanation of each component in a multidisciplinary unit. Examples are from a multidisciplinary unit plan on the topic, *Principal Deserts of the United States*. Although that unit is planned for students in the fifth grade, it can be adapted for other middle school grade levels. The examples are intended only to illustrate the planning process. A few examples for each component in the process are included with the explanations; the complete unit plan appears at the end of this chapter.

Selecting a Topic, Theme, or Problem

Explanation of the task: Topics selected for students in the upper elementary grades and middle school should be kept broad to increase opportunities for student participation. Excellent planning guides that have been developed by state departments of education and the National Council for the Social Studies can help in the selection process. In long-term planning, we should consult statewide and local curriculum guides and lists of learning standards to assist us in making decisions about the topics to be taught. Often, a prescribed course of study must be met, especially for the middle school (Kellough & Kellough, 2003).

Multidisciplinary topics can also be selected from disciplines other than those included in the social studies curriculum. Post, Ellis, Humphreys, and Buggey (1997) show examples of several topics with an environmental focus. Environmental topics are interesting to most students in the upper elementary grades and middle school, and they always involve several disciplines. Regardless of the source of topics, several criteria may be helpful when making final decisions about the topics that need to be taught:

- Topics that address specific learning standards and are required by the state should be included where they fit most naturally.
- The topic should be broad and inclusive. However, time constraints for teaching the unit, if any, should be considered because they may influence the type of topic that can be investigated (Criteria for Selection of Class Research Topics, 1966).

- To be sufficiently motivating, the topic selected should be of inherent interest to the students whenever possible. The scope of the study should also be flexible enough to allow for differences in individual interests, multiple intelligence areas, and learning styles.
- The unit topic should involve all the disciplines that can help to inform it.
- The availability of resource materials needed by students to investigate the topic should be considered. Required reading materials should be selected according to the students' independent reading levels.
- A topic should help to broaden students' understanding of their multicultural world and strengthen their sense of social justice and responsibility. The example below shows the topic, grade level, and estimated length of the *Deserts* unit.

Topic: Principal Deserts of the United States

Level: Grade 5

This unit plan is designed specifically for students in the fifth grade, and it can be adapted for students in the sixth or seventh grades.

Estimated Unit Length: 5–6 weeks

Determining the Unit General Objectives

Explanation of the task: Prepare a list of general objectives. General objectives include the knowledge, skills, and dispositions that the unit will aim to develop. Any general objectives that are listed must be consistent with and elaborate the intent of the unit learning standards. The following are examples:

General Objectives
This unit will assist in developing the following knowledge (understandings), skills, and dispositions.

Knowledge
Students will understand that:
The discovery of desert regions in the United States impacted the lives of Native Americans who were living in those regions at the time they were discovered by others.

Skills
Students will improve their ability to:
Design investigations.

Dispositions
Students will:
Work cooperatively and courteously with others in group situations.

Determining the Unit Content Learning Standards

Explanation of the task: After selecting a topic for the unit, prepare a list of the content learning standards that the unit will address. Content learning standards are long-term goals. They are selected from national, state, and local level lists prepared by professional organizations, state departments of education, and other generic standards typical of those prepared by school districts. The standards give direction to the study and suggest the important understandings and skills that will be developed and assessed. Because they are comprehensive, a unit may not address all aspects of a standard; those that are listed must at least be partly addressed in the unit. Two examples from the *Deserts* unit follow.

Learning Standards

This unit will contribute to developing aspects of the following learning standards.

Students will:

- Identify issues and problems in the past and analyze the interests, values, perspectives, and points of view of those involved in the situation *(Historical Thinking Standards/*

Grades 5-12, Standard 5.A, National Center for History in the Schools/UCLA http://nchs. ucla.edu).

- Develop critical sensitivities such as empathy and skepticism regarding attitudes, values, and behaviors of people in different historical contexts *(National Council for the Social Studies/ Middle Grades II.e, reprinted by permission).*

Preparing the Essential Questions of the Unit

Explanation of the task: Prepare essential questions and other questions that reflect the general objectives—knowledge, skills, and dispositions—of the unit, and define specifically what students should gain from their study. Essential questions must also be consistent with the unit learning standards. Two examples from the *Deserts* unit follow.

Essential Questions

The following questions form the basis of the *Deserts* study:

- How, when, and by whom were the principal deserts in the United States discovered?

- How did discovery of the desert regions impact Native American people who had been living in them?

Preparing the Unit Assessment Plan

Explanation of the task: The assessment plan for a multidisciplinary unit describes the specific requirements of students that will be assessed during the study. Those assessments demonstrate how well students are able to respond to the essential questions of the unit and the extent to which they have met the learning standards and general objectives.

The assessments need to show how well students can apply their new knowledge in practical ways with applications, interpretations, creative work, original designs and models, art projects, journals, presentations, experiments, and so on. Similar to the interdisciplinary unit assessments that were described in Chapter 3, multidisciplinary studies also usually include examinations, papers, and observations of students. Each assessment should link to one or more of the unit essential questions. An example follows.

Assessment Plan

Committee Reports Each committee must present a report to the class about the desert region it studied that includes information about its discovery, early inhabitants, size, location, temperature variations, rainfall, plant life, animal species, crops produced, mineral deposits, historical sites, national parks, famous musicians, and famous artists. *(The accuracy and completeness of each committee's report will provide for assessment of the students' ability to locate and report this information. The committee reports will be assessed using rubrics.)*

Preparing the Unit Learning Plan

The unit learning plan includes two parts. First, a chart is constructed that outlines a list of possible student research committees, areas for committee research, and disciplinary teachers' instructional tasks for the teacher or teachers. Second, brief descriptions of each disciplinary teacher's instructional tasks in the unit chart are prepared.

Constructing the Unit Chart

Explanation of the task: A multidisciplinary unit plan chart substitutes for the type of web design included in interdisciplinary unit plans. When constructing the unit chart, the topic should be clearly stated, with titles of the student research committees to be organized for the study. The information that each of the committees should attempt to locate is included on the chart to provide the committees with an outline of material that may be possible to collect.

The chart also includes specific lessons and activities listed by discipline. These comprise the learning plan for the unit. In elementary classes, the classroom teacher assumes the responsibility for most instruction but may be able to arrange with art and music teachers to help with those aspects of the study. In a departmentalized school, the responsibilities are divided among the different team teachers and their respective disciplines. Optionally, lists can be prepared instead of constructing a unit chart because the chart for some topics can become overcrowded and difficult to read. A partially completed chart for the *Deserts* unit is shown in Figure 4.2. Only a sample of the kinds of information are included in the example. The entire unit chart can be found in the completed *Deserts* unit at the end of this chapter.

Preparing Descriptions of Disciplinary Teachers' Instructional Tasks

Explanation of the task: Instead of designing complete instructional plans in the multidisciplinary unit plan design, brief descriptions of the disciplinary teachers' instructional tasks indicated in the unit chart can be written. The descriptions only suggest the lesson

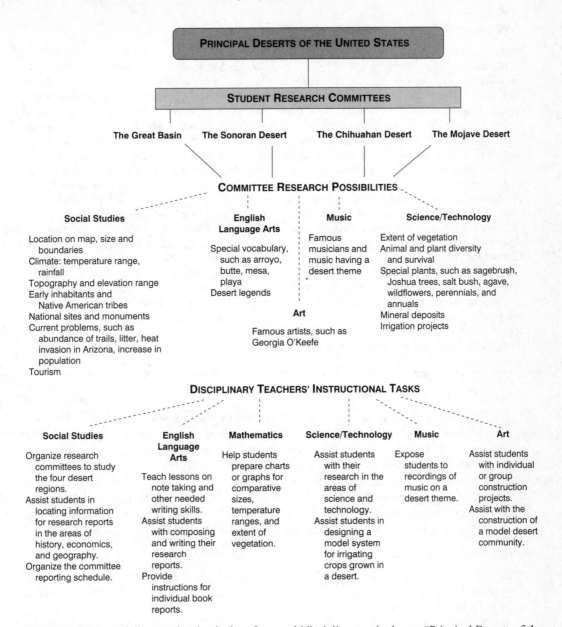

FIGURE 4.2 A partially completed unit chart for a multidisciplinary unit plan on "Principal Deserts of the United States."

plans that need to be developed by the classroom teacher or various members of the teaching team. Using the descriptions, complete lesson plans can be designed when they are needed. (Note that lesson planning is discussed in Chapter 5. In that chapter, there are guidelines for lesson planning using several different procedural protocols for different types of lessons.) Examples of an instructional plan and an activity from the *Deserts* unit follow.

Learning Plan
Instruction

Introduce the unit and organize student research committees. The first lesson in this unit will introduce the Deserts unit and organize students for their committee work. The lesson is in two parts and will take two class periods to accomplish. The first part of the lesson will be a guided viewing of a PowerPoint presentation that introduces the students to the four largest desert regions in the United States—the Great Basin, Chihuauha Desert, Mojave Desert, and Sonoran Desert. (The guided viewing protocol is explained in Chapter 5 along with an example lesson plan.) Following the presentation, students will be told that the class will be divided into committees that will study each of the four deserts regions. The students will be given an opportunity to consider which of the regions they have seen in the presentation that they would like to investigate and then be asked to list the four regions in order of preference. Using the students' lists, committees will be formed.

Activities

Research committees. Student committees will be formed to investigate each of the four desert regions of the unit study. Each committee will have six to eight student members. Composition of the group should be planned carefully, considering factors such as leadership, learning styles, social factors, the students' ability to share responsibilities, and their individual talents, interests, and academic capabilities. It will be important to ensure that all members of each committee share in both the research and reporting responsibilities. Develop a "buddy" system in committees that include special-needs students, who often leave the classroom during regular times devoted to research or other class activities. Those who leave for special assistance programs can be paired with others in their committee groups who will review with them the committee's work during their absence.

Listing the Unit Materials

Explanation of the task: The materials needed for the unit are separated into two lists: (a) materials that will be used with or for students and (b) informational resources for the teacher. It is not necessary to list every item. A simple listing of the kinds of texts and trade books; computer software; teacher-prepared presentations; DVD and videotape programs; and other materials are sufficient for the unit plan. These materials rapidly become dated, and items are usually available each time the unit is retaught. Addresses of Internet resources (URLs) and names of people who have been helpful as consultants or as guest speakers can be listed. Most of the usual art and other consumable materials need not be listed. Several examples follow.

Materials
Instructional Materials

- Art materials for projects and report covers
- Deserts: Geology and resources. United States Geological Survey. Retrieved from www.usgs.gov/science/
- Sufficient quantities of social studies and science textbooks from a variety of publishers (four to six copies of each)

Informational Resources
The following is a sample of materials available. A search for "deserts of the United States" will yield numerous other sources that are available on the Internet for students and teachers.

- *Desert USA.* (n.d.). Retrieved from http://www.desertusa.com
- *Digital desert.* (n.d.). Retrieved from http://aeve.com/digitaldesertt/ddpi/lalol.html
- Ring E. (2005). *Drylands.* Detroit, MI: Blackbirch Press.

Multidisciplinary Unit Plan Example

The following is an example of a complete multidisciplinary unit plan.

Topic: Principal Deserts of the United States

Level: Grade 5

This unit plan is designed specifically for students in the fifth grade, but it can be adapted for students in the sixth or seventh grades.

Estimated Unit Length: 5–6 weeks

Learning Standards

This unit will contribute to developing aspects of the following learning standards.

Students will:

- Develop critical sensitivities such as empathy and skepticism regarding attitudes, values, and behaviors of people in different historical contexts *(National Council for the Social Studies/Middle Grades II.e, reprinted by permission).*

- Identify issues and problems in the past and analyze the interests, values, perspectives, and points of view of those involved in the situation *(Historical Thinking Standards/ Grades 5-12 Standard 5.A, National Center for History in the Schools/UCLA http://nchs. ucla.edu).*

- Interpret data presented in timelines by designating appropriate equidistant intervals of time and recording events according to the temporal order in which they occurred *(Historical Thinking Standards/Grades 5-12 Standard 1.E, National Center for History in the Schools/UCLA http://nchs.ucla.edu).*

- Elaborate mental maps of locales, regions, and the world that demonstrate understanding of relative location, direction, size, and shape *(National Council for the Social Studies/Content Standards/Social Studies/ Middle Grades III.a, reprinted by permission).*

- Understand how human actions modify the physical environment *(National Geography Standards Standard 14/Geography Education Standards Project. 1994. Geography for*

Life: National Geography Standards, 1994, Washington, DC: National Geographic Research and Exploration).

- Read a wide range of print and non-print texts to build an understanding of texts, of themselves, and of the cultures of the United States and the world to acquire new information; to respond to the needs and demands of society and the workplace; and for personal fulfillment. Among these texts are fiction and nonfiction, classic and contemporary works *(National IRA/NCTE Standards for the English Language Arts, Standard 1, reprinted with permission of the International Reading Association www.reading .org).*

- Respond critically to a variety of works in the arts, connecting the individual work to other works and to other aspects of human endeavor and thought *(Arts Standard 3, by permission of the New York State Education Department).*

- Use a variety of technological and informational resources to gather and synthesize information and to create and communicate knowledge *(National IRA/NCTE Standards for the English Language Arts, Standard 8, reprinted with permission of the International Reading Association www.reading.org).*

- Know how to use maps and other geographic representations, tools, and technologies to acquire, process, and report information *(National Geography Standards Standard 1/Geography Education Standards Project. 1994. Geography for Life: National Geography Standards, 1994, Washington,*

(continued)

DC: National Geographic Research and Exploration).

- Actively engage in the processes that constitute creation and performance in the arts dance, music, theatre, and visual arts and participate in various roles in the arts *(Arts Standard 1, by permission of the New York State Education Department).*
- Recognize the distinguishing features and needs of various animal and plant species.
- Construct records of data they collect and explain patterns observed in those records.
- Raise questions and issues to generate inquiries and conduct investigations.
- Be able to use technology to create plans and original constructions.

General Objectives

This unit will assist in developing the following knowledge (understandings), skills, and dispositions.

Knowledge

Students will understand that:

- The discovery of desert regions in the United States impacted the lives of Native Americans who were living in those regions at the time they were discovered by others.
- The principal desert regions in the United States vary in significant ways, such as size, location, natural resources, life forms, temperature, and rainfall.
- Plants and animals in desert regions are those that are adapted to the severe conditions of a desert climate.
- Irrigation projects have enabled the adaptation of desert regions for farming and have contributed to the growth in the population of desert regions.
- Major problems face our deserts today, including heat invasion in Arizona, an over-abundance of trails, litter, threats to animal and plant life, and the dramatic increase in population.
- The works of writers, artists, and musicians have been influenced by living in a desert region.

Skills

Students will improve their ability to:

- Design investigations
- Locate and read informational sources

- Collect and record data from informational sources
- Read and interpret maps
- Prepare group and individual reports of research
- Construct charts and graphs to show patterns in collected data
- Create art with various media
- Design and construct models
- Write essays
- Follow the conventions of grammar, syntax, spelling, and punctuation when writing

Dispositions

Students will:

- Work cooperatively and courteously with others in group situations
- Gain sensitivity to the problems exploration of new regions can cause people living in those regions
- Develop the desire to search for understanding
- Increase their interest in inquiring

Essential Questions

The following questions form the basis of the *Deserts* study:

- How, when, and by whom were the principal deserts in the United States discovered?
- How did discovery of the desert regions impact Native American people who had been living in them?
- How can the major desert regions in the United States be distinguished from one another?
- In what ways have plant and animal species adapted to life in the principal desert regions of the United States?
- What natural resources do the principal deserts in the United States possess?
- How do irrigation projects work, and what effects have they had on the principal desert regions in the United States?
- What problems do the principal desert regions in the United States face today?
- In what ways has living in a desert region affected the work of famous writers, artists, and musicians?
- What precautions should people take for survival in a desert?

Learning Plan
Unit Chart
(See Figure 4.3.)
Disciplinary Teachers' Instructional Tasks

Instruction: Introduce the unit and organize student research committees. The first lesson in this unit will introduce the Deserts unit and organize students for their committee work. The lesson is in two parts and will take two class periods to accomplish. The first part of the lesson will be a guided viewing of a PowerPoint presentation that introduces the students to the four largest desert regions in the United States—the Great Basin, Chihuauha Desert, Mojave Desert, and Sonoran Desert. (The guided viewing protocol is explained in Chapter 5 along with an example lesson plan.) Following the presentation, students will be told that the class will be divided into committees that will study each of the four deserts regions. The students will be given an opportunity to consider which of the regions they have seen in the presentation that they would like to investigate and then be asked to list the four regions in order of preference. Using the students' lists, committees will be formed.

At the second class session, students will be given their committee assignments. The list of essential questions for the unit will be shared with students to assist them in their investigations. The committees will then meet and be asked to accomplish three tasks—to select a committee chair and recorder, to make a list of any additional questions they may have about the desert region they will be studying, and to divide the research responsibilities among the committee members. During the committee meeting time, the teacher will circulate to assist where needed. The recorder for each committee will be responsible for handing in a record of the committee's decisions at the end of the period.

Introduce and review related literature. Select and introduce to the students books on the desert theme, such as *America's Deserts* by Marianne D. Wallace (1996).

Conduct a field trip to a local museum of natural history (if available). Prepare students for a field trip to a local museum of natural history. A list of important questions should be prepared by the students and teacher to guide their time at the field site. On the day

of the trip, students should have a list of the questions with them for reference as they try to gain answers at the museum. After returning to the classroom, conduct a discussion using the same questions to elicit any answers the students have gained from the trip. Students should include any new information gained in their notebooks for reference.

Teach skills lessons on letter-writing and note-taking. Some students will need to write away for information via regular mail or e-mail. Either teach a lesson to all the students to show them an appropriate form for business correspondence, and/or assist individuals who need to write for information during the unit. Review and then continue the series of letter-writing and note-taking lessons started during the previous units.

Teach locational skills. Assist the students in locating information for their topics throughout the study. Some formal locational skills lessons may need to be taught. It may be possible to ask the school librarian (or media specialist) to assist in teaching a series of lessons on locating reference materials in the library or media center. In a departmentalized team, the English language arts teacher can assume this responsibility. Assist any students who need help in locating information from authentic sites on the Internet. A classroom computer connected to the Internet with LCD projection will be used to demonstrate searching for information and checking for authenticity of Internet sources.

Assist students in preparing a timeline showing the discovery of the four deserts. After the students have had time to investigate their desert sub-topic for approximately two weeks, conduct a lesson on timelines to show historical information. For most students at this level, only a review of timelines will be needed. Ask the four student committees to provide any information they have gleaned about the early discovery of each desert by European settlers. If any committee has not yet found such information, they will need to have some time to research it before continuing with the preparation of a timeline. Once all committees have the dates needed for the timeline, have the students prepare and post the timeline in the classroom.

Help students experiment with sand painting. Show Internet sites, such as the Penfield Gallery of Indian

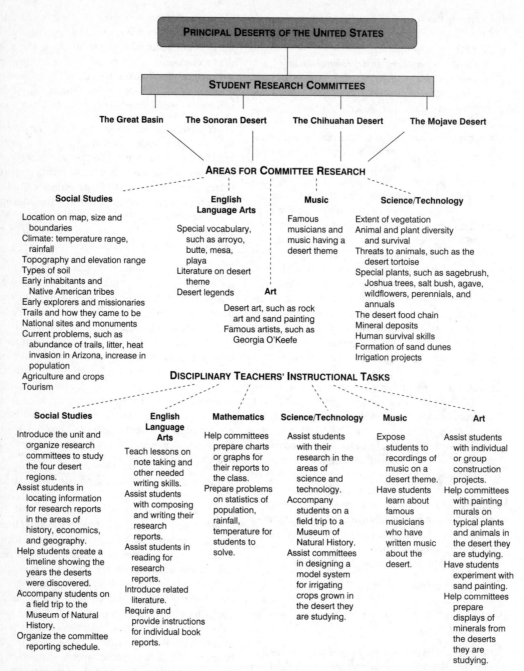

PRINCIPAL DESERTS OF THE UNITED STATES

STUDENT RESEARCH COMMITTEES

The Great Basin   The Sonoran Desert   The Chihuahan Desert   The Mojave Desert

AREAS FOR COMMITTEE RESEARCH

Social Studies

Location on map, size and
    boundaries
Climate: temperature range,
    rainfall
Topography and elevation range
Types of soil
Early inhabitants and
    Native American tribes
Early explorers and missionaries
Trails and how they came to be
National sites and monuments
Current problems, such as
    abundance of trails, litter, heat
    invasion in Arizona, increase in
    population
Agriculture and crops
Tourism

**English
Language Arts**

Special vocabulary,
    such as arroyo,
    butte, mesa,
    playa
Literature on desert
    theme
Desert legends

Art

Desert art, such as rock
    art and sand painting
Famous artists, such as
    Georgia O'Keefe

Music

Famous
    musicians and
    music having a
    desert theme

Science/Technology

Extent of vegetation
Animal and plant diversity
    and survival
Threats to animals, such as the
    desert tortoise
Special plants, such as sagebrush,
    Joshua trees, salt bush, agave,
    wildflowers, perennials, and
    annuals
The desert food chain
Mineral deposits
Human survival skills
Formation of sand dunes
Irrigation projects

DISCIPLINARY TEACHERS' INSTRUCTIONAL TASKS

Social Studies

Introduce the unit and
    organize research
    committees to study
    the four desert
    regions.
Assist students in
    locating information
    for research reports
    in the areas of
    history, economics,
    and geography.
Help students create a
    timeline showing the
    years the deserts
    were discovered.
Accompany students on
    a field trip to the
    Museum of Natural
    History.
Organize the committee
    reporting schedule.

**English
Language
Arts**

Teach lessons on
    note taking and
    other needed
    writing skills.
Assist students
    with composing
    and writing their
    research
    reports.
Assist students in
    reading for
    research
    reports.
Introduce related
    literature.
Require and
    provide instructions
    for individual book
    reports.

Mathematics

Help committees
    prepare charts
    or graphs for
    their reports to
    the class.
Prepare problems
    on statistics of
    population,
    rainfall,
    temperature for
    students to
    solve.

Science/Technology

Assist students
    with their
    research in the
    areas of
    science and
    technology.
Accompany
    students on a
    field trip to a
    Museum of
    Natural History.
Assist committees
    in designing a
    model system
    for irrigating
    crops grown in
    the desert they
    are studying.

Music

Expose
    students to
    recordings of
    music on a
    desert theme.
Have students
    learn about
    famous
    musicians
    who have
    written music
    about the
    desert.

Art

Assist students
    with individual
    or group
    construction
    projects.
Help committees
    with painting
    murals on
    typical plants
    and animals in
    the desert they
    are studying.
Have students
    experiment with
    sand painting.
Help committees
    prepare
    displays of
    minerals from
    the deserts
    they are
    studying.

FIGURE 4.3   Unit chart for a multidisciplinary unit plan on "Principal Deserts of the United States."

(continued)

Arts at penfieldgallery.com/sand.shtml, and help the students to learn the original purpose and significance of the paintings. Students can then design and try using colored sand to paint a design. Teachers of elementary classes may be able to elicit the assistance of the art specialist in their schools for this activity.

Provide for individual inquiry.   Some students may have interests in subtopics that do not relate directly to the committee's work. Encourage these individuals to pursue their interests, and provide opportunities for them to report their findings.

Activities:

Research committees.   Student research committees will be formed to investigate each of the four desert regions of the unit study. Each committee will have six to eight student members. Composition of the group should be planned carefully, considering factors such as leadership, learning styles, social factors, the students' ability to share responsibilities, and their individual talents, interests, and academic capabilities. It will be important to ensure that all members of each committee share in both the research and reporting responsibilities. Develop a "buddy" system in committees that include special-needs students, who often leave the classroom during regular times devoted to research or project activities. Those who leave for special assistance programs can be paired with others in their committee groups who will review with them the committee's work during their absence.

The committees will be informed of the essential questions of the unit as the basis for their research; however, each committee can add other questions that they would like to include in their investigation. After they have completed their research, the committees will be responsible for reporting their findings to the class at the end of the unit. These reports will provide the culminating activity for the unit. The reports will be scheduled for each committee when research activity is nearing completion. The committees will be encouraged to report in different ways. Possible reporting methods include the following:

- Panel discussions
- Demonstrations
- Skits
- Dramatic presentations
- PowerPoint presentations
- Explanations of displays, constructions, and murals

After each report, all students will participate in summarizing the information presented by the committee and note that information in their notebooks. (Note that at the end of the study, a unit examination will be given that is based mainly on the committee reports.)

Guidelines for the content of committee reports will be provided for students. Each report should include information about the discovery of the desert; early inhabitants; the size and location of the desert; variation in temperature and rainfall; predominant plant and animal species; crops produced; mineral deposits; historical sites and national parks; famous musicians, artists and other residents; and current problems in that region. Each committee should also prepare the following displays for their reports:

- A list of items needed for survival in the desert it is studying. Encourage students to use the Internet for this kind of information because it is readily available at sites, such as DesertUSA.com.
- Charts or graphs of data such as the extent of vegetation, rainfall, and temperature variations in each of the four deserts.
- A model showing how an irrigation works to supply water for desert farming. The committees can opt to create a three-dimensional model with materials, such as a salt and flour mixture, painting a mural of a project, and so on.
- A mural showing plant and animal species found in the region being studied. In elementary classes, it may be possible to involve the art specialist for this activity.
- A display of minerals found in the region it is investigating. The display can be a simple collection of photographs of the minerals, or if available, samples of the actual minerals.

Individual portfolios.   Require each student to maintain a portfolio in which they place reports of

(continued)

the research for which they assumed responsibility for their committee. Other items that will be included are book reviews, individual sketches for murals, the unit examination, and other individual contributions to committee research. Students who can should prepare their reports in writing. (Note that students who have difficulty preparing written reports should have alternatives, such as designing a construction or project, preparing a PowerPoint presentation or a demonstration.) Encourage each student to use art media for a project that reflects understandings gained from their individual research. Provide a form to guide the reporting process. The form should include information about the questions that the student was researching, answers to these questions, and the sources consulted for their research. Ask students to include the following information:

> *Topic:*   The committee topic and the subtopic for which the student was responsible.
> *Questions:*   The question(s) the student used to guide his or her research.
> *Findings:*   This section will vary in complexity according to each student's abilities. A simple list of findings, written in the student's words, may be adequate for some. Others will be able to write several paragraphs or pages. Students using alternate reporting methods will need to give verbal explanations to communicate what they have learned.
> *References:*   Depending on each student's abilities, the documentation format can vary from a simple list of the books and other materials used to a more sophisticated and complete documentation format.

Individual book reports.   Require each student to read and prepare a review of a book from the library (either fiction or nonfiction) related to desert life. The book can be either prose or poetry. Students will need to write a book review that encourages other students to read it, or they can prepare a story map or plot profile for a work of fiction. Rubrics will be used to assess individual book reports.

Unit examination.   After all committees have reported at the end of the unit, students will take a unit examination comprised of questions on the information presented in the four committee reports.

Assessment Plan

Committee Reports   The four committee reports at the conclusion of the study of *Principal Deserts of the United States* will provide the culminating activity of the unit. The various requirements for those presentations offer opportunities to assess the unit objectives as follows:

- Each committee must present a report to the class about the desert region it studied that includes information about its discovery, early inhabitants, size, location, temperature variations, rainfall, plant life, animal species, crops produced, mineral deposits, historical sites, national parks, famous musicians, and famous artists. *(The accuracy and completeness of each committee's report will provide for assessment of the students' ability to locate and report this information. The committee reports will be assessed using rubrics.)*
- Each committee report must include a graph or chart showing temperature range and rainfall in the desert region studied and explain the graph or chart to the class as a part of its final report. *(The accuracy of the charts and graphs and explanations will demonstrate the students' ability to construct and explain charts and graphs to show patterns in the data they have collected.)*
- Each committee will paint a mural of the major plant and animal species found in the desert region studied and explain the mural to the class as a part of its final report. *(The mural will demonstrate the students' ability to make use of art media to present a visual summary of the information they have gathered about plants and animals in the desert studied. The mural and explanation of it will be assessed for completeness, accuracy, and clarity.)*
- Each committee will develop a model of an irrigation project and explain the model during its presentation to the class. *(The accuracy of the model and the verbal explanation presented to the class will provide for assessment of the students' ability to design and construct models as well as their understanding of the significance of irrigation in desert regions.)*

- Each committee will prepare a display of minerals found in the region it is investigating. *(The display will demonstrate the students' ability to locate information on mineral deposits found in the desert region studied and to present a visual display of that information.)*

Other Assessments

- The students will submit portfolios that include individual reports of the research they completed as a part of their committee responsibility, a book review, and sketches for murals. The reports will be written following the format provided to students. Special needs students will have alternate methods for preparing their reports. *(The individual student reports will demonstrate each student's ability to locate, read, and summarize the information they gained for their individual committee research responsibilities. The reports will be assessed using rubrics tailored to the instructions provided for the students.)*
- Each student will prepare a review of a fiction or nonfiction book that is related to the desert topic. *(The book review will demonstrate students' ability to locate, read, and critically review a topical book. Rubrics will be used to assess the book reviews.)*
- All students will take a unit examination at the conclusion of the study that includes questions on information presented in the committee reports. One test item will ask students to write an essay from the viewpoint of a Native American living on a desert during the period of discovery by new settlers. The essay should include reactions to what students have learned about the loss of land and exposure to unfamiliar people and their new ideas for land use that Native American tribes experienced. Rubrics will be used to assess essays. *(The examination will provide information demonstrating the extent to which the students have gained knowledge and understanding of the four principal desert regions they have studied.)*

Materials

Instructional Materials

- Art materials for projects and report covers
- Deserts: Geology and resources. United States Geological Survey. Retrieved from www.usgs.gov/science/
- Sufficient quantities of social studies and science textbooks from a variety of publishers (four to six copies of each)
- Trade books from the school and public libraries on U.S. desert regions
- Computer software and related CD–ROM titles
- Computer technological services and consultation on the Internet for sources of information
- DVDs and videotapes on U.S. deserts
- Travel agency brochures that highlight desert vacation areas

Informational Resources The following is a sample of materials available. A search for "deserts of the United States" will yield numerous other sources that are available on the Internet for students and teachers.

Butcher, R. D. (1976). *The desert*. New York: Viking Press.

Desert USA. (n.d.). Retrieved from http://www.desertusa.com

Digital desert. (n.d.). Retrieved from http://aeve.com/digitaldesertt/ddpi/lalol.html

Mails, T. E. (1998). *The Pueblo children of the earth mother*. New York: Marlowe.

McMahon, J. A. (1997). *Deserts*. New York: Knopf.

The North American deserts. (n.d.). Retrieved from http://www.desertusa.com/glossary.html

Ring E. (2005). *Drylands*. Detroit, MI: Blackbirch Press.

Social and environmental aspects of desertification. Retrieved from www.usgs.gov/science/

Waldman, C. (1985). *Atlas of the North American Indian*. New York: Facts on File.

ACTIVITY

Study the web design in Figure 4.4. It is from an interdisciplinary unit plan on the American Revolution, a topic taught at the middle school level.

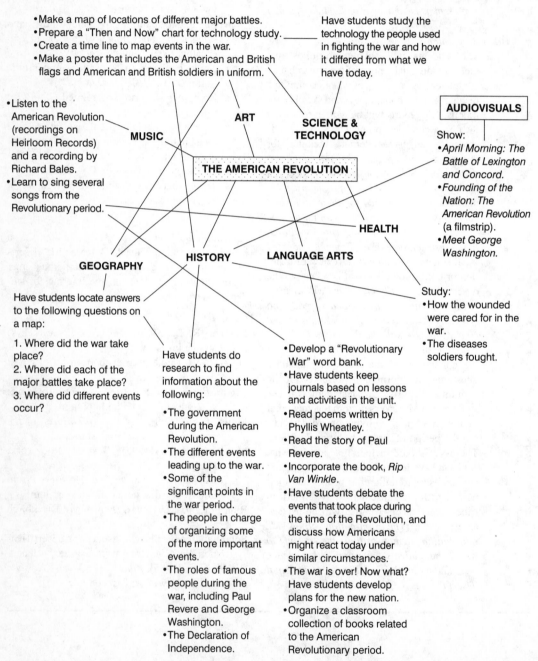

• Make a map of locations of different major battles.
• Prepare a "Then and Now" chart for technology study.
• Create a time line to map events in the war.
• Make a poster that includes the American and British flags and American and British soldiers in uniform.

Have students study the technology the people used in fighting the war and how it differed from what we have today.

ART

SCIENCE & TECHNOLOGY

MUSIC

• Listen to the American Revolution (recordings on Heirloom Records) and a recording by Richard Bales.
• Learn to sing several songs from the Revolutionary period.

THE AMERICAN REVOLUTION

AUDIOVISUALS

Show:
• *April Morning: The Battle of Lexington and Concord.*
• *Founding of the Nation: The American Revolution* (a filmstrip).
• *Meet George Washington.*

HEALTH

GEOGRAPHY

HISTORY   **LANGUAGE ARTS**

Have students locate answers to the following questions on a map:

1. Where did the war take place?
2. Where did each of the major battles take place?
3. Where did different events occur?

Have students do research to find information about the following:

• The government during the American Revolution.
• The different events leading up to the war.
• Some of the significant points in the war period.
• The people in charge of organizing some of the more important events.
• The roles of famous people during the war, including Paul Revere and George Washington.
• The Declaration of Independence.

• Develop a "Revolutionary War" word bank.
• Have students keep journals based on lessons and activities in the unit.
• Read poems written by Phyllis Wheatley.
• Read the story of Paul Revere.
• Incorporate the book, *Rip Van Winkle.*
• Have students debate the events that took place during the time of the Revolution, and discuss how Americans might react today under similar circumstances.
• The war is over! Now what? Have students develop plans for the new nation.
• Organize a classroom collection of books related to the American Revolutionary period.

Study:
• How the wounded were cared for in the war.
• The diseases soldiers fought.

FIGURE 4.4   Web design for an interdisciplinary unit on "The American Revolution (middle school level).

The design is prepared for an interdisciplinary unit; therefore, it does not indicate how it could be taught as a multidisciplinary study by a team of middle school teachers. Convert the many ideas for lessons and activities into a multidisciplinary unit chart which assigns responsibility for the different lessons and activities to individual team members. Plan your chart according to the information outlined in this chapter.

Work in a small group to complete this activity. Each member of the group should assume the role of one of the team members—social studies, English (literacy), mathematics, science, mathematics, art, and so on. Work together to develop the chart.

REFERENCES

Criteria for selection of class research topics. (1966, April 28). *Our 3 C's—Characteristic curricular concepts, 12*(12). (Union Free School District No. 25, Merrick, NY)

Kellough, R. D., & Kellough, N. G. (2003). *Teaching young adolescents: A guide to methods and resources* (4th ed.). Upper Saddle River, NJ: Pearson/Merrill Prentice Hall.

Piaget, J., & Inhelder, B. (1969). *The psychology of the child.* New York: Basic Books.

Post, T. R., Ellis, A. K., Humphreys, A. H., & Buggey, L. J. (1997). *Interdisciplinary approaches to curriculum: Themes for teaching.* Upper Saddle River, NJ: Pearson/Merrill Prentice Hall.

Santrock, J. W. (2008). *Children* (8th ed.). Boston: McGraw-Hill.

Wallace, M. L. (1996). *America's deserts: Guide to plants and animals.* Golden, CO: Fulcrum Kids.

Wiggins, G., & McTighe, J. (2005). *Understanding by design* (2nd ed.). Alexandria VA: Association of Supervision & Curriculum Development.

SUGGESTED READINGS

The supplemental readings listed below provide additional background material on the selected topics related to the discussion in this chapter.

Cooperative Learning

Chard, S. C., & Flockhart, M. E. (2002, November). Learning in the park. *Educational Leadership, 60*(3), 53–56.

Johnson, D. W. (1999). *Learning together and alone: Cooperative, competitive, and individualistic learning.* Boston: Pearson/Allyn & Bacon.

Johnson, D. W., Johnson, R. T., & Holubec, E. J. (1994). *Cooperative learning in the classroom.* Alexandria, VA: Association for Supervision and Curriculum Development.

Joliffe, W. (2007). *Cooperative learning in the classroom: Putting it into practice.* Thousand Oaks, CA: Sage Publications.

Lyman, L., Foyle, H., & Azwell, T. (1993). *Cooperative learning in the elementary classroom.* Washington, DC: National Education Association.

Mason, E. (1972). *Collaborative learning.* New York: Agathon Press.

Rottier, J., & Ogan, B. J. (1991). *Cooperative learning in middle-level schools.* Washington, DC: National Education Association.

Snodgrass, D. M. (2000). *Collaborative learning in middle and secondary schools.* Larchmont, NY: Eye On Education.

Objectives

Davies, I. K. (1976). *Objectives in curriculum design.* London: McGraw-Hill.

Dick, W., Carey, L., & Carey, J. O. (2009). *The systematic design of instruction* (7th ed.). Upper Saddle River, NJ: Pearson/Merrill Prentice Hall.

Gronlund, N. E. (2009). *Gronlund's writing instructional objectives* (8th ed.). Upper Saddle River, NJ: Pearson/Merrill Prentice Hall.

Kibler, R. J., Cegala, D. J., Barker, L. L., & Miles, D. T. (1981). *Objectives for instruction and evaluation* (2nd ed.). Boston: Pearson/Allyn & Bacon.

Mager, R. (1997). *Preparing instructional objectives: A critical tool in the development of effective instruction* (3rd ed.). Atlanta, GA: Center for Effective Performance.

Portfolios

Grosvenor, L. (1993). *Student portfolios.* Washington, DC: National Education Association.

O'Neil, J. (1993, September). The promise of portfolios. *Update, 35*(7), 1–5.

Reigeluth, C. M. (1987). *Instructional theories in action: Lessons illustrating selected theories and models.* Hillsdale, NJ: Erlbaum.

Middle School

Messick, R. G., & Reynolds, K. E. (1992). *Middle level curriculum in action.* New York: Longman.

Stevenson, C., & Carr, J. F. (Eds.). (1993). *Integrated studies in the middle grades.* New York: Teachers College Press.

Wadsworth, B. J. (1978). *Piaget for the classroom teacher.* New York: Longman.

Projects

Weinland, T. P., & Protheroe, D. W. (1973). *Social science projects you can do.* Upper Saddle River, NJ: Prentice Hall.

CHAPTER

5 Lesson Planning Strategies for Interdisciplinary Instruction

Cooperative planning between an art specialist and classroom teacher.

OVERVIEW

Chapter 5 is designed for teachers who plan lessons and activities involved in interdisciplinary studies. The discussions of lesson planning processes and protocols and the lesson plan examples can also be useful for teachers who use other approaches to education at the elementary and middle school levels. The chapter includes the following:

- Learning and developmental principles for instructional planning
- Using Bloom's Taxonomy to determine cognitive levels of objectives, questions, and directions
- Formats used to prepare written lesson plans

- Explanations of learning standards, general objectives, key questions, and behavioral objectives included in lesson plans
- Critical elements in a lesson plan procedure
- Protocols used to design some lesson plan procedures

Learning and Developmental Principles for Lesson Planning

Successful teachers have always attended to the literature and research on the psychology of learning and development. In a 1993 discussion of developmentally appropriate teaching practices, Wakefield offers a strong argument for attending to child development and learning theory when planning for instruction. Others emphasize the need to understand the major principles of learning and their implications for the instructional processes (Mayer, 2008; Ryan, Cooper, and Tower, 2008). The important question is this: What are preliminary considerations regarding learning and development when we design instructional plans for students in elementary and middle schools? The following are several important principles to consider.

Principle: Learners Construct Their Own Knowledge.   Learners are able to construct knowledge most efficiently when they have opportunities to engage in personal experiences and when they have opportunities to interact with other people. This principle is central to Piaget's (1963) adaptation theory, which strongly suggests the importance of including concrete, direct experiences in learning situations. For example, when possible, students should be given opportunities for experiences, such as the following:

- Working with manipulative materials
- Conducting their own experiments
- Visiting field sites where they can become directly involved with authentic materials and environments that are not accessible in their classrooms or where they can study genuine artifacts related to the topics they are studying

Activities that encourage students to listen to others' viewpoints and to reflect on their own include the following:

- Cooperative learning projects and other group activities
- Debates and panel discussions
- Simulations
- Instructional games
- Whole-class discussions
- Learning centers that involve activities requiring working with other students

Principle: New Knowledge Builds upon Existing Knowledge.   In 1973, Kamii offered a detailed discussion of the relevance of the principle that new knowledge can only be built on a learner's existing knowledge base. This pedagogical principle is also based on Piagetian theory. When beginning to plan, we must know whether students have sufficient background knowledge for the concepts to be developed in a lesson. This determination can often be made near the beginning of the lesson by doing the following:

- Raising questions that help to determine what the students already know
- Providing a brief review of what students have learned about an ongoing study to help bridge the way to the new concepts to be taught in the new lesson

These practices will also provide us with information about what our students know or believe they know about a topic before the lesson continues. Occasionally, we may discover that the new lesson needs to be delayed until sufficient background knowledge is developed.

Principle: Intrinsic Interest Is More Effective than Extrinsic Motivation. We know that when students are interested, learning is easier for them. Observation of students and conversations with them over time can provide information about their individual and group interests. Sometimes, we can capitalize on specific interests of individual students during an interdisciplinary study. For example, we can suggest that an individual student conduct research on a subtopic of special interest that is related to a study the class is pursuing. Individuals can be invited to lead others in small-group studies and to present the results of their research to the class. Learning centers can be designed with activities that appeal to students' interests.

Principle: Concept Development Is Facilitated by Holistic Studies. In chapter 1, it was explained that research on the human brain suggests that concept development is facilitated by holistic, unified, interdisciplinary studies. This is a primary factor on which interdisciplinary instruction is based and on which the planning of lessons and units are structured. Although integration of the disciplines is appropriate for students at all levels, Jensen (2005) suggests that a holistic study may be "more useful for older students than younger ones" (p. 96). Jensen bases this statement on his belief that older students will have developed a greater fund of knowledge to help them form associations among the disciplines more easily. However, holistic studies are also appropriate for younger children as long as they study topics appropriate for their developmental level and have adequate concrete experiences to help them detect the interrelatedness of the disciplines.

Principle: The Learning Processes Are Important for Learning How to Learn. The idea that learning processes are important in all academic pursuits clearly suggests that to help students master the various processes needed for learning throughout life, we need to provide them with opportunities such as these:

- Experiencing the steps in the inquiry process as they conduct their own research on topics that are appropriate for their developmental levels
- Applying the scientific method of investigation and conducting their own experiments in science
- Practicing the various learning processes through activities provided in a learning center

Students who become skilled at the processes of learning are likely to be better equipped to become independent learners in the future.

Principle: Differentiated Instruction Is Essential for Promoting Learning in All Students. Today, any list of important teaching concerns must include attention to the many different ways students learn. Hall (2002) provides an exceptionally clear and comprehensive overview of *differentiated instruction* that not only promotes this idea but gives us practical ways to manage it in our classrooms. In Chapter 1, Sternberg's (1997) and Gardner's theories regarding students' differing intelligences suggest that attention to individual cognitive strengths and working styles can enable more students to succeed in school. However, Gardner has expressed his desire that his theory not be misinterpreted and that teachers seek appropriate applications of his theory in their practices (Viadero, 1995). For example, even though students have differing strengths in the nine multiple intelligence areas, certainly not all intelligences can or need to be addressed in a single lesson. Instead, lesson plans constructed over time should attempt to include opportunities for students to use their strongest intelligence areas to learn and show what they have learned.

Although the theories are similar, Gardner does not equate his MI theory with *learning styles* theory. Definitions of learning styles tend to vary; however, most suggest that they are the unique, individual strengths, preferences, and approaches students use as they attempt to acquire knowledge. Implications of learning styles theory suggest that when planning for instruction, we should consider practices that will help our students gain knowledge in different ways. For example, students can sometimes be offered choices, such as the following:

- Students who are researching a topic might be given a choice of writing a conventional paper or reporting in some other way—a computer presentation, a demonstration, a performance, a panel discussion, and so on. In the lower elementary grades, students might paint a mural or construct a diorama to show what they have learned.
- Learning center activities can also offer opportunities for students to apply their individual learning styles and multiple intelligences by engaging in independent, hands-on activities, particularly in mathematics, science, and art.

In summary, organizing instructional plans that generate student interest and foster their participation is an important concern in the teaching and learning processes. Attention to students' developmental and individual learning preferences can help to ensure that students become more involved in the lessons and activities that are designed for them.

Using Bloom's Taxonomy to Determine the Cognitive Levels of Instruction

Teachers determine the questions, standards, and instructional objectives of their lessons, units, and learning center activities. When planning the procedure of a lesson, we often find that we need to raise questions and give directions that range in level of difficulty. Questions may vary considerably from those that elicit fundamental, factual information to those that involve higher levels of thought.

How can we estimate the difficulty levels of our objectives, questions, and directions? Perhaps the most widely recognized classification system designed to help teachers determine the cognitive levels of the lessons they plan is Bloom's Taxonomy. Bloom (1956) outlined a six-level taxonomy to help determine the relative difficulty of instructional objectives. The taxonomy is also helpful for classifying questions, directions, and test items. A brief outline of Bloom's Taxonomy in the cognitive domain follows.

Level 1: Knowledge

Objectives and questions at level 1 require students to provide limited, memorized, factual responses. Genuine understanding may or may not be demonstrated in students' responses. Questions at this level usually require simple, convergent responses.

Examples

- What is the name of the largest city on the West Coast of the United States?
- What is the meaning of the word *irrigation*?
- Who is the author of *The Deerslayer?*

Level 2: Comprehension

Understanding is required at the comprehension level. When responding to questions at this level, students may need to explain, summarize, translate, and give examples to demonstrate their understanding.

Examples

- Write a summary of the main points in this article.
- Explain how an irrigation system works in a desert area.
- Give an example of a crustacean.

Level 3: Application

Students must use processes, problem-solving, and research skills to determine their responses at the application level of the taxonomy. This level is exceptionally important because it is in applying what they know and understand that we are able to assess students' *real* understandings.

Examples

- Now that you have recorded the daily temperature on this graph for the past three weeks, what does the record appear to indicate?
- Sort these rocks into the three classifications we just studied.
- Solve these new mathematics problems using the process you have just studied.

Level 4: Analysis

Analysis requires interpreting, noting inferences, thinking beyond the literal level when reading, detecting cause-and-effect relationships, and drawing conclusions. Analytical questions usually invite more divergent responses.

Examples

- What are some reasons why our experiment with plants failed?
- What reasons can you give for the boy's actions in this story?
- Why do you think it is important to exercise our right to vote?

Level 5: Synthesis

Questions and directions for students at level 5 often ask for creative and divergent responses. New, or original, thinking is required to produce plans, raise hypotheses, predict, or produce original proposals, designs, art, or music.

Examples

- Devise a plan that will help to minimize the environmental problems caused by the increasing number of people settling in desert areas today.
- Write a poem that shows how you feel in the spring.
- Construct a diorama that demonstrates some aspect of what you have learned about your study of ancient Greece.

Level 6: Evaluation

Students make judgments at level 6. They decide ratings and express opinions based on standard or personal criteria.

Examples

- Does this essay on desert life include accurate information about current problems experienced by the people who live there?
- Which of these two plans to save endangered animals is better, or more likely to be effective?
- Do you like abstract art?

(Follow evaluation questions with "Why or why not?" to elicit the students' analysis and reasoning for their judgment.)

Lesson Plan Formats Used for Interdisciplinary Instruction

Designing the plans for lessons and activities included in an interdisciplinary study is one of our most serious concerns. In addition to planning lessons that involve literacy, science, and social studies concepts, we also plan for a variety of activities, such as group discussions, cooperative group and committee work, panel discussions, dramatizations, simulations, and role-playing.

Each lesson or activity in a unit needs to contribute to the development of its standards and general objectives. Wiggins and McTighe (2005) also emphasize the need to address *enduring understandings* in all planning. (See examples of enduring understandings in Chapter 1, Figure 1.2.) Teachers who are new to the interdisciplinary approach usually find that, at first, it is helpful to include considerable detail, especially when developing the steps they plan to follow in the lesson procedure.

Most lesson planning formats are similar; all include sections for listing learning standards, objectives, materials, and procedures. Some also include other sections, such as general objectives and key questions. The procedure is the heart of a lesson plan because it provides a detailed outline of the lesson step-by-step. It includes information about the role of the teacher, and may also provide notes about the anticipated actions and reactions of students during the lesson.

In some lesson plans, the procedure section is divided into distinct subsections, including motivation, development, and closure. Cooper (2006), Ornstein and Lasley (2004), Reiser and Dick (1996), and Roberts and Kellough (2008) use subdivisions for the procedure section in their lesson plan formats. Segmenting the procedure section in this way can help to highlight important groups of steps in a lesson plan. For example, in the *Five-Step Lesson Plan* (Hunter, 2004), the procedure is subdivided into six parts: *anticipatory set, motivation, application, guided practice, closure,* and *follow-up activities*. The Five-Step Lesson Plan, which is explained later in this chapter, is particularly well suited for planning skills-oriented lessons. Other formats that do not segment the procedure section may be easier to adapt for lessons in history, literature, science, and for planning committee work or conducting field trips. Borich (2007); Post, Ellis, Humphreys, and Buggey (1997); and the backward design lesson plan format outlined by Moore (2005) tend not to segment the procedure section of the lessons they describe.

The procedure section for lessons in this text is not segmented; instead, it is flexible enough to accommodate planning most kinds of lessons and activities needed for interdisciplinary and multidisciplinary studies. Although *essential questions* are appropriate for units of study, "lessons are simply too short to allow for in-depth exploration of essential questions" (Wiggins & McTighe, 2005, p. 8). Instead of listing essential questions, the lesson plan format in this text includes a place for *key questions*. Key questions are short-term questions that indicate the specific intent of the lesson and target a lesson assessment plan. See the complete lesson plan outline for lessons that will be presented in this text in Figure 5.1.

Listing the various components of the lesson plan can differ from the outline shown here in order to accommodate individual preferences. For example, some teachers prefer to list the materials section before the procedure. The lesson plan topic, grade level, estimated time, and materials need little explanation. More information about learning standards, key questions, general objectives, behavioral objectives, the procedure, and assessment plan will be provided next.

FIGURE 5.1 Lesson plan outline.

Topic:

Level:

Estimated Time:

Learning Standards:

General Objectives:
    Knowledge
    Skills
    Dispositions

Key Questions:

Behavioral Objectives:

Procedure:

Assessment Plan:

Materials:

Learning Standards, General Objectives, Key Questions, and Behavioral Objectives

Unit and lesson plans both include lists of learning standards, and some teachers add their own general objectives. Lesson plans include specific, short-term, *behaviorally* stated objectives. They can also incorporate key questions.

Learning Standards and General Objectives

Learning standards and general objectives are similar; both are comprehensive and often long-term goals toward which a lesson contributes. Although both learning standards and general objectives suggest the main objectives of a lesson, their sources differ. *Learning standards* are developed at national and state levels; committees of teachers and administrators may also prepare generic learning standards for use in their school districts. Learning standards communicate clearly and provide for a degree of uniformity from teacher to teacher and school to school. Using learning standards, we can help to ensure that our students are introduced to similar content regardless of where they attend school.

General objectives differ from learning standards in that they are written by individual teachers for a particular group of students. General objectives for any lesson may vary considerably from one teacher to another. Even when the same topic is studied using the same materials, teachers may emphasize knowledge (major understandings), skills, and dispositions (attitudes and affective concerns) to be developed by a particular lesson.

Although a unit can address a number of learning standards and general objectives, a single lesson can address relatively few. The obvious reason for this is that a lesson is much narrower in scope than a unit and is usually taught over a short period of time. Lesson plans should include the content learning standards that they address. General objectives are listed to help specify the knowledge (understandings), academic skills, and dispositions that the lesson will foster. When deciding on the learning standards and general objectives to include in a lesson plan, we need to consider three domains or categories: cognitive (or content to be learned), affective (dispositions—attitudes and affective concerns), and process objectives (ways of knowing). Examples of each category appear next.

Examples

Content learning standard: Students analyze the geographic, political, economic, religious, and social structures of the early civilizations of Ancient Greece *(California Learning Standard, World History and Geography: Ancient Civilizations 6.4. by approval, California Department of Education).*

General knowledge objective: Students will understand that a democratic government involves a legislative system of checks and balances.

General skill objective: Students will improve their ability to outline material from informational sources.

General dispositional objective: Students will share in the use of materials.

In addition to learning standards, other categories, such as performance standards, curriculum standards, and delivery standards are usually included in national, state, and local standards lists. Sweeny (1999, p. 64) explains the differences in these categories: *performance standards* describe "how well students must know and do specific assessment tasks." Teachers can use the performance suggestions to help assess students' progress toward meeting content learning standards. *Curriculum standards* are written for teachers to "define how teachers will reach desired results" and what teachers will need to teach. *Delivery standards* outline what teachers "must know and do if students are to perform at the desired level."

Subdivisions of learning standards, which may be called *performance indicators* or *benchmarks*, also accompany most national, state, and local lists. These are useful in helping to select the specific content learning standards that relate directly to the knowledge, skills, and dispositions listed in the general objectives of the lesson plan.

Examples

The following examples of performance indicators are related to New York State Social Studies Standard 1: Students will "use a variety of intellectual skills to demonstrate their understanding of major ideas, eras, themes, developments, and turning points in the history of the United States and New York" *(by permission of the New York State Education Department).*

Performance indicator (elementary level):   Students will "explain those values, practices, and traditions that unite all Americans."

Performance indicator (middle school level):   Students will "interpret the ideas, values, and beliefs contained in the Declaration of Independence and the New York State Constitution, and United States Constitution, Bill of Rights, and other important historical documents."

Performance indicators narrow the scope of content learning standards; they help to clarify if a particular standard reflects the general objectives of the lesson. However, they are not as clear as key questions and behavioral objectives for explaining the specific, short-term objectives of a lesson.

Key questions.   Key questions can be included in a lesson. Key questions "define tasks, express problems, and delineate issues" (Elder & Paul, 2002, p. 3). They reflect the process of inquiry, which always begins with questioning. Students can be involved in finding answers to key questions at all levels of Bloom's Taxonomy. Listing the key questions to be addressed in a lesson is also another logical way to express the objectives of the lesson. The best key questions are those that are stimulating, require use of background knowledge and personal experiences, involve students, and suggest an assessment plan for the lesson. Several examples of key questions follow.

- How can we support our answers to questions raised about a reading selection?
- How can the painting of a mural inform others of our findings from research?
- What can we do to show support for a friend?
- Why should a citizen exercise his/her right to vote?
- What is an appropriate form for a business letter?
- How should we construct a birdhouse for a wren?

Note that each key question is short-term, specific, and comparatively narrow in scope. Let's consider the last example above. After teaching the lesson on wrens, we could simply ask students to explain verbally how to construct the birdhouse. *(This is at the knowledge or possibly comprehension level of Bloom's Taxonomy.)* However, the key question suggests that we want to know if students would actually be able to construct a birdhouse suitable for a wren *(an application level task).* Therefore, we need to see if the students can just do that, possibly by having students draw plans for the birdhouse or even better, actually construct one. A *behavioral objective* would then be written so that it provides a way to assess students who complete this task.

Behavioral Objectives: Short-Term Goals

Short-term objectives usually conform to the format and terminology associated with *behavioral* objectives. Behavioral objectives provide measures of assessment for the lesson. Following are three questions to consider when writing behavioral objective statements:

1. What standards and key questions are being addressed in the lesson?
2. How will the students demonstrate that they have met the standards? What specific performances will be expected of students to demonstrate that they can respond to the key question? Performances are indicated by verbs describing observable student behaviors. Several examples of verbs that are acceptable for writing behavioral objectives are: *list, define, label, describe, translate, explain, demonstrate, perform, compare, classify, design, summarize, select,* and *compare.* All of these behaviors

can be observed. Examples of verbs that are not acceptable are: *know, understand, learn,* and *apply.* These verbs do not clearly indicate an observable behavior.

3. How well are the students expected to demonstrate the behavior? How well will they need to perform what they are required to do? What is the standard that needs to be reached in order to pass the objective?

Behavioral objective statements can be written in a single sentence that includes (a) for whom the lesson is planned, (b) the behavior indicating that students have met the standards and key questions addressed in the lesson, (c) the special conditions (if any) under which these behaviors should be performed, and (d) how well the students must perform to meet the standards successfully. Examples of three behavioral objectives follow.

- After a trip to the zoo *(describes a condition),* each student *(tells for whom the objective is intended)* will complete a drawing of one animal observed at the zoo and dictate a sentence for each picture that includes at least one fact learned about the animal as a result of the field trip *(explains the specific behaviors to be demonstrated by the students). Note that the degree of acceptable performance for this objective for kindergarten or early first-grade level is implied to be 100 percent.*
- Given a compass and five written directions to follow *(the conditions),* each student *(for whom the objective is intended)* will accurately follow four of the five directions *(the behavior to be demonstrated and degree of acceptable performance; upper elementary grade level).*
- After completion of a unit on the theme Emerging African Nations *(the condition),* the students *(for whom the objective is intended)* will pass a comprehensive unit test on major concepts developed in the unit *(the behavior to be demonstrated)* with at least 75 percent accuracy *(the degree of acceptable performance; middle school level).*

The Lesson Plan Procedure

Critical Elements in the Procedure Section of a Lesson

As we gain experience in planning, we usually modify our planning strategies and tend to use shorter formats that fit our individual needs and teaching styles. Even so, it is important to consider, at least mentally, the steps that we will follow when teaching the lesson, and we need to ensure that several *critical elements* are always included in the lesson procedure.

While designing the procedure section of a lesson plan, we should try to visualize what will occur at each step. One way to do this is to imagine recording the lesson with a video camera while trying to anticipate student responses and reactions as the lesson proceeds. Recognizing possible student behaviors—their reactions, interpretations, and potential misinterpretations—before teaching the lesson can help to allay some of our fears about what to do when the unexpected occurs during the lesson.

Regardless of how the procedure section is set up, it needs to include several elements which are critical to the potential success of the lesson. Others have stressed the importance of similar elements (Duplas, 2008; Ryan, Cooper, and Tauer, 2008). The following are *critical elements* that should be included in any lesson procedure:

- A clear introduction to the lesson and its purpose to help students to focus their thinking on the lesson topic
- A connection between students' current background knowledge and the concepts or skills to be developed by the new lesson
- Questions and/or other techniques that cause cognitive conflict in students' minds, which help them to realize they have something new to learn
- A step or steps at which the behavioral objective of the lesson can be assessed
- Closure to the lesson

Critical Element: An Introduction.   The lesson should be clearly introduced to help students focus their thinking on the lesson topic or problem and to inform them about what they should be able to do to show they have gained the desired results. This can often be accomplished informally. For example, a brief statement, such as "Today, we are going to begin studying more about the planet Mars" or another explanation can let students know what the lesson will be about or what the activity will involve. Students should then be told what they will be expected to do if they have understood the objective of the lesson.

Critical Element: A Connection with Students' Background Knowledge.   Help students to make connections between the new lesson and what they already know about the topic. This should happen early in the lesson procedure. Possible ways to accomplish this include the following:

- Reviewing what has been studied or learned previously about the topic
- Reminding students about what they have been taught about the topic
- Asking students what they know about the new topic

Occasionally, we may need to provide a preliminary experience or an entire lesson to help prepare students for new concepts and to develop adequate background for the information to be included in a new lesson.

Critical Element: Questions and Other Techniques that Produce Cognitive Conflict. Students construct their own knowledge, and the construction process cannot begin nor will students become interested in learning anything new until they first realize that something they do not know is of importance to them. This constructivist viewpoint strongly suggests that motivation must develop from within. Therefore, instead of assuming the role of motivator, we need to help our students become aware of the need to develop some new knowledge or skill. In each lesson procedure, we must introduce cognitive conflict to help students realize that there is something they do not already know; then the process of acquiring new knowledge can begin. We can introduce cognitive conflict in a number of ways, including the following examples:

FIGURE 5.2   A convergent question-and-response pattern.

1. Asking important questions during the lesson relating to the concept(s) to be developed
2. Having students observe a discrepant event—something they will have difficulty in explaining immediately
3. Providing purposes for students or eliciting purposes from the students before a reading, listening, or viewing experience or before they observe a demonstration

Because questioning strategies are fundamental in presenting conflict, we need to become skilled at formulating both convergent and divergent question types. *Convergent* questions generally require a relatively narrow range of responses from students, whereas *divergent* questions are relatively open-ended and often encourage students to think critically and creatively. Models of the two question types are shown in Figures 5.2 and 5.3.

Examples (convergent questions)

- Name two treaties that have involved European nations during the last two centuries.
- Please define *amphibian*.
- What is the second largest city in the world?
- In what country is the Congo River located?
- Which mathematics process is needed to solve these equations?

Examples (divergent questions)

- Can you think of a way to improve our local system of mass transit?
- How did you feel when you listened to the recording of "Appalachian Spring"?
- What do you think this line in the poem means?
- What do you find especially interesting in this piece of art?

Holding a discussion during a lesson is often critical to helping students process the new concepts introduced in the lesson, particularly when stimulating, thoughtful questions are raised (Caram & Davis, 2005; Cooper & Kiger, 2008; DuPlass, 2008; Macbeth, 2003). Therefore, preparing for class discussions is an important step in the design of most lesson plans.

Some discussions arise spontaneously. Others we plan to include in a formal lesson in reading or another discipline. A discussion can even involve a lengthy debate about some

FIGURE 5.3   A divergent question and response pattern.

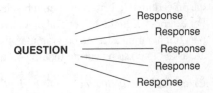

specific issue or problem. To help students focus on the lesson topic and to ensure more productive discussions, the following suggestions may be helpful:

- Before beginning any discussion, or raising a question that will stimulate discussion, try to ensure that students have sufficient general background knowledge about the topic.
- Before the discussion, remind students of the rules that have been established for good discussions, such as raising one's hand before answering to allow more students opportunities to contribute. Interrupting a discussion to talk about rules distracts the group from the point of the discussion. If possible, ignore students who call out or who make unnecessary noise when raising their hands; instead, immediately call on another student.
- Maintain an emotional climate in the classroom that is conducive to a discussion. Students who feel safe from ridicule or sarcasm by other students or their teacher are likely to be more willing to contribute. They may also be more willing to risk making mistakes when answering questions.
- Decide in advance how to handle students who never volunteer to participate. Sometimes, a simple nod will invite a shy student to contribute. Make decisions about whether or not to call on students by name if they do not volunteer. Some teachers believe that calling on students gives them an invitation to participate. Other teachers believe that calling on a student by name may be intimidating and even may increase the chance that these students will not volunteer in the future. In addition, other students in the group may believe that they do not need to offer to respond when another student is called on for an answer.
- Raise only one question at a time. Silence does not necessarily indicate that students have failed to understand the question. They may need a few moments to consider a possible response. Wait for at least four or five seconds before restating the question or raising another.
- Ask both convergent and divergent questions. Questions that require students to recall information are easy to prepare. However, it is important to plan questions that require students to think critically and creatively.
- When a student responds with a vague answer to a question, ask for some clarification. Often, simply asking the student something like "Can you tell us more?" or "Can you give us an example?" will invite a clearer response.
- Summarize or ask students to summarize periodically during a discussion. Doing so will help to maintain focus on the main topic.

These general suggestions may help to make discussions during lessons more productive as well as make them more interesting for students.

Critical Element: Assess the Behavioral Objectives of the Lesson.   At some step or steps in the procedure of a lesson, it should be clear that the behavioral objectives are being assessed. For example, if in the behavioral objective students are required to underline all the verbs in a paragraph during a lesson on grammar, there should be a step in the procedure where students are asked to do so, ensuring that the objective can be assessed.

Critical Element: Bring Closure to the Lesson.   At the end of the lesson, the design of the procedure needs to include a way to bring the lesson or activity to closure. This important step helps students to summarize what they have gained during the lesson. Closure can be accomplished in a variety of ways including those that follow.

- Reviewing with students what they have learned
- Having one student or several students summarize what they believe they have learned
- Holding a discussion about the students' different projects—drawing pictures, designing murals, preparing dioramas, constructing with papier-mâché or another art media, presenting a drama or dance performance—that reflect the concepts they have gained from completion of the project

Other Considerations for Planning the Lesson Procedure

In addition to the critical elements outlined in the previous page, the following are also important to consider when planning the lesson procedure.

Follow Appropriate Methods, Techniques, and Protocols: The method, approach, or technique used to structure the lesson procedure should be appropriate for the objectives of the lesson. For example, in the course of an interdisciplinary study, it may be helpful to have students read a selection from an article or other content material on the unit topic. It is appropriate to follow a *guided reading* protocol for this kind of lesson. (Guided reading is explained and illustrated with an example lesson later in this chapter.) If a skill, such as letter writing or outlining, is being taught, following the *Five-Step Lesson* protocol is suitable. (The Five-Step protocol is also explained and illustrated with an example lesson later in this chapter.)

Anticipate Possible Student Reactions and Responses: At various steps in the lesson procedure, students may be asked to respond in some way. For example, if a question is raised, students' possible responses can be noted in the lesson plan. Although students' anticipated responses and reactions are not typically included in lesson plan procedures, doing so can help minimize problems that arise from unexpected reactions when the lesson is taught.

Address the Principles of Learning, and Consider Students' Learning and Working Styles: We should consider students' different learning and working styles when planning steps in the lesson procedure. Students' multiple intelligences, interests, and talents can often be addressed if they have been considered when preparing the lesson procedure.

Include Sufficient Detail: All steps in the procedure should be well detailed and clear enough so that another teacher would be able to follow the plan if necessary.

Sequence the Procedure Steps in a Logical Order: The sequence of the procedure should be clear, logical in order, and easy to follow.

In summary, attention to the preceding critical elements and other considerations for designing lesson procedures can help to ensure a greater degree of success when the lesson is taught. Productive instructional sessions are more likely to occur when the procedure section of a lesson plan:

- Provides a clear introduction to the lesson and helps students focus their thinking on the lesson theme.
- Helps students make connections to what they already know about the lesson topic.
- Stimulates thinking with questions and other techniques that cause conflict in students' minds.
- Provides for assessment of the lesson objectives.
- Brings closure to the lesson.

Finally, lessons are more likely to be successful when lesson plans follow appropriate methods, techniques, and protocols; attend to principles of learning and include notes about possible student reactions and responses; attend to students' different working and learning styles; provide enough detail; and are carefully sequenced.

Protocols for Planning Some Lesson Procedures

In most professions, there are protocols for some procedures. For example, in the medical profession, surgeons follow protocols for surgery, and in the legal profession, lawyers and judges have established procedural protocols for many deliberations. Many lessons and activities that are taught in elementary and middle schools can be planned by following established protocols that have evolved in the teaching profession. In teaching, a lesson *protocol* is a specific procedure that has been found to work well in practice over time and that includes all of the critical elements discussed in previous page.

We have learned that some specific instructional procedures—or protocols—work better than others for different types of lessons. There are activities, such as simulations and role playing that have well-established procedures. The following are seven lesson planning protocols that can be used when planning the kinds of lessons that are used frequently during the teaching of an interdisciplinary study.

1. Guided reading: For many lessons in reading
2. The survey, question, read, recite, review (SQ3R) technique: For independent study of a reading selection
3. Guided listening: To help students attend and gain more from a listening activity
4. Guided viewing: To help students attend and gain more from viewing visual materials
5. The know, want to know, learned (KWL) technique: For establishing purposes and organizing for any kind of study
6. The Five-Step Lesson: A protocol especially useful for skills instruction
7. The scientific method: For lessons in which students undertake science experiments

Each of the seven protocols are explained and illustrated with examples below.

A Protocol for Guided (Directed) Reading Instruction

Guided reading is also known as directed reading, the directed reading activity (DRA), and the directed reading–thinking activity (DRTA) (Stauffer, 1969). Guided reading has been used successfully by teachers in teaching reading for many years (Cooper & Kiger, 2008). According to Heilman, Blair, and Rupley (2002), this protocol is generally followed in most commercial reading textbook series. It is a logical approach to use for many instructional reading activities and is especially suitable for reading content material in connection with interdisciplinary studies. The four steps in the protocol are the following:

1. *Pre-reading and Introduction to the Selection to Be Read:*   Students are helped to make a connection between what they will be reading and their current background knowledge. Important new vocabulary and concepts are introduced. It is usually best to include only the essential new vocabulary and concepts that we believe students will not be able to decode or comprehend successfully on their own. Students may lose interest if too much time is spent at this step in the protocol. Also, we want to encourage students to use the word analysis skills they have developed to attack new words they meet and to use context and other comprehension clues to understand new concepts that are included in new reading materials.

2. *Guided Silent Reading of the Selection:*   We need to set specific purposes for reading the new selection; this is especially important when students are being helped to read material at their instructional level, which may be difficult for them (Tovani, 2005). Sometimes, we can involve students in setting their own purposes. If the selection is long, it can be subdivided into shorter sections for silent reading. Vacca and Vacca (2008) suggest that students in the middle elementary grades can usually read passages of approximately 500–900 words. Younger students should be assigned somewhat shorter passages at a time. To set a purpose, the teacher can raise a specific question that can be answered only after the passage is carefully read. Students can often set their own purposes by deciding what they would expect to find in the reading, or they may be asked to predict what they believe will occur in the selection before they read silently to determine if their predictions are accurate.

3. *Discussion Following Silent Reading and Oral Re-reading to Support Responses to Questions:*   After students have finished reading the selection (or part) silently, questions are raised relating to the main purpose set for reading. If students have made predictions, they can be asked about the accuracy of their predictions. During the discussion, students should be asked to read a sentence or short part of the selection orally that supports their answers to the questions that are raised or a part that confirms their predictions. In the primary grades, it may be necessary to have students re-read more of the selection orally to determine their word analysis skill levels. However, asking students to read an entire selection orally after they have read it silently is not usually necessary beyond beginning reading levels. Doing so not only prolongs the activity, but it can also interrupt the flow of information or narrative, reduce overall understanding of the reading material, and even destroy students' interest. Students generally read silently when reading on their own and when taking examinations; therefore, it seems logical to encourage them to read silently and be prepared to support their answers during instructional sessions. If we do not encourage the practice of reading silently for comprehension, students may be at some disadvantage when they must do so on standardized tests. The guided reading protocol may, in fact, be of considerable help to students who need to improve their scores on such tests.

4. *Follow-up Skills and Enrichment Activities:*   Practice with skills on worksheets or in workbooks may be helpful for some students after reading a selection. However, other activities, such as creative writing, outlining a selection, preparing a dramatization based on a narrative selection, or writing a short report of content material, may be more beneficial and engender greater student interest.

Guided reading encourages students to read the way most of us read through life— silently, as we follow a narrative or search for information in reference books and other content materials. Following is a sample lesson plan that follows the guided reading protocol. It assists students with reading a selection on the purchase of the Louisiana Territory during an interdisciplinary study of Westward Expansion. This unit develops an important understanding that westward expansion in the United States affected relations between Native Americans and white settlers as well as, internationally, other nations.

Example Lesson Plan Following the Guided Reading Protocol

Topic: The Louisiana Purchase

Level: Grade 5

Estimated Time: 35–40 minutes

Learning Standards

- Students understand U.S. territorial expansion between 1801 and 1861 and how it affected relations with external powers and Native Americans *(National Council for the Social Studies/National Social Science, U.S. History Standard 5-12.1, reprinted by permission).*
- Students will use a variety of intellectual skills to demonstrate their understanding of major ideas, eras, themes, developments, and turning points in the history of the United States and New York *(New York State Social Studies Standard 1, by permission New York State Education Department).*
- Use a variety of technological and informational resources to gather and synthesize information and to create and communicate knowledge *(National IRA/NCTE Standards for the English Language Arts, Standard 8, reprinted with permission of the International Reading Association www.reading.org).*

General Objectives

Knowledge   Students will understand that the Louisiana Purchase marked the beginning of the period of westward expansion in the United States.

Skill   Students will improve their comprehension of materials when reading for information.

Key question

Why was the purchase of new territories during the period of westward expansion—particularly Louisiana—historically important to the growth of the United States?

Behavioral Objectives

- After reading a selection on the Louisiana Purchase, students will state at least three reasons included in the selection regarding why this purchase was significant in the history of the United States.
- Students will support their responses by orally reading appropriate sections from the text.

Procedure

NOTES

Pre-Reading

Steps 1–5:

Students are helped to make a connection between what they will be reading and their current background knowledge. They are introduced to the topic of the new selection to be read.

1. Remind the students that they have been studying the early growth of the United States and that they have learned that several large land purchases contributed to the westward expansion of U.S. borders. Explain that they are now ready to learn more about some of these purchases and their effects.
2. Ask the students if they can recall the names of some of the purchases.
   Students may recall the names of several that they have heard about, such as Texas, Louisiana, Alaska, and others.
3. Tell the students that today they will be reading about the purchase of the Louisiana Territory and that a short selection from a book on the purchase has been duplicated for them to read.
4. Explain that the selection is the introductory chapter from the book *The Louisiana Purchase*, by James A. Corrick.
5. Explain that the selection will help them to understand why the Louisana Territory purchase was so important in U.S. history.

Steps 6–8:

New vocabulary and concepts are introduced.

6. Ask students if they know the meaning of the word "territory".
   Students may respond that it means land *or something that belongs to someone.* Explain if needed.
7. Ask the meaning of *real estate.*
   Students should suggest that this has to do with land or the value of land. Explain if necessary.
8. Write the word *impact* in a sentence on the chalkboard: "The purchase of the Louisiana Territory had a considerable impact on the expansion of the United States." Ask students what they think the word *impact* means in this sentence.
   Students should indicate that it means an effect on the expansion.
9. Distribute the reading selection to each student.

Guided Silent Reading

Steps 10–11:

Students preview the selection using the headings, and a purpose is set for silent reading of the selection.

10. Ask the students to read the boldface headings silently so that they will have a general idea about the kinds of information the selection includes.

11. When students have finished examining the headings, say, "Now, I would like you to read the selection. As you read, try to note some of the reasons why the Louisiana Purchase had such a significant impact on U.S. history. You can take notes if doing so will help you to recall the reasons you find in the text. Turn the selection over on your desk when you have finished reading so that I will know when most of you have completed the reading."

Discussion

Steps 12–13:

Discussion follows silent reading. Questions are raised that are related to the purpose established in step 11. The behavioral objective and key question of the lesson are checked at step 12.

12. When most students have completed the reading, ask the class for the reasons they found. Note these reasons on the chalkboard. As students offer their contributions, ask them also to locate and read orally a sentence or two that supports what they contribute.

    The major reasons provided by the students should include the following:

    - This was the first purchase of new territory by the United States, and because no provision was made for such purchases in the Constitution, the purchase of Louisiana established the right of the federal government to acquire new property. This right also strengthened the power of the federal government.
    - The purchase nearly doubled the size of the United States.
    - It opened the way for thousands of people to begin exploring the West.
    - The territory was rich in ores for mining, and the land provided an expanse of farmland for agricultural development.
    - It gave the United States complete control of the Mississippi River.

13. Raise other related questions, such as the following:

    - Why was control of the Mississippi River important?

    Students should respond with the idea that the river was needed for economic reasons, for transportation, and for exploration.

    - What were the borders of the Louisiana Territory?

    Students should reply that the exact borders were not clear.

    - What groups of people lived in the new territory?

    Students should say that Native Americans, blacks, and white settlers lived there.

■ What are some of the states that were part of the Louisiana Territory?

Students should include Oklahoma, Colorado, North and South Dakota, Wyoming, Kansas, Iowa, Minnesota, Missouri, Montana, and Louisiana.

Closure

Step 14:

The lesson is brought to closure with a summary of what students have gained from the selection.

14. Bring the lesson to closure by asking the students what they believe they learned from this reading.
    Students will include the idea that the purchase of the Louisiana Territory was exceptionally important to the westward expansion of the United States.
15. Ask students to copy the reasons listed on the chalkboard into their notebooks for future reference.

Assessment Plan

The behavioral objectives and the key question of this lesson require students to suggest reasons why the Louisiana Purchase was significant and to support those reasons by selecting and reading orally an appropriate passage in the text. Assessment of the behavioral objectives and key question are accomplished at step 12 in the lesson procedure.

Material

Corrick, J. A. (2001). The Louisiana Purchase. San Diego, CA: Lucent Books. (Copies of pages 10–14 will be needed for each student.)

SQ3R: The Survey, Question, Read, Recite, Review Protocol for Independent Reading

A technique related to guided reading is SQ3R. Students learn to apply the steps in the protocol independently because the teacher is not present. SQ3R is self-guided reading. The five steps in SQ3R are as follows:

1. *Survey:* Students learn to look over the selection they will be reading and try to recall what they know about the topic. Titles, headings, subheadings, illustrations, photographs, captions, and introductory paragraphs are examined.
2. *Question:* The teacher is absent, so students raise specific questions to guide their reading. They can learn to turn boldface headings into questions to help with this step.
3. *Read:* Students read the selection, keeping in mind the questions they raised.
4. *Recite:* Students try to answer their questions after reading. They prepare notes for later review.
5. *Review:* Students check their notes to review what they gained from the reading material.

A Protocol for Guided Listening

A guided listening protocol is similar to guided reading. It provides direction for students when material is read to them or when they are listening to a speaker or some recorded material. These are lessons that are frequently found in interdisciplinary studies. To follow this protocol, we need to do the following:

- Help students make the necessary cognitive connection with the topic of the material they will hear.
- Clarify new concepts or vocabulary included in the listening activity.
- Help students attend to the material they will be hearing by providing or eliciting from students a purpose or purposes for listening.
- Hold a discussion following the listening session to determine what students have gained from listening.

The example lesson plan below follows the guided listening protocol and is designed to introduce students in a fourth grade to their new interdisciplinary study of Alaska. Important understandings addressed in this lesson are that lifestyles in world communities are influenced by environmental and geographic factors and that culture and experience influence perceptions of places and regions in the United States, Canada, and Latin America.

Example Lesson Plan Following a Guided Listening Protocol

An Eskimo Story
By Audrey Asaro and Smithe Jean-Baptiste

Topic: Eskimos of Alaska (This lesson is a guided listening activity that introduces students to a multidisciplinary unit on the study of Alaska.)

Level: Grades 4–5

Estimated Time: 30–45 minutes

Learning Standard
Students understand ways in which environment influences life and culture in diverse world regions.

General Objectives
Knowledge   Students will understand that there are cultural differences among people living in different regions of the United States.

Skill   Students will improve in their ability to listen for information.

Key questions
- How does geography influence the lifestyle of Alaskan Eskimo people?
- How does the lifestyle of Alaskan Eskimos differ from ours?
- In what ways is it similar?

Behavioral Objective
After listening to a reading of the book, *The Seasons and Someone,* each student will suggest one new fact gained about Alaskan Eskimos or their lifestyle.

Procedure
In preparation for this lesson, a map of the western hemisphere should be displayed, and a small collection of materials on this topic should be available in the classroom. Have the students meet in a section of the classroom conducive to listening, where they will listen to a reading of *The Seasons and Someone,* by Virginia Kroll. This book is about a young Eskimo girl and her family.

NOTES

Pre-Listening

Steps 1–4:

Students are helped to recall what they already know about the topic. This establishes the needed connection to the reading material they will hear.

1. When ready for the lesson, ask students what they know about the Eskimo people.
   Students will probably reply that Eskimos are people who live in the cold weather of the North, that they live in igloos, and that they are people of the snow.
2. Ask if students know the part of the United States where Eskimos are living.
   Some students may know that Eskimos live in the state of Alaska.
3. Ask if students know any other parts of the world where Eskimos are living.
   Some students may cite the North Pole and Canada. Some may not know.
4. Ask for volunteers to point out Alaska, Greenland, Canada, and the parts of Asia where Eskimos live. Assist students as needed in finding these locations.

Step 5:

Students are given specific purposes for listening to the selection.

5. Before beginning to read the story, ask students to listen carefully to learn about the family's living environment, how it is similar or different from ours, what their homes are like, the kinds of clothing they wear, and the kinds of animals they have. List these purposes on the board or on a chart for students' reference during the reading.
6. Begin the oral reading with the author's note. The note explains that Eskimos inhabit the northernmost areas of the world, areas that have the coldest and most bitter weather. The note also gives some information about Eskimo beliefs, customs, and homes. Ask students if they have any questions. Respond as needed; then continue.
7. During the reading, stop occasionally to show students the beautiful illustrations of Eskimos life and their environment. Also, ask for any questions, and remind students about the list of purposes for listening.

Discussion Following Listening

Steps 8 and 9:

Students' written responses at step 8 and the discussion in step 9 will provide for assessment of the lesson objective.

8. After the story is completed, begin assessing what students have gained from the listening activity by asking each student to take a few minutes to write what he or she learned about Eskimos in Alaska. Refer to the list on the board as an outline.

Closure

Step 9:

The lesson is brought to closure.

9. After students have made a list of their understandings, bring closure to the lesson by asking each student to tell one thing he or she learned about this Eskimo family from listening to the story that is either alike or different from our lifestyle or how the geography influences their lives.

Students should include references to the geography and the cold climate which influence the homes they live in, the clothing they wear, and the foods they eat. It is expected that students will mention animals that live in the environment, such as oxen, seals, birds, and polar bears.

10. To conclude the lesson, do the following:

   - Tell the students to keep in mind all they learned from this story about one Eskimo family, and explain that this lesson begins a new study during which they will be working in committees to complete research on Alaska for the next several weeks.

   - Direct students' attention to the materials that have been collected on Alaska for their use. Explain that they may look at these materials to get some ideas about what they may be able to learn about Alaska.

   - Ask students to begin thinking about what they would like to learn about Alaska as they begin the study. Explain that after they have had a few days to look over the materials and to think about what they would like to learn, they will prepare an outline and list of research questions to help guide their research.

Assessment Plan

The behavioral objective of this lesson asks students to suggest facts they have learned about Eskimos or their lifestyle after listening to a reading selection. Assessment of the behavioral objective is accomplished at steps 8 and 9 of the lesson procedure during which it will be possible to also assess if the key questions of the lesson have been addressed.

Materials

   - Kroll, V. L. (1994). *The seasons and someone*. San Diego, CA: Harcourt Brace.
   - A collection of materials on Alaska and Eskimos
   - Large maps of the United States and the world

A Protocol for Guided Viewing

A guided viewing protocol is also similar to guided reading, but it provides direction for students when they are watching a DVD or videotaped program, a computer presentation, a film, or a filmstrip for some specific information. The following steps are included in the guided viewing protocol:

   - Students are helped to make the necessary cognitive connection with the topic of the material they will be viewing.
   - New concepts or vocabulary that will be included in the visual material are introduced.
   - Specific purposes for viewing are given to direct students' attention and help them focus on the visual presentation.
   - Discussion is held with the students to determine what they have gained from the viewing activity.

Guided viewing encourages students to watch attentively as they follow a narrative or search for information in visual materials. See the sample lesson plan below which follows the guided viewing protocol. It is a lesson that introduces students to a new interdisciplinary study on the exploration of outer space and addresses important undertstandings that scientific investigation often involves considerable failure before success and that new scientific discoveries can stimulate important turning points in history.

Example Lesson Plan Following a Guided Viewing Protocol

Topic: Exploring Space, a lesson that introduces a multidisciplinary unit on the exploration of outer space

Level: Middle school—Adaptable for grades 6–8

Estimated Time: 30–40 minutes

Learning Standard
Students investigate key events and developments and major turning points in world history to identify the factors that brought about change and the long-term effects of these changes *(Standard 2, New York State Social Studies Learning Standards. Reprinted by permission of the New York State Education Department).*

General Objectives
Knowledge
- Students will understand significant events, such as the launching of the Soviet Union Sputnik and experimenting with sending animals and finally, humans into space.
- Students will understand that the space age in the United States included many failures before success.

Skill Students will improve in their ability to extract information from visual presentations.

Key Questions
- Why did the exploration of space take such a long time before it experienced any success?
- What critical events occurred during the Space Age (1947–1961) that brought about advances in the exploration of outer space?

Behavioral Objective
After viewing a DVD documentary presentation on the Space Age (1947–1961), students will list in a class discussion at least three significant events in the history of space exploration and infer that considerable failure occurred before success.

Procedure
In preparation for this lesson, have all equipment ready in advance—a computer with a DVD-ROM drive, an LCD projector, and a chart on which to record students' contributions following the presentation.

NOTES

Pre-Viewing

Steps 1–2:

Students are helped to establish a connection to the information presented in the material to be viewed.

1. Say, "You know that U.S. scientists have been exploring outer space." Ask if students know some of the accomplishments of the U.S. space program.
   Students are likely to recall that U.S. astronauts landed on the moon, that satellites have been launched, and that we have a space shuttle.

2. Ask students if they know when the first satellite was launched.

Some students may know that it was Sputnik in 1957. Others may not know.

Steps 3–4:

Students are introduced to the lesson topic and the presentation.

3. Explain that we are beginning a new study about the exploration of outer space and that, today, students will view a DVD presentation that includes information about the Space Age in the twentieth century.

4. Explain that in the presentation, they will see film clips of significant events that occurred during the Space Age.

Guided Viewing

Steps 5–6:

Students are given specific purposes for viewing the DVD program.

5. Introduce the DVD presentation. Say, "As you view the presentation, look for some of the most significant events—the turning points—that took place during the Space Age."

6. Explain that the presentation has a great deal of information and that students may ask to have it paused at times so that they can take notes.

7. Show the presentation. Remind students to watch carefully and to take notes about the events they see. (Pause the presentation when students need more time to take notes.)

Discussion Following Viewing

Step 8:

Discussion includes questions designed to assess the behavioral objective of the lesson.

8. After the presentation, hold a discussion about information the students gained from viewing the DVD program, and list contributions on a chart such as the one shown below in Figure 5.4.

Ask the following questions:

■ What were some of the most important events that occurred during the Space Age?

The students will suggest most of the events given in the presentation, including Sputnik in 1957 and the first U.S. satellite in 1958. They may also recall that Gagarin was the first human to travel in space in 1959.

FIGURE 5.4 Chart on which to record contributions after viewing of a DVD presentation called The Space Age: 1947–1961.

Space Age Exploration
1947–1961

Important events:

First living things in space:

Why launching the first satellite took so long:

Other information:

■ What living things were sent into outer space before any humans rocketed into orbit?

Students should mention rats, dogs, and monkeys.

■ Why do you think it took such a long time for the first U.S. satellite to be launched?

Students should have noticed that failures occurred in the space program before the first successful satellite was launched.

■ Do you recall any other information that was included in the presentation?

Students may have noted that outer space begins at 250 kilometers above the earth and that the temperature in outer space is −273°C.

Closure

Step 9:

The lesson is brought to closure with a summary of the information gained by viewing the DVD program.

9. Summarize the lesson by reviewing the students' contributions recorded on the chart.

10. Remind students that their new study will include conducting research on space exploration, and ask what the first step will be in conducting their research.
Responses should indicate the need for questions to guide their research.

11. Conclude the lesson by asking students to prepare at least two questions to guide their research before the next session.

Assessment Plan

The behavioral objective of this lesson requires that students must state at least three significant events in the history of space exploration during a class discussion of the program. They also need to suggest that there was considerable failure that caused delays in early space exploration. The behavioral objective and key questions are assessed at step 8 in the lesson procedure.

Materials

■ *A century to remember: The great events of the 20th century* [*DVD CD-ROM*]. (1999). St. Laurent, Quebec, Canada: Mendacy Entertainment Group.
■ LCD projector and screen
■ Chart paper

KWL: The Know, Want to Know, Learned Protocol

The KWL technique was initially designed to assist students with reading comprehension (Ogle, 1986). Today, it is also commonly used to help students organize for research or to prepare plans for a field trip. Before the lesson, the teacher prepares three large charts or sections of chalkboard, each of which has one of the letters *K, W,* and *L* at the top. Students' responses will be recorded under each letter. The charts form the three columns needed for the protocol. The charts or board sections must be large enough to be easily read and to accommodate the responses of all students. The KWL protocol includes the following five steps:

1. Students are asked to list what they know about a topic, and their ideas are written in the *K* column. Ogle (1986) suggests that two steps be included in the *K* section. First, students are given an opportunity to suggest all that they know or think they know about a topic. To stimulate student thinking during this initial brainstorming,

   > . . . ask volunteers after they have made their contributions, "Where did you learn that?" or "How could you prove that?" By not simply accepting the statements that students offer but probing to make them think about the sources and substantiveness of their suggestions, you challenge both contributors and the rest of the class to a higher level of thinking. (p. 566)

   Second, students are helped to find common categories among the information they have suggested. For example, if several students have mentioned several different foods that an animal eats, "foods" can become one of the common categories; similarly, other categories can include those in which students have suggested more than one item.

2. In the *W* section, students are asked to list what they would like to learn as they research the topic. The students set the main purposes of their study. As students contribute to the *K* and *W* sections during the initial lesson, their contributions are written on the chart in complete sentences.

3. Students copy the first two sections for reference as they conduct research to determine whether what they thought they knew about the topic in the *K* section is accurate and to find answers to questions in the *W* section of the chart. The *W* and *L* sections will often require considerable time to complete.

4. Time is provided for the students to gather information, to find answers to their questions, and to locate support for the information recorded in the *K* column. This step will require a number of active research periods.

5. As the students gain information, they enter it in the third—what was learned, or *L* section. The information included in this section helps students to confirm or modify the information they have included in the *K* section of the chart, to realize what they have learned about a topic, and what they have been unable to learn relative to the questions they raised initially. The students can then try to determine where to search for additional information.

Below is a sample lesson plan on the season of spring which follows the KWL protocol. This lesson is designed to introduce the interdisciplinary unit of study that is prepared in Chapter 3. This lesson engages students' thinking about the changes brought about during the spring season, and the students are involved in helping to raise the questions to be investigated.

Example Lesson Plan Following a KWL Protocol

Topic: Spring

Level: Grade 2

Estimated Time: 20–25 minutes

Learning Standards

Students understand that seasons of the year, weather, and climate are determined by physical changes in the environment.

Students raise questions and issues to generate inquiries and conduct investigations.

General Objectives

Knowledge   Students will understand that research can begin with the raising of a question or questions.

Skill   Students will gain experience with using the KWL technique to guide the study of a topic.

Disposition   Students will be respectful of others while participating in discussions.

Key question

What do we already know about spring, and what do we want to learn about it?

Behavioral Objective

Students will complete the *K* and *W* sections of a *KWL* chart by generating a list of what they think they know about the season of spring and suggesting at least five questions that will be used to help guide their study of their new unit on spring.

Procedure

In preparation for the lesson, three sections of the chalkboard, dry erase board, or large charts will be needed for the three columns. Use vertical lines to separate the columns, and leave a space at the top on which to write headings for the *K, W,* and *L* sections, as shown in Figure 5.5.

FIGURE 5.5   A *KWL* Chart.

What We Know	What We Want to Know	What We Learned

Because this lesson will involve discussion, before beginning the lesson, remind students about rules for participation.

NOTES

1. Select a day for the field trip in advance, and secure the necessary permissions. Invite two adults from the list of parent volunteers to assist with supervision on the walk. The field trip will be taken after this introductory lesson, which is designed to prepare the students for their walk.

2. The first lesson begins with a class meeting in the early afternoon during the time regularly devoted to unit studies.

Introduction

Steps 3–6:

Students are asked to recall previous studies involving their local neighborhood and their school. They are asked about the changes they have recently noticed in their neighborhood, and are introduced to the topic of their new study.

3. Begin the lesson by reminding the students that they have been studying their neighborhood this year and that their last unit was called *Our School.* Ask the children to recall some activities from that unit.
   The students may say that they remember drawing a map of the school and visiting and interviewing several people who work in the school: the nurse, the school principal, and a custodian. They may also remember that they learned about these people's jobs, that they saw where the people do their work, and that they were given a chance to see some materials used in these jobs. The children may also recall drawing and labeling pictures of school helpers.

4. Ask the students if they have noticed that the school custodians are beginning to do some work they have not been able to do all winter.
   The students may have noticed that the school custodians are working outside on the grounds.

5. Ask the students if they can think of any reasons why work is beginning outside at this time of year.
   The students may say that it is because the grass is growing and it is warmer. They may also say it is now spring.

6. Explain that they will be studying this new season and that spring is the topic of their new unit.

Discussion

Steps 7–9:

The *K* section of the *KWL* chart is completed. Students suggest signs of spring to look for on their field trip, and their contributions are listed in the *K* section of the *KWL* chart.

7. Ask the students what they already know about the spring season. Use a concept web to record what the children say. (See Figure 5.6 for a concept web showing the children's initial concepts of spring.) Then write their responses in the *K* section of the *KWL* chart.
   Responses may include that it is a special time of the year, a time when the weather gets warmer and they no longer have to wear heavy clothing. They may say the grass and

FIGURE 5.6 A students' concept web for spring.

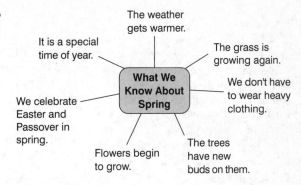

some flowers begin to grow in spring and that the trees have buds. Some children may remember that some important holidays occur during the spring season.

8. Suggest that all of the ideas they have noticed are important ones. Then ask the students if they know that their ideas are actually "signs" of the spring season. Write "sign" on the board, and ask if the children know what it means.
   Children may probably say that a sign is a signal or idea of something. Other similar responses may be given as well.

9. Tell the children that there may actually be other signs of spring they have not yet noticed, and explain that at the end of the week, the class will take a walk along several streets near the school to look for signs of spring in the neighborhood. Then ask, "What signs of spring do you think we will find when we take our walk in the neighborhood?" Write the signs that the students suggest in a list on a large sheet of paper separate from the *KWL* chart.
   The students will be likely to suggest looking for different kinds of flowers and noticing where the grass has begun to turn green. They may also mention looking for birds that have returned after the winter and examining trees and shrubs for signs of new growth.

Step 10:

Students contribute possible questions to the *W* section of the *KWL* chart.

10. Next, ask the students what, in addition to signs of spring, they would like to learn about the spring season. Write any questions they contribute in the *W* section of the *KWL* chart.
    Possible questions include: What other changes occur during the season of spring? How does spring affect us? How can we grow some spring plants? How do spring flowers differ from one another? Do we have a lot of rain in the spring? What holidays do we have in the spring? What are some birds that come back in the spring?

Closure

Steps 11–12:

The lesson is brought to closure with a review of the contributions students have made to the *KWL* chart, and permission slips for their field trip are distributed.

11. To conclude the lesson, summarize briefly by reviewing the *K* and *W* sections of the *KWL* chart, and ask the students to copy information on the chart in their notebooks for later reference.

12. Finally, distribute permission slips and explain that each child must take a permission slip home to be signed. Tell them that the slips must be returned in two days so the class can take the walk.

Assessment Plan

The behavioral objective of this lesson requires students to complete the *K* and *W* sections of a *KWL* chart to record what they believe they already know about the season of spring and to raise questions that will help in the planning of their interdisciplinary study. It may be necessary to add other questions to those the students suggest in order to ensure that the key question, which asks students to provide the most important questions for a study of spring. Step 10 in the procedure of the lesson will ensure this assessment.

Materials

Chart paper and a supply of parental permission slips to distribute to each child in the class

A Protocol for Skills Instruction: The Five-Step Lesson

Skills instruction can follow a fairly traditional outline. A Five-Step Lesson plan (Hunter, 2004) is especially appropriate for teaching skills lessons. The protocol includes the following five elements:

1. An *anticipatory set,* during which the teacher sets the purpose for the lesson, introduces students to the concepts that the lesson will include, and helps students to make the needed connections between their present skills and the new skill to be developed.

2. The *presentation* of the lesson, in which the teacher uses various techniques to present a model of the skill to be developed. The teacher demonstrates the skill for the students.

3. *Guided practice,* in which students are assisted with practice applications of the new skill.

4. *Independent practice,* in which students practice the new skill they have just been taught. Following the lesson, additional practice is assigned.

5. *Closure,* in which students are helped to summarize what they learned about the new skill and its applications during the lesson.

See the sample lesson plan below on the skill of outlining. This is an important skill for all students. Developing skill in outlining information found in various sources as students explore interdisciplinary and multidisciplinary studies is essential.

Example Lesson Plan Following the Five-Step Protocol

Learning How to Outline

Topic: An introduction to outlining

Level: This lesson is adaptable for students from Grade 3–8.

Estimated Time: 30–45 minutes

Learning Standard
Use a variety of technological and informational resources to gather and synthesize information and to create and communicate knowledge *(National IRA/NCTE Standards for the English Language Arts, Standard 8, reprinted with permission of the International Reading Association www.reading.org).*

General Objective
Skill   Students will learn to use outlining to assist them in extracting information from print sources and preparing written reports.

Key question
How can information be extracted from original print and other media sources, summarized, and reported without plagiarizing those sources?

Behavioral Objectives
■ After a demonstration and guided practice in outlining paragraphs from a social studies textbook, each student will outline the main ideas and supporting details from a five-paragraph textbook selection.

■ After developing a five-paragraph outline, students will explain the process involved in outlining informaton from a reading source.

Procedure
Select reading material for this lesson that is appropriate for the grade and reading level of the students. A social studies textbook at the grade level of students will usually be appropriate because it will include information on topics that are investigated for interdisciplinary or multidisciplinary studies.

NOTES

Anticipatory Set

Steps 1–2:

Students are asked to explain the methods they currently use to recall information for their research when using reading materials, and they are introduced to the lesson topic.

1. Ask the students what they do when they are researching a topic and want to remember information they find in books or other reading materials.
   Students are likely to say they copy some of the sentences from the readings into their notebooks.
2. Explain that the purpose of this lesson is to help them to learn more about how to record such information without copying it and that they will be learning how to outline information they find in a book, in an article, or in a document on the Internet.

Presentation

Step 3–5:

The teacher demonstrates outlining for students and invites them to observe and participate in a discussion of the main topic and details in a paragraph used for the demonstration.

3. Invite the students to watch as you demonstrate a way to outline paragraphs in a reading selection. (Using an LCD or an overhead projector, project a selection that includes three or four paragraphs of content material, preferably a page from the students' social studies textbook. The topic should be one that students are currently investigating.)

4. Direct students' attention to the title and first paragraph of the selection. Have students read the first paragraph silently; then ask one student to read it orally for the class. (Note that although you are demonstrating at this point in the lesson, students should be involved in the thought process as much as possible.)

5. Hold a brief discussion of the content of the paragraph. Ask students what they think is the main point of the paragraph. Phrase the main idea for the students, and demonstrate how to begin the outline by writing the main idea on the chalkboard next to a Roman numeral I.

Step 6–8:

Demonstration continues. Students are asked to suggest other details and important points in the paragraph as the teacher demonstrates how to include those points in the outline.

6. Ask students to suggest other important points they recall from the paragraph. Phrase these points, and write each under the main idea, using uppercase letters—*A, B, C,* and so on.

7. Continue demonstrating how to outline each succeeding paragraph in the projected sample, following steps 4 and 5.

8. Ask students to look at the outline and to explain how the outline differs from the text selection.
   Students should note that the outline is shorter than the selection, that it includes the most important information, that the wording is different, and that nothing from the text has been copied directly.

9. If necessary, demonstrate the process with a second projected selection.

Guided Practice

Step 10:

Guided practice begins.

10. If students appear to understand what has been demonstrated, continue by helping them to apply the skill to a new selection.
    a. Ask the students to read the selection silently.
    b. Ask the students to determine the main idea and other related information for each paragraph in the projected selection.
    c. Guide the students in their wording of the outline.
    d. Continue to guide students as they outline additional projected selections if needed.

Independent Practice

Steps 11–12:

Independent practice begins.

11. Direct students to a selection in their social studies textbooks. Follow the same procedure outlined in step 10 to guide students through the outlining procedure. Use more than one selection if needed. If students appear to understand the process, continue with step 12.

12. Ask students to individually outline a new five-paragraph selection from their textbooks.

13. Collect the students' outlines after they have had sufficient time to prepare them so that you can assess their success and understanding of the process.

Closure

Step 14:

The lesson is brought to closure with a review of the outlining process students have just been taught.

14. After the outlines have been collected, ask the students to explain the process involved in outlining information they locate in reading materials.
    Students should explain that the process begins with a careful reading of the selection. Next, each paragraph is analyzed for its main idea and important information related to that idea. Finally, the students should explain that they need to write the outline of these points in their own words and without copying directly from the text.

15. Tell the students they will have further practice with outlining but that the most important practice will be the outlining they need to do when they are researching the topics they are studying.

Assessment Plan

The behavioral objectives of this skills lesson requires students to prepare an outline of a five-paragraph selection from a text and to describe the outlining process in a class discussion. To assess these objectives, students are required to outline a five-paragraph selection in their text independently at steps 11 and 12, and the outlines are collected for individual assessment at step 13. At step 14, students are asked to explain the outlining process.

Materials

- Several three- to five-paragraph selections of content material prepared for overhead or LCD projection
- Copies of the students' social studies textbooks
- An LCD projector and a computer, or an overhead projector with transparencies prepared in advance

The Scientific Method of Investigation: A Protocol for Some Lessons in Science

Rick Allen (2006) reminds us that standards developed by the "National Research Council in 1996 calls for K-12 students to both understand and be able to do scientific inquiry" (p. 4). The scientific method is a logical choice when a lesson involves students in scientific experimentation. In that procedure, students are guided to follow these five steps:

1. Observe a phenomenon.
2. Suggest hypotheses for the phenomenon.
3. Design a method of testing the hypotheses.
4. Observe the results.
5. Draw conclusions relative to the hypotheses.

The lesson plan that follows is an example of a lesson in which the procedure follows the scientific method of investigation. It is a lesson that provides students with an opportunity to gain insight in the important understanding that variables in the interactive forces between energy and matter affect changes in motion. In this specific lesson, students will learn the scientific principle of the pendulum, that the length of a pendulum is the only variable that can affect its swing rate.

Example Lesson Plan Following the Scientific Method of Investigation

Topic: The Pendulum

Level: Grade 3 or 4

Estimated Time: 20–30 minutes

Learning Standard

Students will develop an understanding of the scientific method of investigation and be able to apply it to investigations in science.

General Objective

Knowledge   Students will understand that it is only the length of a pendulum that affects its swing rate.

Skill   Students will gain experience in solving problems in physical science by following the scientific method of investigation.

Disposition   Students will develop a positive attitude about failure when investigating in science.

Key question

How can the swing rate of a pendulum be changed?

Behavioral Objective

After experimentation with a pendulum, students will state in discussion that it is the length of a pendulum that affects its swing rate.

Procedure

Set up a simple pendulum before the lesson following the directions in the materials section below.

NOTES

Step 1:

Students observe the model pendulum and recall objects they know that swing.

Step 2:

Students are introduced to the topic of the new unit.

Steps 3 and 4:

Students learn how to count pendulum swings and determine the base swing rate of the pendulum.

1. Swing the model pendulum, and ask the students if this reminds them of anything they have seen before.
   Students may be reminded of swings on the playground and clocks that they have seen. Some students may suggest that it is like a "pendulum." However, because other students may not be familiar with the word pendulum, you may need to clarify its meaning.

2. While the pendulum is swinging, tell the students this: "Today, we are beginning a new unit in which we will be involved in completing several investigations. The first will be a study involving a pendulum."

3. Ask the students if they can think of a way to determine how fast the pendulum is swinging.
   Timing and counting will probably be suggested.

4. Because the students will not know how to count pendulum swings to determine the swing rate, demonstrate how to count the swings—one swing for each back-and-forth movement.

Decide on how long to time the pendulum swings. Have one student keep time while others count silently; then, record the basal swing rate on the board.

Steps 5 and 6:

Students are invited to hypothesize, to suggest ways they think will make the swing rate of the pendulum increase, and their suggestions are listed.

5. Say, "I wonder if there is a way to make the pendulum swing faster." List the students' suggestions—their hypotheses—on the board under the basal swing rate.
   The students may suggest pushing it harder, starting it from a higher position, adding or subtracting weights, and perhaps lengthening or shortening the pendulum.

6. Ask how they can determine if any of their ideas will make the pendulum swing faster.
   The students should suggest that they will need to try each suggestion—to experiment.

Steps 7:

Using their own hypotheses, students experiment to determine if any of their ideas will increase the swing rate of the pendulum.

7. Provide time for experimentation. Ideally, the pendulum should be set up in a corner of the classroom where all students will have an opportunity to experiment during several days. A schedule, either a sign-up sheet or a list of names, should be posted near the pendulum. Students will need to work in pairs to test their hypotheses—one child to time the swings and one to count. The students should record their hypotheses and the results of each test in their notebooks or on a specially designed worksheet. If you decide that the experimentation should be completed as a whole-class activity (for safety or other reasons), some students should be invited to assist with timing and counting. Others should be reminded to observe carefully.

Step 8:

Closure is brought to the lesson; the key question and behavioral objective of the lesson are checked.

8. After the experimentation is completed, engage the class in a discussion. Ask, "What have you found that causes the pendulum to swing faster?"
   The response should include the idea that only shortening the pendulum will increase its swing rate.

9. Collect any student's records—notebooks or worksheets—of their experimentation.

Step 10:

The questions raised at step 10 require students to apply their new information about pendulums to authentic situations.

10. Indicating each of the hypotheses—on the board—that failed to increase the swing rate of the pendulum, ask the following five questions:
    - Can anyone explain why you thought that would work? (This question helps the students to analyze their thinking about each hypothesis.)
    - How do you suppose we could correct a clock with a pendulum that is losing time?
    - If you want your backyard swing to swing faster, what would you have to do to it?
    - Do you think there is any other way to make a pendulum swing faster?
    - What will we have to do to make the pendulum swing slower?

Assessment Plan

The behavioral objective of this lesson requires that students explain how the swing rate of a pendulum can be made to change. The objective and students' ability to respond accurately to the key question of the lesson are assessed at step 8 in the lesson procedure.

Materials

- A simple pendulum (Use a stick, a ruler, or an unsharpened pencil taped securely to a tabletop so that it overhangs the top by about 6 inches; a 30-inch length of string tied and wrapped several times around the end of the stick; a large paper clip, opened and attached to one end of the string; several weights, such as metal washers of equal size and weight, placed on the open end of the paper clip; and several additional weights for experimenting.)
- Masking tape
- A timer with a second hand

Other Procedures

Procedures suitable for demonstrations, applications, and practice sessions can involve combinations of the preceding protocols. For example, a lesson might begin with a directed listening activity, having students listen to a short selection or book. The listening activity may lead to the preparation of a *KWL* chart to introduce some research the students will be undertaking. Follow-up activities might make use of additional protocols.

Summary

This chapter has reviewed principles of learning and development that are important for planning interdisciplinary and multidisciplinary units. Bloom's Taxonomy, a six-level classification system, and questioning techniques have been outlined and illustrated with examples.

An overview of lesson planning has included explanations of planning formats, learning standards, general objectives, key questions, and behavioral objectives. Critical elements in the procedure section of any lesson plan have also been listed and explained. Several lesson planning protocols for teachers who plan for interdisciplinary instruction have been outlined and illustrated with example lesson plans. Chapter 6 will include basic information on assessment for interdisciplinary and multidisciplinary instructional plans.

ACTIVITY

Ms. Benson, a sixth-grade teacher, has designed an interidisciplinary unit on an interesting and unusual theme, *Mysteries*. A web design (see Figure 5.7) shows a number of interesting lessons and activities that she plans to include in the study.

Select one of the lessons or activities and plan a complete lesson plan following one of the protocols reviewed in this chapter. Be sure that the protocol followed is appropriate for the type of lesson or activity you select.

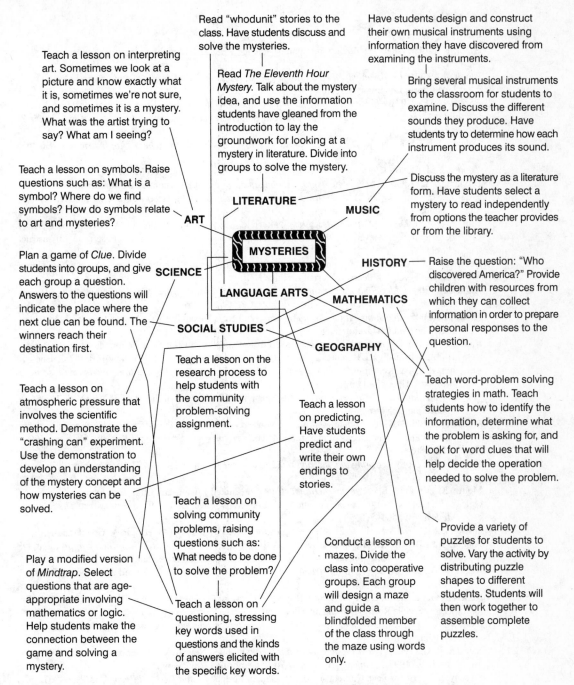

Read "whodunit" stories to the class. Have students discuss and solve the mysteries.

Read *The Eleventh Hour Mystery*. Talk about the mystery idea, and use the information students have gleaned from the introduction to lay the groundwork for looking at a mystery in literature. Divide into groups to solve the mystery.

Have students design and construct their own musical instruments using information they have discovered from examining the instruments.

Bring several musical instruments to the classroom for students to examine. Discuss the different sounds they produce. Have students try to determine how each instrument produces its sound.

Teach a lesson on interpreting art. Sometimes we look at a picture and know exactly what it is, sometimes we're not sure, and sometimes it is a mystery. What was the artist trying to say? What am I seeing?

Teach a lesson on symbols. Raise questions such as: What is a symbol? Where do we find symbols? How do symbols relate to art and mysteries?

Discuss the mystery as a literature form. Have students select a mystery to read independently from options the teacher provides or from the library.

LITERATURE

MUSIC

ART

MYSTERIES

SCIENCE

HISTORY

Raise the question: "Who discovered America?" Provide children with resources from which they can collect information in order to prepare personal responses to the question.

Plan a game of *Clue*. Divide students into groups, and give each group a question. Answers to the questions will indicate the place where the next clue can be found. The winners reach their destination first.

LANGUAGE ARTS

MATHEMATICS

SOCIAL STUDIES

GEOGRAPHY

Teach a lesson on the research process to help students with the community problem-solving assignment.

Teach a lesson on predicting. Have students predict and write their own endings to stories.

Teach word-problem solving strategies in math. Teach students how to identify the information, determine what the problem is asking for, and look for word clues that will help decide the operation needed to solve the problem.

Teach a lesson on atmospheric pressure that involves the scientific method. Demonstrate the "crashing can" experiment. Use the demonstration to develop an understanding of the mystery concept and how mysteries can be solved.

Teach a lesson on solving community problems, raising questions such as: What needs to be done to solve the problem?

Conduct a lesson on mazes. Divide the class into cooperative groups. Each group will design a maze and guide a blindfolded member of the class through the maze using words only.

Provide a variety of puzzles for students to solve. Vary the activity by distributing puzzle shapes to different students. Students will then work together to assemble complete puzzles.

Play a modified version of *Mindtrap*. Select questions that are age-appropriate involving mathematics or logic. Help students make the connection between the game and solving a mystery.

Teach a lesson on questioning, stressing key words used in questions and the kinds of answers elicited with the specific key words.

FIGURE 5.7   An interdisciplinary unit plan web design for "Mysteries", a sixth grade study.

REFERENCES

Allen, R. (2005, August). Moving elementary science from afterthought to inquiry. *Education Update* *48*(8), 4.

Bloom, B. S. (1956). *Taxonomy of educational goals, by a committee of college and university examiners.* New York: Longmans, Green.

Borich, G. D. (2007). *Effective teaching methods* (6th ed.). Upper Saddle River, NJ: Pearson/Merrill.

Caram, C. A., & Davis, P. B. (2005, Fall). Inviting student engagement with questioning. *Kappa Delta Pi Record, 42*(1), 19–23.

Cooper, J. D., & Kiger, N. D. (2008). *Literacy assessment: Helping teachers plan instruction.* Boston: Houghton Mifflin.

Cooper, J. M. (2006). *Classroom teaching skills* (8th ed.). Boston: Houghton Mifflin.

DuPlass, J. A. (2008). *Teaching elementary social studies* (2nd ed.). Boston: Houghton Mifflin.

Elder, L., & Paul, R. (2002). *A miniature guide to the art of asking key questions.* Dillon Beach, CA: Foundation for Critical Thinking.

Hall, T. (2002). *Differentiated instruction.* Wakefield, MA: National Center on Accessing the General Curriculum. Retrieved March 5, 2008 from http://www.cast.org/publications/ncac/ncac_diffinstruc. html

Heilman, A. W., Blair, R. R., & Rupley, W. H. (2002). *Principles and practices of teaching reading.* Upper Saddle River, NJ: Pearson/Merrill Prentice Hall.

Hunter, R. (2004). *Madeline Hunter's mastery teaching: Increasing instructional effectiveness in elementary and secondary schools.* Thousand Oaks, CA: Corwin Press.

Jensen, E. (2005). *Teaching with the brain in mind* (2nd ed.). Alexandria, VA: Association for Supervision and Curriculum Development.

Kamii, C. (1973). Pedagogical principles derived from Piaget's theory: Relevance for educational practice. In M. Schwebel & J. Raph (Eds.), *Piaget in the classroom* (pp. 199–215). New York: Basic Books.

Kellough, R. D., & Kellough, N. G. (2003). *Middle school teaching: A guide to methods and resources* (4th ed.). Upper Saddle River, NJ: Pearson/Merrill Prentice Hall.

Learning standards for social studies. (1996). Albany: The University of the State of New York/The State Education Department.

Macbeth, D. (2003). Hugh Mehan's learning lessons reconsidered: On the differences between the naturalistic and critical analysis of classroom discourse. *American Educational Research Journal, 40*(1), 239–280.

Mayer, R. E. (2008). *Learning and instruction* (2nd ed.). Upper Saddle River, NJ: Pearson/Merrill Prentice Hall.

Moore, K. D. (2009). *Effective instructional strategies* (2nd ed.). Thousand Oaks, CA: Sage.

Ogle, D. M. (1986). K-W-L: A teaching model that develops active reading of expository text. *The Reading Teacher, 39,* 564–570.

Ornstein, A. C., & Lasley, T. J. (2004). *Strategies for effective teaching* (4th ed.). Boson: McGraw-Hill.

Post, T. R., Ellis, A. K., Humphreys, A. H., & Buggey, L. J. (1997). *Interdisciplinary approaches to curriculum: Themes for teaching.* Upper Saddle River, NJ: Prentice Hall.

Reiser, R. A., & Dick, W. (1996). *Instructional planning: A guide for teachers* (2nd ed.). Boston: Pearson/ Allyn & Bacon.

Roberts, P. L., & Kellough, R. D. (2008). *A guide for developing interdisciplinary thematic units* (4th ed.). Upper Saddle River, NJ: Pearson Education.

Ryan, K., Cooper, J. M., & Tauer, S. (2008). *Teaching for student learning: Becoming a teacher.* Boston: Houghton Mifflin.

Stauffer, R. G. (1969). *Teaching reading as a thinking process.* New York: Harper & Row.

Sternberg, R. J. (1997). *Thinking styles.* New York: Cambridge University Press.

Sweeny, B. (1999, Winter). Content standards: Gate or bridge? *Kappa Delta Pi Record, 35*(2), 64–67.

Tovani, C. (2005, October). The power of purposeful reading. *Educational Leadership, 63*(2), 48–51.

Vacca, R. T., & Vacca, J. L. (2008). *Content area reading: Literacy and learning across the curriculum* (9th ed.). Boston: Pearson/Allyn & Bacon.

Viadero, D. (1995, November 8). Expert testimony. *Education Week*, pp. 33–34.

Wakefield, A. P. (1993). Developmentally appropriate practice: "Figuring things out." *The Educational Forum, 57*(2), 134–143.

Wiggins, G., & McTighe. (2005). *Understanding by design* (2nd ed.) Alexandria, VA: Association for Supervision and Curriculum Development.

SUGGESTED READINGS

The supplemental readings listed below are additional resources on specific topics related to the lesson planning processes discussed in this chapter.

Learning Standards and Instructional Objectives

Many excellent resources are available for more information on learning standards and instructional objectives including the following. Note that descriptive documents on standards can also be located on the Internet at the Mid-continent Research for Education and Learning Web site: http://www.mcrel.org.

Arends, R. I. (2009). *Learning to teach* (8th ed.). Boston: McGraw-Hill.

Behavioral verbs for writing objectives in the cognitive, affective and psychomotor domain. Retrieved from http://www.isst-d.org/2007conference/Wordingforobjectives.pdf

Dembo, M. H. (1994). *Applying educational psychology in the classroom* (5th ed.). New York: Longman.

Dick, W, Carey, L., & Carey, J. O. (2009). *The systematic design of instruction* (7th ed.). Upper Saddle River, NJ: Pearson/Merrill.

Gronlund, N. E. (1991). *Stating objectives for classroom instruction* (4th ed.). New York: Macmillan.

Guskey, T. R. (2001). Helping standards make the grade. *Educational Leadership, 59*(1), 20–27.

Harris, D. E., & Carr, J. F. (1996). *How to use standards in the classroom.* Alexandria, VA: Association for Supervision and Curriculum Development.

Holt, L. C., & Kysilka, M. (2006). *Instructional patterns: Strategies for maximizing student learning.* Thousand Oaks, CA: Sage.

Kibler, R. J., Cegala, D. J., Barker, L. L., & Miles, D. T. (1981). *Objectives for instruction and evaluation* (2nd ed.). Boston: Pearson/Allyn & Bacon.

Mager, R. (1997). *Preparing instructional objectives: A critical tool in the development of effective instruction* (3rd ed.). Atlanta, GA: Center for Effective Performance.

Marchesani, R. J. (2007). *The field guide to teaching: A handbook for new teachers.* Upper Saddle River, NJ: Pearson/Merrill Prentice Hall.

Ormrod, J. E. (2009). *Essentials of educational psychology* (2nd ed.). Upper Saddle River, NJ: Pearson/Merrill/Prentice Hall.

Schmoker, M., & Marzano, R. J. (1999, March). Realizing the promise of standards-based education. *Educational Leadership, 56*(6), 17–21.

Wilson, M., & Tienken, C. (2001). Using standards to improve instruction. *Kappa Delta Pi Record, 38*(2), 82–84, 88.

Writing Learning Objectives. Retrieved January 20, 2009 from http://www.acoem.org/uploadedFiles/Continuing_Education/Joint_Sponsorship/Learning%20Objectives.doc

Zook, K. B. (2001). *Instructional design for classroom teaching and learning.* Boston: Houghton Mifflin.

Learning Styles

Dunn, R. S. (1994). *Teaching young children through their individual learning styles: Practical approaches for grades K–2.* Boston: Pearson/Allyn & Bacon.

Dunn, R., & Dunn, K. (1992). *Teaching elementary students through their individual learning styles: Practical approaches for grades 3–6.* Boston: Pearson/Allyn & Bacon.

Dunn, R. S., & Dunn, K. (1993). *Teaching secondary students through their individual learning styles: Practical approaches for grades 7–12.* Boston: Allyn & Bacon.

Fizzell, R. (1984). The status of learning styles. *The Educational Forum, 48*(3), 303–312.

Kagan, D. (1987). Cognitive style and instructional preferences: Some inferences. *The Educational Forum, 51*(4), 393–403.

Learning styles and the brain. (1990). *Educational Leadership, 48*(2), 4–81.

O'Neil, H. F., & Spielberger, C. D. (1979). *Cognitive and affective learning strategies*. New York: Academic Press.

Phye, G. D., & Andre, T. (Eds.). (1986). *Cognitive classroom learning*. Orlando, FL: Academic Press.

Piaget, J. (1963). *Judgment and reasoning in the child*. Totowa, NJ: Littlefield, Adams.

Five-Step Lesson Plan

Elements of effective instruction: The Madeline Hunter model. (n.d.). Retrieved August 16, 2008 from http://www.humboldt.edu/~tha1/hunter-eei.html#eei

Questioning Strategies

The following sources provide additional information on questioning and discussion.

Orlich, D. C., Harder, R. J., Callahan, R. C., & Gibson, H. W. (2001). *Teaching strategies: A guide to better instruction* (6th ed.). Boston: Houghton Mifflin.

Ormrod, J. E. (2008). *Educational psychology: Developing learners* (6th ed.). Upper Saddle River, NJ: Pearson/Merrill/Prentice Hall.

Wilen, W. W. (Ed.). (1987). *Questions, questioning techniques, and effective teaching*. Washington, DC: National Education Association.

Lesson Plan Formats

Lesson design and performance models. (n.d.). Retrieved August 2, 2008 from http://www.foothill.net/~moorek/lessondesign.html

Scientific Method

Carin, A. A. (2001). *Teaching science through discovery* (9th ed.). Upper Saddle River, NJ: Pearson/Merrill Prentice Hall.

6 Assessment Planning for Interdisciplinary Instruction

Students taking an end-of-unit examination.

OVERVIEW

This chapter reviews aspects of assessment for interdisciplinary and multidisciplinary units, lessons, and activities. The focus of this chapter is on the following:

- Assessment and interdisciplinary instruction
- Using authentic assessment techniques with interdisciplinary instruction
- Using rubrics with interdisciplinary instruction
- Using examinations with interdisciplinary instruction
- Writing valid and reliable test items

Assessment and Interdisciplinary Instruction

Assessment of unit and lesson objectives and the evaluation of student achievement are as important in the interdisciplinary instructional approach as with other teaching methods. Although they are sometimes thought to be synonomous, Arends (2009) clarifies the differences between *assessment* and *evaluation*. Assessment includes all the information we gather through various techniques while evaluation indicates "making judgments, assigning value, or deciding on worth" (p. 211). For example, an examination is an assessment tool, but the actual grade a student earns as a result of taking it results in an *evaluation* of the student's achievement on that examination.

Assessment strategies need to be decided early in the process of planning a lesson or an interdisciplinary or multidisciplinary study. The strategies and techniques we use must relate directly to the objectives and learning standards of a specific instructional plan. In Chapters 3 and 4 on unit planning and Chapter 5 on lesson planning, assessments were determined immediately after the unit or lesson objectives had been determined and before specific procedures were outlined. This sequence differs from conventional practice by placing assessment decisions second instead of the final step in the process of designing both units and lessons. The rationale for this sequence is simply that it is difficult to plan ways to help students achieve our objectives unless we know what students will have to do in order to demonstrate that they have mastered those objectives.

There are two general assessment categories—*formative* and *summative*. Assessing students' progress *during* the teaching process, while concepts are still forming, is called *formative assessment*. Shepard (2005) links formative assessment to the Vygotskian concepts of *scaffolding* and *zone of proximal development* because "it is a dynamic process in which supportive adults or classmates help learners move from what they already know to what they are able to do next . . ." (p. 66). "Formative assessments can vary significantly, both in terms of the activities that qualify as assessments and the timing of those activities" (An "Insider's View," 2007, p. 3). Techniques that can serve as formative assessment measures with interdisciplinary and multidisciplinary units include reviewing the material that students have previously studied in the unit, raising questions about what has been taught, conducting quizzes, and observing the ways students work on various tasks and in their committee work.

Other assessment techniques are used at the end of instruction. Typical of those are final examinations and reports of various kinds. Assessments at the conclusion of instruction are referred to as *summative*. Those techniques help to determine the extent to which students have met the intended standards and objectives of their units and provide for the final evaluation.

Even though assessment is primarily our responsibility as teachers, we need to recognize the importance of involving students in the process. Popham (2006, February) emphasizes the student role when he defines meaningful assessment as assessment *for* learning as opposed to assessment *of* learning. He explains that "the aim... is to empower students to monitor their own progress toward clearly understood goals" (p. 82). Knowing their objectives can "give students a performance target to aim for" (Wilcox, 2006, p. 1). Therefore, both teachers and students have an investment in the process. In interdisciplinary and multidisciplinary studies, students are routinely involved in planning their studies; they can also be encouraged to help decide ways the objectives of their studies will be assessed.

The Purposes of Assessment

While both formative and summative assessment techniques determine the extent to which students have achieved the objectives of instruction, the same techniques can help in diagnosing where students have difficulty with some particular material and the extent to which teaching has been effective.

Diagnosis: Both summative and formative assessment techniques can be used in the ongoing diagnosis of students' areas of strength and relative weakness. The purpose of all diagnosis is to help improve learning by designing or redesigning instruction to better meet individual student's needs. The interdisciplinary approach typically involves individual conferences with students and committees to determine how well the students are proceding with their research and projects. Those conferences can yield information about strengths and limitations for both individuals and groups of students, information that will indicate the need for some specific instruction in the future.

Teaching Effectiveness: Assessment can also help us to learn about the effectiveness of our own teaching. We can use the results of both summative and formative assessment techniques for this purpose. We can note what students have gained from their research by monitoring their oral presentations and individual written reports. We can make use of students' examination scores; however, if we do, it will be important to view those results in combination with our knowledge of the students and informal observations of their work before drawing any tentative conclusions about our teaching.

Assessment Techniques: The Need for Variety

Although most educators agree that some form of assessment is needed in order to evaluate student progress and achievement, not all agree on the techniques to use for different purposes. Ellis (2009) urges teachers to become familiar with several approaches to assessment because experience has not proven that one is better than another. Sternberg (1999) also suggests that "different kinds of assessment . . . complement one another . . . . There is no single 'right' kind of assessment" (p. 51). Instead, all assessment strategies need to be appropriate to the grade level, subject matter, development levels, and skills abilities of the students (Dick, Carey, & Carey, 2009; Jacobs, 1997). Perhaps, as Guskey (2003) suggests, those that are "best suited to guide improvements in students . . . [are those] that teachers administer on a regular basis in their classrooms" (p. 7).

Wiggins and McTighe (2006) define three types of assessments as those that check for "understanding (such as oral questions, observations, and dialogues); traditional quizzes, tests, and open-ended prompts; and performance tasks and projects" (p. 152).

The interdisciplinary approach makes use of all of those techniques. Rubrics can be designed to assess various student products, demonstrations, and oral presentations. Quizzes may be administered during a study, and examinations are usually given at the conclusion of each unit.

Traditionally, examinations and quizzes have been used more than other assessment tools; however, most paper-and-pencil tests are limited to assessing students' verbal and logical–mathematical achievement. To limit assessment to formal and informal tests is inconsistent with the interdisciplinary approach because it fails to recognize the value of student products, such as papers, projects, and performances in the process. It also ignores the value of including students in the assessment *process* (Wexler-Sherman, Gardner, & Feldman, 1988); it leaves the responsibility for assessment solely on the shoulders of teachers, with students playing a passive role (Johnston, 1987).

As mentioned in Chapter 5, behaviorally stated instructional objectives have also been used for many years in lesson and activity plans. Behavioral objectives are useful for short-term purposes in lesson planning and for measuring progress in the development of specific skills. Although they help to determine the effectiveness of a lesson, behavioral objectives are the only factor to be considered in the overall assessment process.

If we consider the importance of assessing individual student progress in areas other than linguistic and logical–mathematical, neither examinations nor behavioral objectives are totally adequate. For example, we may believe that interdisciplinary or multidisciplinary unit activities should foster improvement in dispositions that will result in better cooperation and interpersonal skills among our students. To assess progress in these areas, we need to observe students directly. Thus, using a test would not be the logical choice. By the same token, testing is not helpful for determining students' interests and attitudes or feelings about their own work or individual progress. Realistically, examinations rarely invite student participation in the assessment process. However, *authentic* assessment techniques do include students in the process.

Using Authentic Assessment Techniques with Interdisciplinary Instruction

Many teachers collect representative examples of students' work in folders to use when they are preparing reports and conferring with parents. Students, as well as teachers, can be involved in assembling these folders, which represent the work produced by students day-to-day. When students take part in selecting the items to be included, their folders are referred to as *portfolios*. The portfolio can then become a resource for ongoing assessment of each student's progress during the course of a unit study.

A portfolio is an *authentic assessment* device because it includes examples of students' actual work and surveys of their interests, feelings, and attitudes. It can often indicate growth in areas for which examinations tend to be ineffective. Portfolios prepared by students—or cooperatively by students and teachers—can include many kinds of materials that are useful in the overall assessment process. Johnston (1992) suggests that a student's portfolio is analogous to an artist's portfolio because the student has the opportunity to include "work that he/she sees fit to display and talk about to others" (p. 129). The following list indicates some of the more common materials found in student portfolios that are assembled during the course of an interdisciplinary or multidisciplinary study.

- Notes and memos about their individual research, projects, and committee work
- Student journals in which they record their observations and analyses of what they have gained from instruction, projects, and work on committees; what they feel they have understood and not understood
- Teacher journals and observations of individual student progress, needs, and committee participation
- Surveys of students' feelings and attitudes about their interests and participation in their unit studies
- Students self-evaluations of their papers, projects, and committee work
- Records that are kept during individual pupil–teacher conferences that occur during the research phase of a unit
- Formal and informal quizzes, tests, and examinations administered throughout a unit of study
- Audio and video recordings; individual and committee oral reports and recitations

Selecting materials for a portfolio needs to be a thoughtful process. The materials that are included should provide for balance, with examples that represent the learning processes as well as student products. Work samples should include notes students take during the research phase of a unit, drafts of papers or other products in progress as well as those that have been completed (Pappas, Kiefer, & Levstik, 1999). We need to develop criteria for guiding students in the selection of the samples they include. Clear criteria will also help students understand how their materials will be evaluated and weighted in the overall assessment process. The roles others will have in the evaluation process, including parents, should be made clear (Borich, 2007). Research on the portfolio technique indicates that portfolios have a positive effect on the improvement of instruction and an impact on the insights that students develop about their academic strengths and weaknesses (O'Neil, 1993).

When students are responsible for maintaining their portfolios or parts of the portfolios they prepare during their unit studies, they can monitor their own development and progress. If students are asked to provide notations on the materials that they include in their unit portfolios, the process becomes even more reflective for them. Shore and Grace (2005) suggest that this encourages students to use important strategies such as "questioning, discussing, guessing, proposing, analyzing, and reflecting" (p. 11).

Thus, unit portfolios can be exceptionally useful authentic assessment tools for use with interdisciplinary and multidisciplinary studies because they provide concrete evidence to help assess students' mastery of the unit objectives. Portfolios also provide a vehicle for reflection and interaction between students and teachers, and they add concrete evidence that can be combined with formal examinations in the overall evaluation process.

Using Rubrics with Interdisciplinary Instruction

During the course of an interdisciplinary or multidisciplinary unit, students prepare reports and projects of different kinds, including written and oral reports, art projects, constructions, panel discussions, exhibits, experiments, and so on. Methods of assessing these student products should be as thoughtful and objective as possible. Although subjectivity cannot be eliminated entirely, using clearly defined criteria in the assessment and evaluation processes can help to minimize it. One of the most effective tools for this purpose is using rubrics that clearly define grading criteria.

Rubrics are scoring tools that are prepared before an assignment is given and that can be used to assess and evaluate a completed student product. If the same assignment has been given in the past and samples of the product have been collected, it is useful to study those samples when designing rubrics for similar products. This exercise can help to make delineating the criteria easier and more realistic of what students can be expected to do with the assignment.

Rubrics indicate quality gradations for each criterion they include. Student products—papers, projects, performances, constructions, and so on—are then examined for compliance with the criteria. Having the criteria to apply in advance of the grading process can help to make that process easier and fairer. When designing rubrics, some teachers examine work samples of previous students to help them decide the criteria that will be reasonable for a particular student product.

There is considerable support for involving students in the assessment process, a key element of interdisciplinary instruction. For example, Goodrich (1997) has suggested that use of rubrics may "improve student performance, as well as monitor it, by making teachers' expectations clear and by showing students how to meet these expectations" (p. 14). In an experimental writing program, Porcaro and Johnson (2003) found that requiring students to use rubrics in the form of writing checklists motivated the students to "look critically at their work" as they edited their papers (p. 78). Thus, it is clear that rubrics can assist teachers with the grading process and that when shared with students in advance, can provide students with clear expectations for their work.

In some schools, sets of rubrics are available for teachers to use to assess student products in various disciplines or subject areas. For example, the Chicago Public Schools provide a *Rubric Bank* (2007). Another source available on the Internet is *Kathy Schrock's Guide for Educators* (Schrock, 2007) which offers rubrics that can be helpful.

An example of rubric construction is shown in Figure 6.1. This set of rubrics will be used to assess the reports that a group of students will be writing on endangered animals. Note that the format in the example can be used to design rubrics for other products and grade levels.

In the example, the rubrics for evaluating student reports on endangered animals indicate that each report must include a clear introduction, provide information about why the animal is endangered, and include two possible ways to correct the problem that are supported by the student's research findings. The reports will be examined for organization, clarity, and writing quality. This set of rubrics has three classifications—Excellent (3 points), Satisfactory (2 points), and Needs Improvement (1 point). Each criterion is rated, and the total is divided by 15 for a percentage grade. Rubrics are not all prepared in

FIGURE 6.1   Example Rubric for written reports on an endangered animal.

RUBRICS FOR A REPORT ON AN ENDANGERED ANIMAL				
		Rating Scale		
Criteria	*3* *Exceptional*	*2* *Satisfactory*	*1* *Needs* *Improvement*	*Rating* *(3–1)*
Introduction	The introduction clearly specifies the endangered animal studied and indicates all of the specific information to be included in the report.	The introduction specifies the endangered animal studied and indicates some of the specific information to be included in the report.	The introduction specifies the endangered animal studied but fails to indicate indicate the specific informa-tion to be included in the report.	
Reason for Endangerment	The report provides a clear, well-detailed explanation about why the animal is endangered.	The report provides a minimal explana-tion about why the animal is endangered.	The reason for the animal's endangerment is not clearly explained.	
Suggestions for Correcting the Problem	Two clearly presented, well-detailed, logical solutions to the animal's endangerment are offered.	One clearly presented, well-detailed, solution is offered for the animal's endangerment.	The solutions presented are unclear and lacking in detail.	
Support	The reasons and solutions presented for the endangerment of the animal are excep-tionally well sup-ported by the student's research.	The reasons and solutions presented for the endangerment of the animal are adequately supported by the student's research.	The reasons and solutions presented for the endanger-ment of the animal are not clearly supported by the student's research.	
Writing	The report is clearly written with no more than one error in grammar and punctuation.	The report is adequately clear with no more than three errors in grammar and punctuation.	The report is not clearly written, or it includes more than three errors in grammar and punctuation.	
			Total Points:	___/15
			Grade:	

the same way as shown in the example: Some include more than three levels, some are simple checklists indicating whether the student has met a specific criteria or not, and others show the level a student has attained but do not assign points.

Using Examinations with Interdisciplinary Instruction

Examinations are most often administered at the ends of interdisciplinary and multidisciplinary unit studies. Most examinations are designed to measure verbal and logical–mathematical achievement; therefore, paper-and-pencil tests are useful for only part of the total assessment process in the interdisciplinary approach. All tests are limited in length for practical purposes, so a single test can provide only a *sample* of all the test items that are possible in assessing the same concepts, standards, and objectives.

Common Test Scores

Two scores can be used when grading interdisciplinary or multidisciplinary unit examinations. The *raw* score is the total number of test items a student answers correctly or the total number of points earned on an examination.

The raw score can easily be converted to a more useful score, the *percentage* score. This score is computed by dividing the number of items a student answers correctly by the total number of items on the examination. The student who answers 22 items correctly on a 30-item examination will earn a score of .73, or 73 percent. The percentage score is one of the most frequently used scores because it allows us to compare and note progress on different examinations.

Two other scores are used primarily with standardized tests. *Percentile* scores are computed to express the rank, or placement, of an individual student in a hypothetical group of 100 students; and *grade equivalent* scores express a student's raw score as a grade level equivalent (e.g., a score of 4.6 means the student has achieved the equivalent of a fourth-grade student after six months in that grade).

Assessment Concerns: Validity and Reliability in Testing

We need to determine whether students have gained the specific knowledge, skills, and dispositions listed as objectives of an interdisciplinary unit. The informal examinations we prepare for our units can be helpful for assessing the degree to which the students have met some of our objectives provided all items on the test are prepared carefully to ensure that they are as *valid* and *reliable* as possible.

Validity.   "Is the test assessing what we intend it to assess?" This is the main question raised in determining the validity of a test. Test validity depends on several factors. First, all test items—the questions—included on a unit examination must address the standards and objectives for which the test is written. For example, if we write a test to help determine whether students have gained specific concepts from an interdisciplinary or multidisciplinary unit on the Middle East, the test items must address only what students have been given the opportunity to learn during the unit study.

A serious factor influencing the validity of a test is its readability. Written tests involve the need to read with full comprehension. If a test is designed to assess students' conceptual knowledge rather than their ability to read and understand, the readability of the questions on the test must be at a level low enough for the students to read independently. Otherwise, the test will be measuring the students' reading ability. Validity can also be affected by the extent to which students have been prepared with readings and other materials during their unit for the questions they will be asked on the test.

Reliability.   Test reliability is also a major concern. We need to ask if the results of the examinations we give are reliable estimates of what students have gained from their unit studies. A test cannot be reliable if it is not valid to begin with; it cannot be reliable if the directions for the test or the questions are unclear. Directions must be clarified in advance and be included on the test paper so that students can refer to them if needed.

Reliability can also be affected by the length of the test and the amount of time allotted for students to complete it. In general, a test will be more reliable if it includes a larger sampling—a greater number of test items. This is accomplished by having enough test items and by allowing students sufficient time to complete these items. For example, except for some essay examinations, a test with only a few test items inadequately samples what students may have gained from their units. Of course, the length of a test must be reasonable for the amount of time allowed to complete it. Teacher-prepared examinations should be designed so that all students can complete them without the pressure of time constraints. Only speed and accuracy tests, which are rarely used in unit testing, need to be restricted with severe time limits.

A relatively simple statistic to use for checking a unit examination is the *split-half correlation*. Computing this statistic involves three easy steps. First, while marking the test results, it is necessary to keep an account of the number of students who have passed each item on the test.

Second, the test is "split in half" between the odd-numbered and even-numbered items. Dividing the test in this way helps to compensate for possible difficulty differences in the levels of questions raised in the first half and second half of an examination. In the following example, the total number for the odd-numbered items is 98, and the total for even-numbered items is 102.

The third step is simply to divide the smaller (odd total in this example) by the larger (the even total) to determine the reliability coefficient, a percentage. In this example, the result is about .96, or 96 percent. The percentage indicates an estimate of the extent to which we can rely on the scores as accurate indicators of the students' mastery of the test content.

Example Test Results for a Group of 25 Students

Item Number	Number of Students Passing
1	22
2	19
3	21
4	15
5	24
6	17
7	19
8	25
9	12
10	26

During the administration of an examination, two additional factors can affect the results of the examination: guessing and cheating. Although guessing may be thought to be a serious concern, it usually is not. Consider a multiple-choice test with four answer choices. If a student has no idea which of the four choices is correct and guesses wildly, the chance of choosing the right answer is only 25 percent. If 10 questions are on the test, the chance of guessing all answers correctly is a negligible 2.5 percent. Most tests have more than 10 items, and most students try to the best of their ability to determine the correct response to each question. Therefore, guessing does not seriously affect the reliability of most test results.

Several precautions will help to minimize the possibility of cheating:

- Ensure that the test is given in a business-like atmosphere free from distractions.
- Provide adequate seating with enough space between desks.
- Supervise your own examinations because students need the security of knowing that their teacher is available to respond to questions.
- Review directions with students before the test begins, and include written directions on the test paper.
- Have students check that they have all pages of the test in the event that a page was missed during collation.
- Use clear, unambiguous language in writing the test items.
- Ensure that the questions are written so that they discriminate accurately between students who know and those who do not know the information required for a correct response.

Writing Valid and Reliable Test Items

The test items that teachers prepare for interdisciplinary and multidisciplinary unit examinations can fall into two general categories:

1. *Supply-type items:* Students provide the answers, as in sentence completion, fill-in, short answer, and essay items.
2. *Objective-type items:* Students are provided with choices from which to select their responses, as in true–false, multiple-choice, and matching formats.

To ensure greater validity and reliability, we need to be sure that our questions are clear and that each test item addresses the standards and objectives of our units. Following are some suggestions for test-item construction with examples for preparing items in each testing format. Using these simple guidelines can help to ensure a higher degree of validity and reliability on unit examinations.

Short answer or fill-in item suggestions:

- Maintain uniformity in the length of all blanks on a completion test to avoid suggesting the length of different words. Make all blanks long enough for the longest answer.
- Include only one blank per test item to avoid the possibility that, in addition to testing for its intended objective, the test will be testing for *closure*—the ability to bridge gaps left in a sentence and to expand on the author's message—or for the ability to use context clues during reading.

Examples

(Poor) A _____ is used in a house to help prevent the _____ of the electrical wiring.

(Better) The overheating of electrical wiring in a house may be prevented if _____ are installed.

- Use one blank, even for names with two words, such as *Los Angeles* and *New York*. Two separate lines may suggest the correct answer.
- Construct the test item so that the blank appears either at or near the end of the statement. If the blank appears early in the sentence, we may be testing students' ability to use closure and context clues in addition to our intended unit objectives.

Examples

(Poor) _____ is the most important product in Brazil.

(Better) The most important product in Brazil is _____.

- Include a key word or phrase that indicates the category to which the answer must belong. For example, if a statement calls for the name of a country, the student will know that unless a country is named, the answer cannot be correct. Indicating the kind of information that must be included in the blank for a fill-in response helps to lessen ambiguity and the possibility of multiple correct answers.

Examples

(Poor) When did the English first arrive in North America?_____

(Better) In what year did the English first arrive in North America? _____

The first example above is poor because a number of possible correct responses that can be written in the blank. For example, the word "when" can suggest a date, or to some students it may mean that they need to provide an historical period or event. The better example specifies that students must supply a year.

- Avoid copying material directly from sources that students have used for their information. Quoting text material for an informal test not only models plagiarism but also encourages students to memorize the text instead of developing genuine concept comprehension.
- Check all test items on a test to determine if one of the questions gives students an answer to another item.
- Always use clear syntax, correct grammar, and accurate punctuation when writing test items.

Essay item suggestions:

- Phrase essay questions so that they clearly indicate the task. Be precise about what and how much information is expected in the response.
- When a test includes several essay items, suggest time allotments for each item to help students budget their time.
- In general, do not offer choices on essay examinations. If each essay item addresses an important standard or objective, it is not logical to offer choices. Any item that is not important should not be included on the exam. However, when the purpose of the test is to determine whether students can write a well-developed essay, students may be given a choice of topics.
- Develop grading criteria—or rubrics—before administering the test. Prepare an outline of what is expected for a complete answer to each essay question and decide how to weigh each essay item before beginning the grading process.
- Use a consistent scoring method: rubrics, a rating scale, rubrics combined with a rating scale, or holistic scoring. Teachers who use *holistic* scoring assign a single numerical score, often using a 10-point scale, in assessing the overall quality of a work. Establish a policy for handling other factors in advance, such as any irrelevant information that students include, and the mechanics of spelling, handwriting, punctuation, grammar, and syntax.
- Read all students' responses to one essay question before reading others; that is, read all students' responses to the first essay question, then continue to read all responses to the second, and so on. Comparing all responses to the same essay question can help to maintain a more even scoring of the responses, especially when we are using a holistic grading method.

Examples

(Poor)   Discuss what you have learned about the British Parliament and the United States Congress.

(Better)   Describe two major differences and one similarity between the British Parliament and the United States Congress.

It is obvious that the first question is poor because there is an absence of clear directions for the student. In fact, if a student had not learned anything much, he or she might just say that. The better question clearly asks for two differences and one similarity between the two systems.

True–false item suggestions:

- Keep the wording succinct and clear in true–false items.
- Avoid broad statements and words, such as *always, never, all, may, seldom, usually,* and so on.
- Use negatives sparingly at all grade levels. If they are used, always draw attention to them with underlining, italics, or bold type. Completely avoid negatives in examinations for children in the primary grades because very young children have considerable difficulty with reversals in thought.
- Avoid ambiguity in the statement. A true–false item should be unequivocally true or false.
- Keep the items as uniform in length as possible.
- Try to balance the numbers of true and false items. When an overbalance of either exists, students may be led to believe they must have answered some questions incorrectly.

Examples

(Poor) _____ Birds eat more than mammals.

_____ Martha and George Washington had two children.

(Better) _____ Considering body weight, birds eat more than mammals do.

_____ Martha and George Washington raised two children.

Multiple-choice item suggestions:

- A multiple-choice test item comprises two parts: a stem and several answer choices. The stem should present enough information so that the answer choices can be relatively short. If students have to read lengthy choices after reading the stem, the questions may actually be testing students' short-term memory. Unless this is the purpose of the test, this memory factor may interfere with the validity of the item.
- Use negatives sparingly, and highlight them if they are used. Avoid negatives in tests for children in the primary grades.
- Avoid determiners, such as *all, some, often, usually,* and so on.
- Use special alternatives such as *all of the above* and *none of the above* sparingly.
- Try to keep the answer choices similar in length to avoid suggesting that any particular answer is the correct one.
- Make sure that all the answer choices are somewhat feasible while ensuring that only one correct answer exists.
- Ensure that all answer choices are grammatically consistent with the stem of the item.

Examples

(Poor)

An example of:

A. an animal that is a mollusk is a whale.

B. an animal that is a mollusk is a clam.

C. an animal that is a mollusk is a crab.

D. an animal that is a mollusk is a lobster.

(Better)

An example of a mollusk is a:
A. whale.
B. clam.
C. crab.
D. lobster.

The poor example includes needless repetition in the answer choices. The better example corrects this problem.

Matching items suggestions:

- Each matching item comprises a set of premises and response choices listed in two columns. The matching set should be relatively short. Requiring students to search through too many choices for an answer may test their short-term memory as well as their knowledge of the material for which the test is intended. This will lower the validity of the test. Try to limit any matching set to seven or fewer premises. Prepare more than one matching set if more items need to be tested.
- The material being tested in a single matching set should be as homogeneous as possible. For example, if the testing is about simple machines, avoid other topics.
- Include as much material in the premises as needed, but keep the length of response choices relatively short to avoid testing short-term memory instead of content.
- Include one or two extra response choices to avoid the certainty that a student who has one answer wrong will have another wrong.

Examples

(Poor)

Column A		Column B
_____	1. Thermometer	A. An instrument that measures humidity
_____	2. Barometer	B. An instrument that measures rainfall
_____	3. Wind vane	C. An instrument that measures wind direction
_____	4. Rain gauge	D. An instrument that measures air pressure
_____	5. Hygrometer	E. An instrument that measures temperature

(Better)

Column A		Column B
_____	1. An instrument that measures wind direction	A. Thermometer
_____	2. An instrument that measures temperature	B. Barometer
_____	3. An instrument that measures humidity	C. Wind vane
_____	4. An instrument that measures rainfall	D. Humidifier
_____	5. An instrument that measures air pressure	E. Hygrometer
		F. Telemeter
		G. Rain gauge

The two columns should be reversed in the poor example above. It is better to read the definitions and then look down the list of possible answer choices, which are short. Also, additional answer choices are needed. These problems are corrected in the better example.

Summary

This chapter has discussed several authentic assessment techniques, including student portfolios that are used to collect samples of a student's completed work and work-in-progress as well as other items that are useful in assessing the student's progress. The preparation of rubrics for grading students' papers, projects, and performances has been explained and illustrated. Explanations and methods of determining test validity and reliability have been provided. Suggestions for the construction of different types of test items have been included and illustrated with examples.

ACTIVITY

Michael DeLaney is an English (literacy) teacher in a middle school. He is a member of a teaching team that designed a multidisciplinary unit on westward expansion in the United States. As a part of their research, students have been studying the history of the Trail of Tears. One of the assessments for the unit is a student essay on this historical event. Mr. DeLaney was responsible for assigning and assessing the essay. He provided students with the following directions during a lesson in which he introduced the assignment:

> *Prepare an essay about the Trail of Tears that is written in the first person from the viewpoint of a Cherokee Native American child of your age. Your essay must include three historical facts you have learned about the event.*

An essay is not an easy student product to evaluate fairly and evenly. However, the use of rubrics for grading essays can help to make the process one that is more consistent from paper to paper. Using the criteria outlined in the requirements of the essay, prepare a set of rubrics to use for grading the students' essays.

REFERENCES

An "Insider's view": What's behind ASCD's focus on formative assessment. (2007, Winter). *ASCD Associate News.* Alexandria, VA: Association for Supervision and Curriculum Development.

Arends, R. I. (2009). *Learning to teach* (8th ed.). Boston: McGraw-Hill.

Borich, G. D. (2007). *Effective teaching methods* (6th ed.). Upper Saddle River, NJ: Pearson/Merrill.

Chicago Public Schools. (2007). *The rubric bank.* Retrieved November 9, 2008 from http://intranet.cps. k12.il.us/assessments/Ideas_and_Rubrics/Rubric_Bank/rubric_bank.html

Dick, W, Carey, L., & Carey, J. O. (2009). *The systematic design of instruction* (7th ed.). Upper Saddle River, NJ: Pearson/Merrill.

Ellis, A. K. (2009). *Teaching and learning elementary social studies* (8th ed.). Boston: Pearson/Allyn & Bacon.

Goodrich, H. (1997). Understanding rubrics. *Educational Leadership, 54*(4), 14–17.

Guskey, T. R. (2003). How classroom assessments improve learning. *Educational Leadership, 60*(5), 6–11.

Jacobs, H. H. (1997). *Mapping the big picture: Integrating curriculum & assessment.* Alexandria, VA: Association for Supervision & Curriculum Development.

Johnston, P. (1987). Teachers as evaluation experts. *The Reading Teacher, 40,* 744–748.

Johnston, P. H. (1992). *Constructive evaluation of literate activity.* White Plains, NY: Longman.

O'Neil, J. (1993). The promise of portfolios. *Update, 35*(7), 1–5.

Pappas, C. C., Kiefer, B. Z., & Levstik, L. S. (2006). *An integrated language perspective in the elementary school* (4th ed.). Boston: Pearson/Allyn & Bacon.

Popham, W. J. (2006). Assessment for learning: An endangered species? *Educational Leadership, 63*(5), 82–83.

Porcaro, J. J., & Johnson, K. G. (2003, Winter). Building a whole-language writing program. *Kappa Delta Pi Record, 39*(2), 74–79.

Schrock, K. (2007). Teacher helpers: Assessment & rubric information. In *Kathy Schrock's guide for educators.* Retrieved September 7, 2008 from http://school.discovery.com/schrockguide/assess.html

Shepard, L. A. (2005). Linking formative assessment to scaffolding. *Educational Leadership, 63*(3), 66–70.

Shores, E. F., & Grace, C. (2005). *The portfolio book: A step-by-step guide for teachers.* Upper Saddle River, NJ: Pearson Education.

Sternberg, R. J. (1999). Ability and expertise. *American Educator, 23*(1), 10–13ff.

Wexler-Sherman, C., Gardner, H., & Feldman, D. H. (1988). A pluralistic view of early assessment: The project spectrum approach. *Theory Into Practice,* 27, 77–83.

Wiggins, G., & McTighe, J. (2006). *Understanding by design* (2nd ed.). Upper Saddle River, NJ: Pearson/ Merrill Prentice Hall.

Wilcox, J. (2006, February). Less teaching, more assessing. *Education Update, 48,*(2), 1ff.

SUGGESTED READINGS

The following readings provide additional background material for the topics included in this chapter.

Assessment Techniques

Burns, D. E., & Purcell, J. H. (2001). Tools for teachers. *Educational Leadership, 59*(1), 50–52.

Eby, J. W., & Martin, D. B. (2006). *Reflective planning, teaching, and evaluation: K–12* (4th ed.). Upper Saddle River, NJ: Pearson/ Merrill Prentice Hall.

Popham, W. J. (2007). *Classroom assessment: What teachers need to know* (5th ed.). Boston: Pearson/Allyn & Bacon.

Popham, W. J. (2008). A misunderstood grail. *Educational Leadership, 66*(1), 82–83.

Popham, W. J. (2009). A process—not a test. *Educational Leadership, 66*(7), 85–86.

Scriffiny, P. L. (2008). Seven reasons for standards-based grading. *Educational Leadership, 66*(2), 70–74.

Seltz, J. A. (2008). Focus on assessment. *Educational Leadership, 66*(1), 92–93.

Authentic Assessment

Arter, J. A., & McTighe, J. (2001). *Scoring rubrics in the classroom: Using performance criteria for assessing and improving student performance.* Thousand Oaks, CA: Corwin.

Campbell, L., Campbell, B., & Dickinson, D. (2004). *Teaching and learning through multiple intelligences* (3rd ed.). Boston: Pearson/Allyn & Bacon.

Charbonneau, M. P., & Reider, B. E. (1995). *The integrated elementary classroom: A developmental model of education for the 21st century.* Boston: Pearson/Allyn & Bacon.

Darling-Hammond, L. (1994). Setting standards for students: The case for authentic assessment. *The Educational Forum, 59*(1), 14–21.

Darling-Hammond, L., Ancess, J., & Falk, B. (1995). *Authentic assessment in action: Studies of schools and students at work.* New York: Teachers College Press.

Engel, B. S. (1994). Portfolio assessment and the new paradigm: New instruments and new places. *The Educational Forum, 59*(1), 22–27.

Grosvenor, L. (1993). *Student portfolios.* Washington, DC: National Education Association.

Houghton Mifflin's Education Place at http://www.eduplace.com.

Lescher, M. L. (1995). *Portfolios: Assessing learning in the primary grades.* Washington, DC: National Education Association.

Moore, K. D. (2009). *Effective instructional strategies: From theory to practice* (2nd ed.). Thousand Oaks, CA: Sage Publications.

Penta, M. Q. (2002). Student portfolios in a standardized world. *Kappa Delta Pi Record, 38*(2), 77–81.

Viadero, D. (1995, April 5). Even as popularity soars, portfolios encounter roadblocks. *Education Week,* pp. 8–9.

Vyzyak, L. (1996). *Student portfolios: a practical guide to evaluation.* Bothell, WA: Wright Group.

Wasserstein, P. (1994, Fall). To do or not to do portfolios: That is the question. *Kappa Delta Pi Record, 31*(1), 12–15.

Rubrics

Cooper, J. D., & Kiger, N. D. (2008). *Literacy assessment: Helping teachers plan instruction* (3rd ed.). Boston: Houghton Mifflin.

Freiberg, H. J., & Driscoll, A. (2005). *Universal teaching strategies* (3rd ed.). Boston: Pearson/Allyn & Bacon.

Ormrod, J. E. (2009). *Essentials of educational psychology.* Upper Saddle River, NJ: Pearson/Merrill.

Ornstein, A. C., & Lasley, T. J. (2004). *Strategies for effective teaching* (4th ed.). Boston: McGraw-Hill.

Recesso, A., & Orrill, C. (2008). *Integrating technology into teaching.* Boston: Houghton Mifflin.

Roberts, P. L., & Kellough, R. D. (2008). *A guide for developing interdisciplinary thematic units* (4th ed.). Upper Saddle River, NY: Pearson/Merrill Prentice Hall.

Saddler, B., & Andrade, H. (2004). The writing rubric. *Educational Leadership, 62*(2), 48–52.

Test Construction

Arends, R. I. (2009). *Learning to teach* (8th ed.). Boston: McGraw-Hill.

Cangelosi, J. S. (1990). *Designing tests for evaluating student achievement.* New York: Longman.

Cooper, J. M. (2006). *Classroom teaching skills* (8th ed.). Boston: Houghton Mifflin.

Dembo, M. H. (1994). *Applying educational psychology in the classroom* (5th ed.). New York: Longman.

Dick, W., Carey, L., & Carey, J. O. (2009). *The systematic design of instruction* (7th ed.). Boston: Pearson/Merrill.

Hoy, A. W. (2008). *Educational psychology* (10th ed.). Boston: Pearson/Allyn & Bacon.

Marchesani, R. J. (2007). *The field guide to teaching: A handbook for new teachers.* Upper Saddle River, NJ: Pearson/Merrill Prentice Hall.

Meisels, S. J., Harrington, H. L., McMahon, P., Dichtelmiller, M. L., & Jablon, J. R. (2002). *Thinking like a teacher.* Boston: Pearson/Allyn & Bacon.

Orlich, D. C., Harder, R. J., Callahan, R. C., & Gibson, H. W. (2001). *Teaching strategies: A guide to better instruction* (6th ed.). Boston: Houghton Mifflin.

Ormrod, J. E. (2009). *Essentials of educational psychology* (2nd ed.). Upper Saddle River, NJ: Pearson/Merrill Prentice Hall.

Ornstein, A. C., & Lasley, T. J. (2004). *Strategies for effective teaching* (4th ed.). Boston: McGraw-Hill.

Popham, W. J. (2006). Diagnostic assessment: A measurement mirage? *Educational Leadership, 64*(2), 90–91.

Popham, W. J. (2006). Needed: A dose of assessment literacy. *Educational Leadership, 63*(6), 84–85.

Popham, W. J. (2008). An unintentional deception. *Educational Leadership, 66*(2), 80–81.

Sample Interdisciplinary Unit Plan Web Designs

Web designs for interdisciplinary unit plans may be constructed in many different ways. The purpose of the sample webs in this appendix (Figures A.1 through A.15) is to show designs that differ stylistically from one another. Because the webs vary in detail, number of lesson and activity planning ideas, and overall quality, the samples are only intended to show alternative ways to construct them.

The essential components are included in all of the web designs. Each includes a central theme and related disciplines to be employed in exploring the theme as well as brief statements or phrases describing the planner's ideas for related lessons and activities. Most of the designs include interconnecting lines that serve to indicate the planner's interdisciplinary thinking about the relationships among the various components.

Each sample represents a graphic design of the learning plan for an interdisciplinary unit. Its design also serves as a succinct reminder of the activities and lessons to be included in the unit when it is taught. Therefore, the diagrams do not give detailed information about learning options, materials, processes, or content that the unit will include. Those details are provided in the *Descriptions of Lessons and Activities* section of the unit plan. Although web designs can include greater detail, doing so tends to make them overcrowded and difficult to read.

The samples indicate only the general level for which the unit topic is appropriate—primary, intermediate, or middle school. Designs for intermediate and middle school levels can be converted to become multidisciplinary units, which are described in Chapter 4.

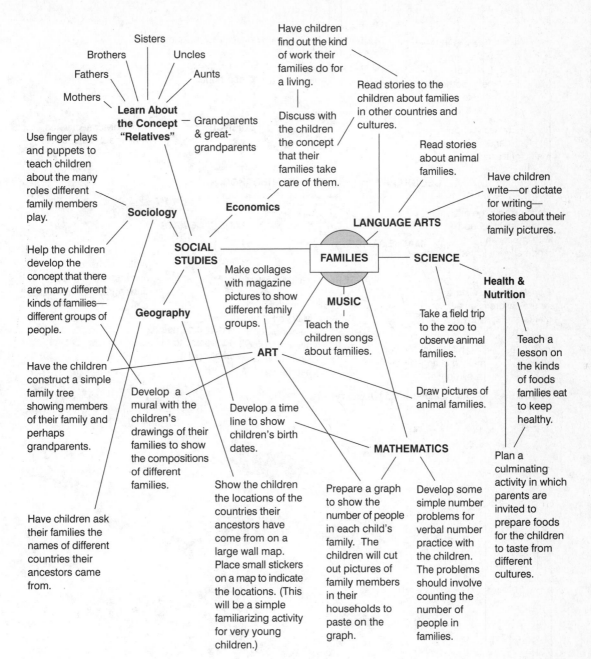

FIGURE A.1 "Families" (primary).

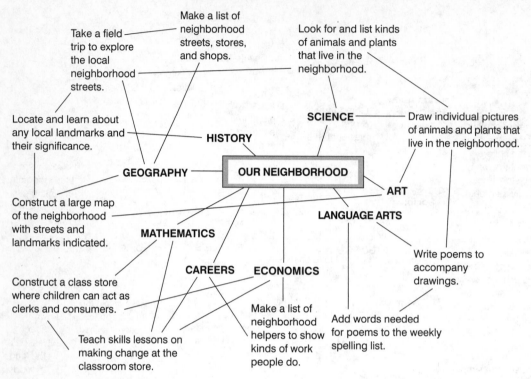

FIGURE A.2   "Our Neighborhood" (primary).

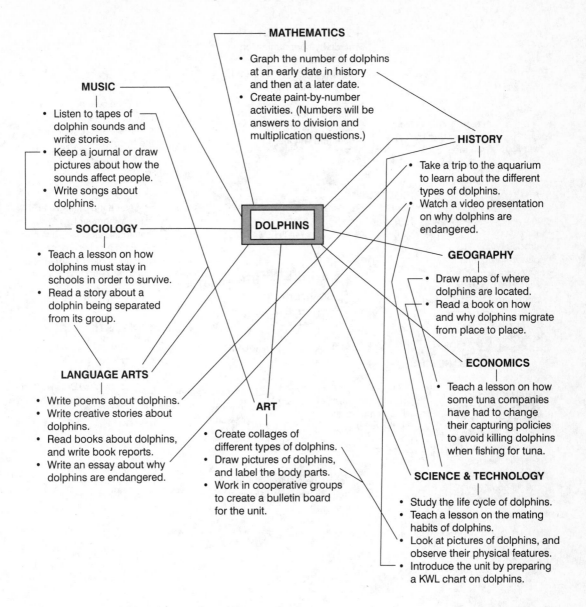

MATHEMATICS
- Graph the number of dolphins at an early date in history and then at a later date.
- Create paint-by-number activities. (Numbers will be answers to division and multiplication questions.)

MUSIC
- Listen to tapes of dolphin sounds and write stories.
- Keep a journal or draw pictures about how the sounds affect people.
- Write songs about dolphins.

HISTORY
- Take a trip to the aquarium to learn about the different types of dolphins.
- Watch a video presentation on why dolphins are endangered.

DOLPHINS

SOCIOLOGY
- Teach a lesson on how dolphins must stay in schools in order to survive.
- Read a story about a dolphin being separated from its group.

GEOGRAPHY
- Draw maps of where dolphins are located.
- Read a book on how and why dolphins migrate from place to place.

ECONOMICS
- Teach a lesson on how some tuna companies have had to change their capturing policies to avoid killing dolphins when fishing for tuna.

LANGUAGE ARTS
- Write poems about dolphins.
- Write creative stories about dolphins.
- Read books about dolphins, and write book reports.
- Write an essay about why dolphins are endangered.

ART
- Create collages of different types of dolphins.
- Draw pictures of dolphins, and label the body parts.
- Work in cooperative groups to create a bulletin board for the unit.

SCIENCE & TECHNOLOGY
- Study the life cycle of dolphins.
- Teach a lesson on the mating habits of dolphins.
- Look at pictures of dolphins, and observe their physical features.
- Introduce the unit by preparing a KWL chart on dolphins.

FIGURE A.3   "Dolphins" (upper primary / intermediate).

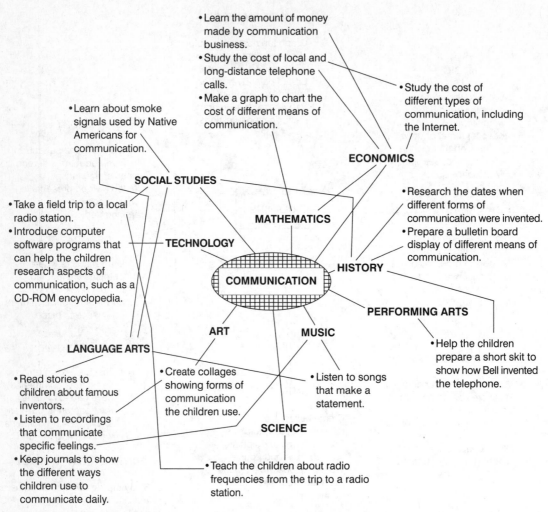

FIGURE A.4   "Communication" (intermediate).

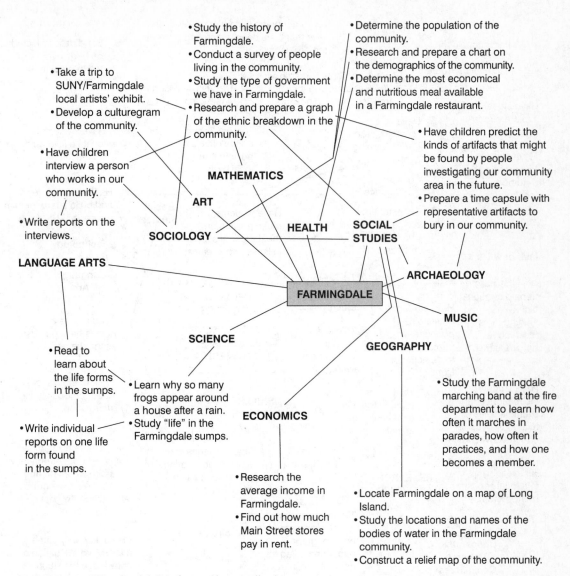

FIGURE A.5 "Farmingdale" (primary / intermediate).

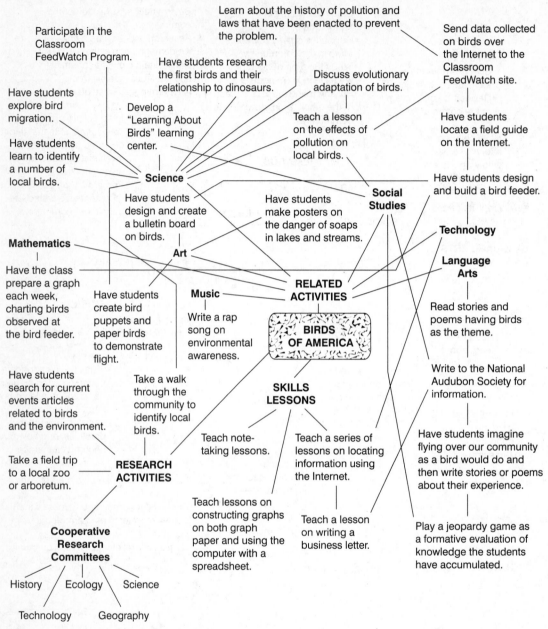

FIGURE A.6   "Birds of America" (intermediate).

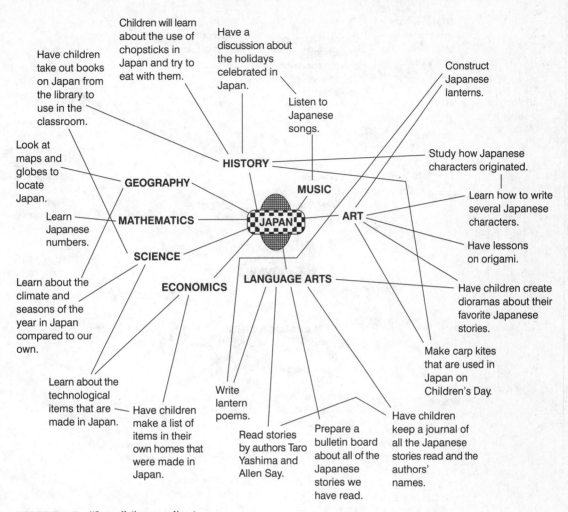

FIGURE A.7 "Japan" (intermediate).

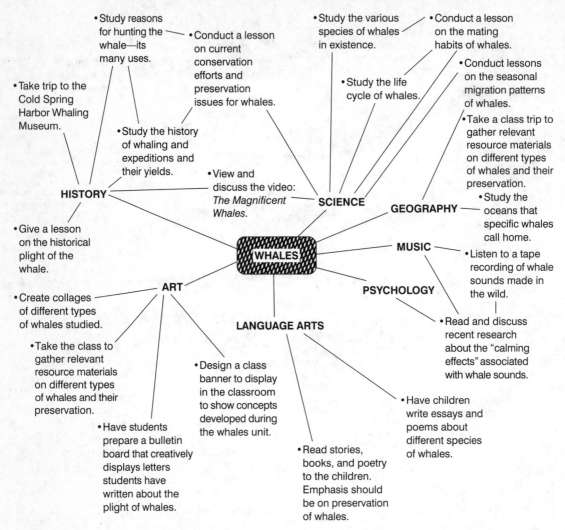

• Study reasons for hunting the whale—its many uses.

• Conduct a lesson on current conservation efforts and preservation issues for whales.

• Study the various species of whales in existence.

• Conduct a lesson on the mating habits of whales.

• Take trip to the Cold Spring Harbor Whaling Museum.

• Study the history of whaling and expeditions and their yields.

• Study the life cycle of whales.

• Conduct lessons on the seasonal migration patterns of whales.

• Take a class trip to gather relevant resource materials on different types of whales and their preservation.

HISTORY

• View and discuss the video: *The Magnificent Whales.*

SCIENCE

GEOGRAPHY

• Study the oceans that specific whales call home.

• Give a lesson on the historical plight of the whale.

WHALES

MUSIC

• Listen to a tape recording of whale sounds made in the wild.

ART

PSYCHOLOGY

• Create collages of different types of whales studied.

LANGUAGE ARTS

• Read and discuss recent research about the "calming effects" associated with whale sounds.

• Take the class to gather relevant resource materials on different types of whales and their preservation.

• Design a class banner to display in the classroom to show concepts developed during the whales unit.

• Have children write essays and poems about different species of whales.

• Have students prepare a bulletin board that creatively displays letters students have written about the plight of whales.

• Read stories, books, and poetry to the children. Emphasis should be on preservation of whales.

FIGURE A.8   "Whales" (intermediate).

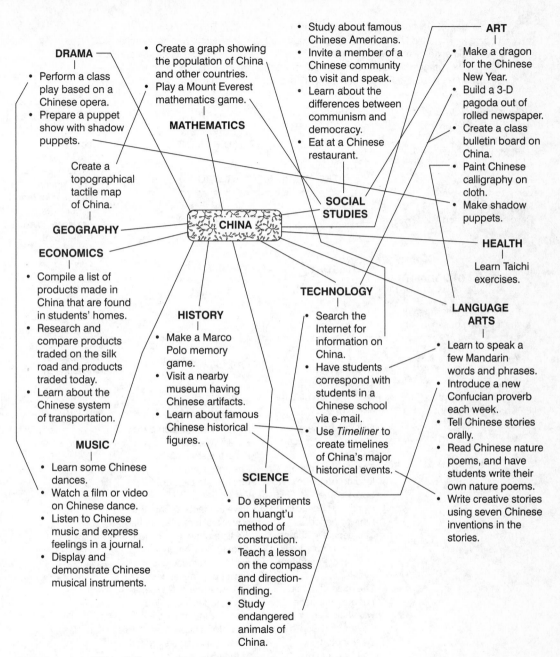

DRAMA
- Perform a class play based on a Chinese opera.
- Prepare a puppet show with shadow puppets.

- Create a graph showing the population of China and other countries.
- Play a Mount Everest mathematics game.

MATHEMATICS

- Study about famous Chinese Americans.
- Invite a member of a Chinese community to visit and speak.
- Learn about the differences between communism and democracy.
- Eat at a Chinese restaurant.

ART
- Make a dragon for the Chinese New Year.
- Build a 3-D pagoda out of rolled newspaper.
- Create a class bulletin board on China.
- Paint Chinese calligraphy on cloth.
- Make shadow puppets.

Create a topographical tactile map of China.

GEOGRAPHY

CHINA

SOCIAL STUDIES

HEALTH
- Learn Taichi exercises.

ECONOMICS
- Compile a list of products made in China that are found in students' homes.
- Research and compare products traded on the silk road and products traded today.
- Learn about the Chinese system of transportation.

HISTORY
- Make a Marco Polo memory game.
- Visit a nearby museum having Chinese artifacts.
- Learn about famous Chinese historical figures.

TECHNOLOGY
- Search the Internet for information on China.
- Have students correspond with students in a Chinese school via e-mail.
- Use *Timeliner* to create timelines of China's major historical events.

LANGUAGE ARTS
- Learn to speak a few Mandarin words and phrases.
- Introduce a new Confucian proverb each week.
- Tell Chinese stories orally.
- Read Chinese nature poems, and have students write their own nature poems.
- Write creative stories using seven Chinese inventions in the stories.

MUSIC
- Learn some Chinese dances.
- Watch a film or video on Chinese dance.
- Listen to Chinese music and express feelings in a journal.
- Display and demonstrate Chinese musical instruments.

SCIENCE
- Do experiments on huangt'u method of construction.
- Teach a lesson on the compass and direction-finding.
- Study endangered animals of China.

FIGURE A.9 "China" (intermediate / middle school).

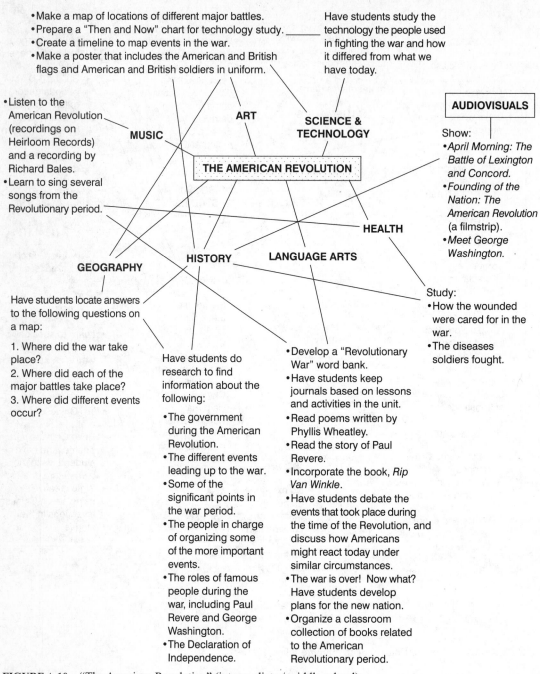

- Make a map of locations of different major battles.
- Prepare a "Then and Now" chart for technology study.
- Create a timeline to map events in the war.
- Make a poster that includes the American and British flags and American and British soldiers in uniform.

Have students study the technology the people used in fighting the war and how it differed from what we have today.

AUDIOVISUALS

Show:
- *April Morning: The Battle of Lexington and Concord.*
- *Founding of the Nation: The American Revolution* (a filmstrip).
- *Meet George Washington.*

- Listen to the American Revolution (recordings on Heirloom Records) and a recording by Richard Bales.
- Learn to sing several songs from the Revolutionary period.

ART

MUSIC

SCIENCE & TECHNOLOGY

THE AMERICAN REVOLUTION

HEALTH

GEOGRAPHY

HISTORY

LANGUAGE ARTS

Have students locate answers to the following questions on a map:

1. Where did the war take place?
2. Where did each of the major battles take place?
3. Where did different events occur?

Have students do research to find information about the following:

- The government during the American Revolution.
- The different events leading up to the war.
- Some of the significant points in the war period.
- The people in charge of organizing some of the more important events.
- The roles of famous people during the war, including Paul Revere and George Washington.
- The Declaration of Independence.

- Develop a "Revolutionary War" word bank.
- Have students keep journals based on lessons and activities in the unit.
- Read poems written by Phyllis Wheatley.
- Read the story of Paul Revere.
- Incorporate the book, *Rip Van Winkle*.
- Have students debate the events that took place during the time of the Revolution, and discuss how Americans might react today under similar circumstances.
- The war is over! Now what? Have students develop plans for the new nation.
- Organize a classroom collection of books related to the American Revolutionary period.

Study:
- How the wounded were cared for in the war.
- The diseases soldiers fought.

FIGURE A.10 "The American Revolution" (intermediate / middle school).

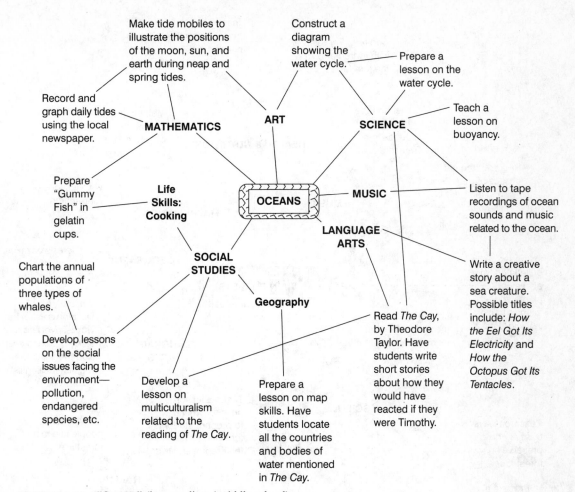

FIGURE A.11 "Oceans" (intermediate / middle school).

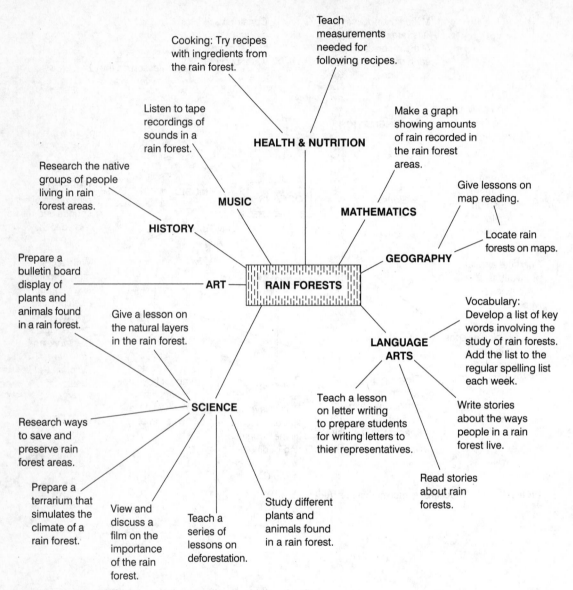

FIGURE A.12 "Rain Forests" (intermediate / middle school).

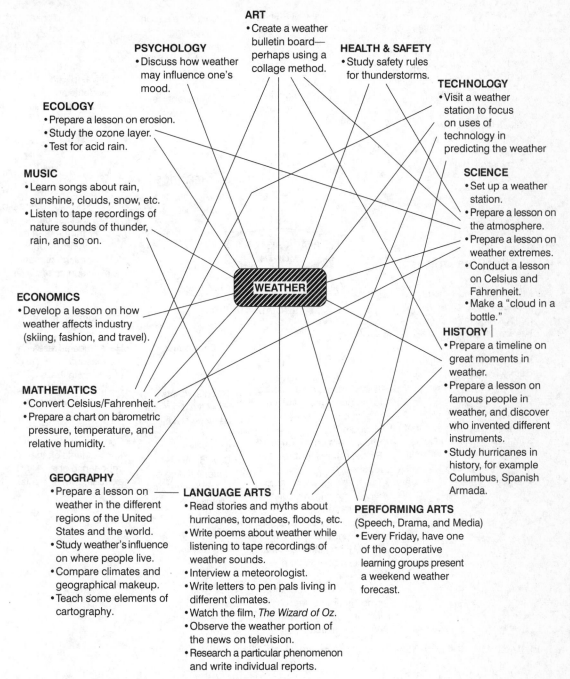

ART
• Create a weather bulletin board—perhaps using a collage method.

PSYCHOLOGY
• Discuss how weather may influence one's mood.

HEALTH & SAFETY
• Study safety rules for thunderstorms.

TECHNOLOGY
• Visit a weather station to focus on uses of technology in predicting the weather

ECOLOGY
• Prepare a lesson on erosion.
• Study the ozone layer.
• Test for acid rain.

MUSIC
• Learn songs about rain, sunshine, clouds, snow, etc.
• Listen to tape recordings of nature sounds of thunder, rain, and so on.

SCIENCE
• Set up a weather station.
• Prepare a lesson on the atmosphere.
• Prepare a lesson on weather extremes.
• Conduct a lesson on Celsius and Fahrenheit.
• Make a "cloud in a bottle."

ECONOMICS
• Develop a lesson on how weather affects industry (skiing, fashion, and travel).

WEATHER

HISTORY
• Prepare a timeline on great moments in weather.
• Prepare a lesson on famous people in weather, and discover who invented different instruments.
• Study hurricanes in history, for example Columbus, Spanish Armada.

MATHEMATICS
• Convert Celsius/Fahrenheit.
• Prepare a chart on barometric pressure, temperature, and relative humidity.

GEOGRAPHY
• Prepare a lesson on weather in the different regions of the United States and the world.
• Study weather's influence on where people live.
• Compare climates and geographical makeup.
• Teach some elements of cartography.

LANGUAGE ARTS
• Read stories and myths about hurricanes, tornadoes, floods, etc.
• Write poems about weather while listening to tape recordings of weather sounds.
• Interview a meteorologist.
• Write letters to pen pals living in different climates.
• Watch the film, *The Wizard of Oz*.
• Observe the weather portion of the news on television.
• Research a particular phenomenon and write individual reports.

PERFORMING ARTS
(Speech, Drama, and Media)
• Every Friday, have one of the cooperative learning groups present a weekend weather forecast.

FIGURE A.13   "Weather" (intermediate / middle school).

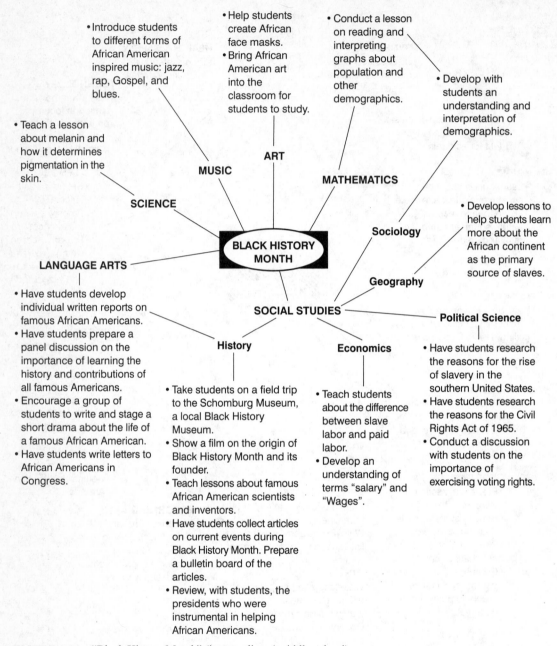

FIGURE A.14 "Black History Month" (intermediate / middle school).

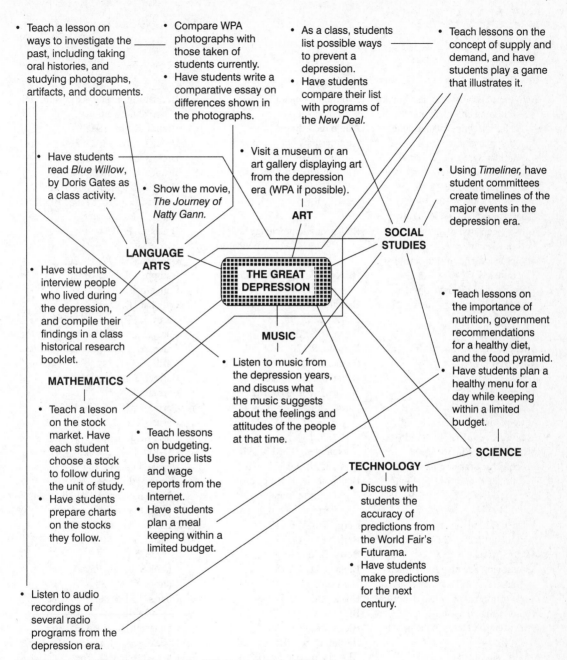

- Teach a lesson on ways to investigate the _____ past, including taking oral histories, and studying photographs, artifacts, and documents.

- Compare WPA photographs with those taken of students currently.
- Have students write a comparative essay on differences shown in the photographs.

- As a class, students list possible ways —— to prevent a depression.
- Have students compare their list with programs of the *New Deal.*

- Teach lessons on the concept of supply and demand, and have students play a game that illustrates it.

- Have students read *Blue Willow,* by Doris Gates as a class activity.

- Show the movie, *The Journey of Natty Gann.*

- Visit a museum or an art gallery displaying art from the depression era (WPA if possible).

ART

- Using *Timeliner,* have student committees create timelines of the major events in the depression era.

LANGUAGE ARTS

SOCIAL STUDIES

THE GREAT DEPRESSION

- Have students interview people who lived during the depression, and compile their findings in a class historical research booklet.

- Teach lessons on the importance of nutrition, government recommendations for a healthy diet, and the food pyramid.
- Have students plan a healthy menu for a day while keeping within a limited budget.

MATHEMATICS

MUSIC

- Teach a lesson on the stock market. Have each student choose a stock to follow during the unit of study.
- Have students prepare charts on the stocks they follow.

- Teach lessons on budgeting. Use price lists and wage reports from the Internet.
- Have students plan a meal keeping within a limited budget.

- Listen to music from the depression years, and discuss what the music suggests about the feelings and attitudes of the people at that time.

SCIENCE

TECHNOLOGY

- Discuss with students the accuracy of predictions from the World Fair's Futurama.
- Have students make predictions for the next century.

- Listen to audio recordings of several radio programs from the depression era.

FIGURE A.15 "The Great Depression" (intermediate / middle school).

INDEX